John Henry Newman

Lectures on the Present Position of Catholics in England

Addressed to the brothers of the Oratory in the summer of 1851

John Henry Newman

Lectures on the Present Position of Catholics in England
Addressed to the brothers of the Oratory in the summer of 1851

ISBN/EAN: 9783337139193

Printed in Europe, USA, Canada, Australia, Japan

Cover: Foto ©ninafisch / pixelio.de

More available books at **www.hansebooks.com**

THE PRESENT POSITION

OF

CATHOLICS IN ENGLAND.

THE ABERDEEN UNIVERSITY PRESS.

ON THE

PRESENT POSITION OF CATHOLICS IN ENGLAND:

Addressed to the Brothers of the Oratory

IN THE SUMMER OF 1851.

BY

JOHN HENRY NEWMAN, D.D.

PRIEST OF THE ORATORY OF ST. PHILIP NERI.

Tempus tacendi, et tempus loquendi.

New Edition.

LONDON
LONGMANS, GREEN, AND CO.
AND NEW YORK: 15 EAST 16th STREET
1893

All rights reserved.

TO THE

MOST REVEREND PAUL,

LORD ARCHBISHOP OF ARMAGH,

AND

PRIMATE OF ALL IRELAND.

My dear Lord Primate,

It is the infelicity of the moment at which I write, that it is not allowed me to place the following pages under the patronage of the successor of St. Patrick, with the ceremony and observance due to so great a name, without appearing to show disrespect to an Act of Parliament.

Such appearance a Catholic is bound to avoid, whenever it is possible The authority of the civil power is based on sanctions so solemn and august, and the temporal blessings which all classes derive from its protection are so many, that both on Christian principles and from motives of expedience it is ever a duty, unless religious considerations interfere, to profess a simple deference to its enunciations, and a hearty concurrence in its very suggestions; but how can I deny of your Grace what may almost be called a dogmatic fact, that you are what the Catholic Church has made you?

Evil, however, is never without its alleviation; and I think I shall have your Grace's concurrence, if in the present instance I recognise the operation, already commenced, of that unfailing law of Divine Providence, by which all events, prosperous or adverse, are made to tend, in one way or other, to the triumph of our Religion. The violence of our enemies has thrown us back upon ourselves and upon each other; and though it needed no adventitious cause to lead me to aspire to the honour of associating my name with that of your Grace, whose kindness I had already experienced so abundantly when I was at Rome in 1847, yet the present circumstances furnish a motive of their own, for my turning my eyes in devotion and affection to the Primate of that ancient and glorious and much enduring Church, the Church of Ireland, who, from her own past history, can teach her restored English Sister how to persevere in the best of causes, and can interchange with her, amid trials common to both, the tenderness of Catholic sympathy and the power of Catholic intercession.

Begging of your Grace for me and mine the fulness of St. Patrick's benediction,

I am, my dear Lord Primate,
Your Grace's faithful and affectionate Servant,

JOHN H. NEWMAN,
Of the Oratory.

THE ORATORY,
Sept. 1851.

PREFACE.

It may be necessary to state, that by "Brothers of the Oratory" are meant the members of an Association or Confraternity of seculars attached, but external, to the Ecclesiastical Congregation, to which the Author belongs. These are the persons to whom the following Lectures are addressed, with a view of suggesting to them, how best, as Catholics, to master their own position and to perform their duties in a Protestant country.

The Author repeats here, what he has several times observed in the course of the Volume itself, that his object has not been to prove the divine origin of Catholicism, but to remove some of the moral and intellectual impediments which prevent Protestants from acknowledging it. Protestants cannot be expected to do justice to a religion whose professors they hate and scorn. It has been objected to the Author, as regards both this and other of his works, that he succeeds better in demolition than in construction; and he has been challenged to draw out a proof of the truth of the Catholic Faith. Persons who so speak, should consider the state of the case more accurately:—that he has not attempted the task to which they invite him, does not arise from any misgiving whatever in his mind about the strength of his cause, but about the disposition of his audience. He has a most profound misgiving about their fairness as judges, founded on his sense of the misconceptions concerning Catholicism which generally pre-occupy the English mind. Irresistible as the proof seems to him to be, so as even to master and carry away the intellect as soon as it is stated, so that Catholicism is almost its own evidence, yet it requires, as the great philosopher of antiquity reminds us, as being a moral proof, a rightly-disposed recipient. While a community is overrun with prejudices, it is as premature to attempt to prove that doctrine to be true which is the object of them, as it would be to think of building in the aboriginal forest till its trees had been felled.

The controversy with our opponents is not simple, but various and manifold; when a Catholic is doing one thing he cannot be doing another; yet the common answer made to his proof of this point is, that it is no proof of that. Thus men shift about, silenced in nothing, because they have not yet been answered in everything. Let them admit what we have already proved, and they will have a claim on us for proof of more. One thing at a time is the general rule given for getting through business well, and it applies to the case before us. In a large and complicated question it is much to settle portions of it; yet this is so little understood, that a course of Lectures might profitably confine itself simply to the consideration of the canons to be observed in disputation. Catholics would have cause to congratulate themselves, though they were able to proceed no further than to persuade Protestants to argue out one point before going on to another. It would be much even to get them to give up what they could not defend, and to promise that they would not return to it. It would be much to succeed in hindering them from making a great deal of an objection till it is refuted, and then suddenly considering it so small that it is not worth withdrawing. It would be much to hinder them from eluding a defeat on one point by digressing upon three or four others, and then presently running back to the first, and then to and fro, to second, third and fourth, and treating each in turn as if quite a fresh subject on which not a word had yet been said. In all controversy it is surely right to mark down and record what has been proved, as well as what has not; and this is what the Author claims of the reader as regards the following Volume.

He claims, and surely with justice, that it should not be urged against his proof that Protestant views of Catholics are wrong, that he has not thereby proved that Catholicism is right. He wishes his proof taken for what it is. He certainly has not proved what he did not set about proving; and neither he nor any one else has any encouragement to go on to prove something more, until what he actually has accomplished is distinctly acknowledged. The obligations of a controversialist lie with Protestants equally as with us.

As regards his Catholic readers, he would ask leave to express a hope that he may not be supposed in his concluding Lecture to recommend to the Laity the cultivation of a controversial temper, or a forwardness and rashness and unseasonableness in disputing upon religion. No one apprehends so clearly the difficulty of arguing on religious topics, consistently with their sacredness and delicacy, as he who has taken pains to do so well. No one shrinks so sensitively from its responsibility, when it is not a duty, as he who has learned by experience his own unavoidable inaccuracies in statement and in reasoning. It is no easy accomplishment in a Catholic to know his religion so perfectly, as to be able to volunteer a defence of it.

The Author has, besides, to apologize to them for having perhaps made some quotations of Scripture from the Protestant version. If anywhere he has been led to do so, it has been in cases where, points of faith not being involved, it was necessary for the argumentative or rhetorical force of the passages in which they occur.

And lastly, he earnestly begs their prayers that he may be prospered and blest in whatever he attempts, however poorly, for God's glory and the edification of His Church.

In Fest. Nativ. B. M. V., 1851.

CONTENTS.

LECTURE		PAGE
I.	PROTESTANT VIEW OF THE CATHOLIC CHURCH	1
II.	TRADITION THE SUSTAINING POWER OF THE PROTESTANT VIEW	42
III.	FABLE THE BASIS OF THE PROTESTANT VIEW	83
IV.	TRUE TESTIMONY INSUFFICIENT FOR THE PROTESTANT VIEW	127
V.	LOGICAL INCONSISTENCY OF THE PROTESTANT VIEW	177
VI.	PREJUDICE THE LIFE OF THE PROTESTANT VIEW	223
VII.	ASSUMED PRINCIPLES THE INTELLECTUAL GROUND OF THE PROTESTANT VIEW	271
VIII.	IGNORANCE CONCERNING CATHOLICS THE PROTECTION OF THE PROTESTANT VIEW	315
IX.	DUTIES OF CATHOLICS TOWARDS THE PROTESTANT VIEW	363

LECTURE I.

PROTESTANT VIEW OF THE CATHOLIC CHURCH.

THERE is a well-known fable, of which it is to my purpose to remind you, my Brothers of the Oratory, by way of introducing to you the subject of the Lectures which I am proposing to deliver. I am going to inquire why it is, that, in this intelligent nation, and in this rational nineteenth century, we Catholics are so despised and hated by our own countrymen, with whom we have lived all our lives, that they are prompt to believe any story, however extravagant, that is told to our disadvantage; as if beyond a doubt we were, every one of us, either brutishly deluded or preternaturally hypocritical, and they themselves, on the contrary, were in comparison of us absolute specimens of sagacity, wisdom, uprightness, manly virtue, and enlightened Christianity. I am not inquiring why they are not Catholics themselves, but why they are so angry with those who are. Protestants differ amongst themselves, without calling each other fools and knaves. Nor, again, am I proposing to prove to you, or to myself, that knaves and fools we are not, not idolaters, not blasphemers, not men of blood, not profligates, not steeped in sin and seared in conscience;

for we know each other and ourselves. No, my Catholic friends whom I am addressing, I am neither attacking another's belief just now, nor defending myself: I am not engaging in controversy, though controversy is good in its place: I do but propose to investigate how Catholics come to be so trodden under foot, and spurned by a people which is endowed by nature with many great qualities, moral and intellectual; how it is that we are cried out against by the very stones, and bricks, and tiles, and chimney-pots of a populous busy place, such as this town which we inhabit. The clearer sense we have of our own honesty, of the singleness of our motives, and the purity of our aims—of the truth, the beauty, the power of our religion, its exhaustless fund of consolation for the weary, and its especial correspondence to the needs of the weak—so much the greater may well be our perplexity to find that its advocates for the most part do not even gain a hearing in this country; that facts, and logic, and justice, and good sense, and right, and virtue, are all supposed to lie in the opposite scale; and that it is bid be thankful and contented, if it is allowed to exist, if it is barely tolerated, in a free people. Such a state of things is not only a trial to flesh and blood, but a discomfort to the reason and imagination: it is a riddle which frets the mind from the difficulty of solving it.

I.

Now then for my fable, which is not the worse because it is old. The Man once invited the Lion to be his guest, and received him with princely hospitality. The Lion had the run of a magnificent palace, in which there were a vast many things to admire. There were large saloons and long corridors, richly furnished and decorated, and filled with a profusion of fine specimens of sculpture and painting, the works of the first masters in either art. The subjects represented were various; but the most prominent of them had an especial interest for the noble animal who stalked by them. It was that of the Lion himself; and as the owner of the mansion led him from one apartment into another, he did not fail to direct his attention to the indirect homage which these various groups and tableaux paid to the importance of the lion tribe.

There was, however, one remarkable feature in all of them, to which the host, silent as he was from politeness, seemed not at all insensible; that diverse as were these representations, in one point they all agreed, that the man was always victorious, and the lion was always overcome. The man had it all his own way, and the lion was but a fool, and served to make him sport. There were exquisite works in marble, of Samson rending the lion like a kid, and young David taking the lion by the beard and choking him. There was the man who ran his arm down the lion's throat, and held him fast by the tongue; and there was that other who, when carried off in his teeth, contrived to pull a penknife from his pocket, and lodge it in the monster's heart. Then there was a lion hunt, or what had been such, for the brute was rolling round in the agonies of death, and his conqueror on his bleeding horse was surveying these from a distance. There was a gladiator from the Roman amphitheatre in mortal struggle with his tawny foe, and it was plain who was getting the mastery. There was a lion in a net; a lion in a trap; four lions, yoked in harness, were drawing the car of a Roman emperor; and elsewhere stood Hercules, clad in the lion's skin, and with the club which demolished him.

Nor was this all: the lion was not only triumphed over, mocked, spurned; but he was tortured into extravagant forms, as if he were not only the slave and creature, but the very creation of man. He became an artistic decoration, and an heraldic emblazonment. The feet of alabaster tables fell away into lions' paws. Lions' faces grinned on each side the shining mantelpiece; and lions' mouths held tight the handles of the doors. There were sphinxes, too, half lion half woman; there were lions rampant holding flags, lions couchant, lions passant, lions regardant; lions and unicorns; there were lions white, black and red: in short, there was no misconception or excess of indignity which was thought too great for the lord of the forest and the king of brutes. After he had gone over the mansion, his entertainer asked him what he thought of the splendours it contained; and he in reply did full justice to the riches of its owner and the skill of its decorators, but he added, "Lions would have fared better, had lions been the artists."

You see the application, Brothers of the Oratory, before I make it. There are two sides to everything; there is a Catholic side of the argument, and there is a Protestant. There is a story of two knights who met together on opposite sides of a monument: one of them praised the gold on the shield of the warrior sculptured upon it, and the other answered that it was not gold, but silver. On this issue they fought; and in the course of the combat they changed places, and were flung, dismounted and wounded, each upon the ground occupied originally by his foe. Then they discovered that the shield was gold on one side, silver on the other, and that both of them were right, and both were wrong. Now, Catholic and Protestant are not both right and both wrong; there is but one truth, not two truths; and that one truth, we know, is in the Catholic Religion. However, without going on just now to the question where the truth lies (which is a further question not to my present purpose), still it is certain, though truth is one, that arguments are many, and there are always two sides in every dispute—I do not say both of them supported by arguments equally cogent and convincing, of course not; still, there *is* a Protestant side, and there *is* a Catholic side—and if you have heard but one of them, you will think nothing at all can be said on the other. If, then, a person listens only to Protestantism, and does not give fair play to the Catholic reply to it, of course he thinks Protestantism very rational and straightforward, and Catholics very absurd; because he takes for granted the Protestant facts, which are commonly fictions, and opens his mind to Protestant arguments, which are always fallacies. A case may be made out for any one or any thing; the veriest villain at the bar of justice is an injured man, a victim, a hero, in the defence made for him by his counsel. There are writers who dress up vice till it looks like virtue: Goethe, I believe, has invested adultery with a sentimental grace; and Schiller's drama of the "Robbers" is said to have sent the young Germans of his day upon the highway. The same has been reported of Gay's "Beggar's

Opera;" and in our own time a celebrated poet has thrown an interest over Cain, the first murderer. Anything will become plausible, if you read all that can be said in its favour, and exclude all that can be said against it.

Thus it comes to pass that, in a measure, every one (as I may say) has his own sphere of ideas and method of thought, in which he lives, and as to which he differs from every one else; and, unless he be a philosopher, he will be apt to consider his own view of things, his own principles, his own tastes, to be just and right, and to despise others altogether. He despises other men, and other modes of opinion and action, simply because he does not understand them. He is fixed in his own centre, refers everything to it, and never throws himself, perhaps cannot throw himself, into the minds of strangers, or into a state of things not familiar to him. So it is especially between country and country: the Englishman thinks his beef and pudding worth all the resources of the French *cuisine;* and the Frenchman thought for certain, until the peace, that he had gained the battle of Trafalgar. Taking men as they are commonly found, one man is not equal to the task of appreciating the circle of ideas and the atmosphere of thought which is the life of another; and yet he will commonly be forward in criticising and condemning it; condemning it, not as having heard what it has to say for itself, but simply and precisely for the very opposite reason, because he has not.

You know it is a favourite device with writers of fiction to introduce into their composition personages of very different characters taking their respective views of one and the same transaction, or describing and criticising each other; the interest which such an exhibition creates in the reader lying in this, that each of the persons in question is living in his own world, and cannot enter into the world of another, and therefore paints that other in his own way, and presents us with a caricature instead of a likeness, though he does not intend it. I recollect an amusing passage of this kind, out of many which might be cited, in one of Sir Walter Scott's tales,[1] which I hope it is not unbecoming to quote, since it is so much to the purpose.

A middle-aged country gentleman and his wife for a while have the care of a very young lady. The host is very matter-of-fact, and his youthful guest, on the other hand, is very romantic; and the humour of the narrative lies in the very opposite judgments passed respectively on the guest by the host, and on the host by the guest. The elderly man, with whom the shadows and illusions of human existence are over, and who estimates things not by their appearance, but by their weight, writing to the father of his young charge with a good deal of kind feeling towards her, and some good-humoured contempt of her flightiness, tells him that she "has much of a romantic turn" in her disposition, with a "little of the love of admiration;" that "she has a quick and lively imagination, and keen feelings, which are apt to exaggerate both the good and evil they find in life;" that "she is generous and romantic, and writes six sheets a week to a female correspondent." "You know," he says, "how I have jested with her about her soft melancholy, and lonely walks at morning before any one is

[1] Guy Mannering.

up, and in the moonlight, when all should be gone to bed, or set down to cards, which is the same thing." And he ends by speaking with some apprehension and dislike of a place of amusement near his grounds, which is "the resort of walking gentlemen of all descriptions, poets, players, painters, musicians, who come to rave and recite, and madden about this picturesque land of ours. It is paying some penalty for its beauties," he adds, "if they are the means of drawing this swarm of coxcombs together."

On the other hand, the young lady, writing to a school acquaintance of her own age, says, " If India be the land of magic, this is the country of romance. The scenery is such as nature brings together in her sublimest moods ; all the wildness of Salvator here, and there the fairy scenes of Claude. I am at present the inmate of an old friend of my father. He is a different, quite a different being from my father, yet he amuses and endures me. He is fat and good-natured, gifted with strong, shrewd sense, and some powers of humour; and having been handsome, I suppose, in his youth, has still some pretension to be a *beau garçon*, as well as an enthusiastic agriculturist. I delight to make him scramble to the top of eminences, and to the foot of waterfalls ; and am obliged in turn to admire his turnips, his lucerne, and his timothy-grass. He thinks me, I fancy, a simple, romantic miss ; so he rallies, hands, and hobbles (for the dear creature has got the gout too), and tells old stories of high life, of which he has seen a good deal ; and I listen, and smile, and look as pleasant and as simple as I can, and we do very well."

This is but a sample of what meets us in life on

every hand; the young have their own view of things, the old have theirs; high and low, trader and farmer, each has his own, by which he measures everything else, and which is proved to be but a view, and not a reality, because there are so many other views just as good as it is. What is true of individuals is true of nations; however plausible, however distinct, however complete the national view of this or that matter may be, it does not follow that it is not a mere illusion, if it has not been duly measured with other views of the same matter. No conclusion is trustworthy which has not been tried by enemy as well as friend; no traditions have a claim upon us which shrink from criticism, and dare not look a rival in the face. Now this is precisely the weak point of Protestantism in this country. It is jealous of being questioned; it resents argument; it flies to State protection; it is afraid of the sun; it forbids competition. How can you detect the sham, but by comparing it with the true? Your artificial flowers have the softness and brilliancy of nature, till you bring in the living article, fresh from the garden; you detect the counterfeit coin by ringing it with the genuine. So is it in religion. Protestantism is at best but a fine piece of wax-work, which does not look dead, only because it is not confronted by that Church which really breathes and lives. The living Church is the test and the confutation of all false churches; therefore get rid of her at all hazards; tread her down, gag her, dress her like a felon, starve her, bruise her features, if you would keep up your mumbo-jumbo in its place of pride. By no manner of means give her fair play: you dare not. The dazzling brightness of her glance, the sanctity beaming from her countenance, the melody of her voice, the grace of her movements, will be too much for you. Blacken her; make her Cinderella in the ashes; do not hear a word she says. Do not look on her, but daub her in your own way; keep up the good old sign-post representation of her. Let her be a lion rampant, a griffin, a wivern, or a salamander. She shall be red or black; she shall be always absurd, always imbecile, always malicious, always tyrannical. The lion shall not draw the lion, but the man shall draw him. She shall be always worsted in the warfare with Protestantism; ever unhorsed and disarmed, ever running away, ever prostrated, ever smashed and pounded, ever dying, ever dead; and the only wonder is that she has to be killed so often, and the life so often to be trodden out of her, and her priests and doctors to be so often put down, and her monks and nuns to be exposed so often, and such vast sums to be subscribed by Protestants, and such great societies to be kept up, and such millions of tracts to be written, and such persecuting Acts to be passed in Parliament, in order thoroughly, and once for all, and for the very last time, and for ever and ever, to annihilate her once more. However, so it shall be; it is, forsooth, our received policy, as Englishmen, our traditional view of things, to paint up the Pope and Papists in a certain style. We have a school of painting all our own. Every character or personage has its own familiar emblem; Justice has her balance, Hope her anchor, Britannia her trident. Again, history has its conventional properties; Richard the First was the lionhearted, and Richard the Third was the crook-back;

William the First was the Conqueror, and William the Third "the pious, glorious, and immortal." These are our first principles; they are unalterable; like the pillars of heaven, touch them, and you bring our firmament down. True or false is not the question; there they are. So it is with the view we take of Popery; its costume is fixed, like the wigs of our judges, or the mace of our mayors. Have not freeborn Britons a right to think as they please? We rule Popery to be what we say it is, not by history, but by Act of Parliament; not by sight or hearing, but by the national will. It is the will of the Legislature, it is the voice of the people, which gives facts their complexion, and logic its course, and ideas their definition.

2.

Now I repeat, in order to obviate misconception, I am neither assuming, nor intending to prove, that the Catholic Church comes from above (though, of course, I should not have become, or be, one of her children, unless I firmly held and hold her to be the direct work of the Almighty); but here I am only investigating how it is she comes to be so despised and hated among us; since a Religion need not incur scorn and animosity simply because it is not recognized as true. And, I say, the reason is this, that reasons of State, political and national, prevent her from being heard in her defence. She is considered too absurd to be inquired into, and too corrupt to be defended, and too dangerous to be treated with equity and fair dealing. She is the victim of a prejudice which perpetuates itself, and gives birth to what it feeds upon.

I will adduce two or three instances of what I mean. It happens every now and then that a Protestant, sometimes an Englishman, more commonly a foreigner, thinks it worth while to look into the matter himself, and his examination ends, not necessarily in his conversion (though this sometimes happens too), but, at least, in his confessing the absurdity of the outcry raised against the Catholic Church, and the beauty or the excellence, on the other hand, of those very facts and doctrines which are the alleged ground of it. What I propose to do, then, is simply to remind you of the popular feeling concerning two or three of the characteristics of her history and her teaching, and then to set against them the testimony of candid Protestants who have examined into them. This will be no proof that those candid Protestants are right, and the popular feeling wrong (though certainly it is more likely that they should be right who have impartially studied the matter, than those who have nothing whatever to say for their belief but that they have ever been taught it), but, at least, it will make it undeniable, that those who do not know there *are* two sides of the question (that is, the bulk of the English nation), are violent because they are ignorant, and that Catholics are treated with scorn and injustice simply because, though they have a good deal to say in their defence, they have never patiently been heard.

1. For instance, the simple notion of most people is, that Christianity was very pure in its beginning, was very corrupt in the middle age, and is very pure

in England now, though still corrupt everywhere else: that in the middle age, a tyrannical institution, called the Church, arose and swallowed up Christianity; and that that Church is alive still, and has not yet disgorged its prey, except, as aforesaid, in our own favoured country; but in the middle age, there was no Christianity anywhere at all, but all was dark and horrible, as bad as paganism, or rather much worse. No one knew anything about God, or whether there was a God or no, nor about Christ or His atonement; for the Blessed Virgin, and Saints, and the Pope, and images, were worshipped instead; and thus, so far from religion benefiting the generations of mankind who lived in that dreary time, it did them indefinitely more harm than good. Thus, the Homilies of the Church of England say, that "in the pit of damnable idolatry all the world, as it were, drowned, continued until our age" (that is, the Reformation), "by the space of above 800 years ... so that laity and clergy, learned and unlearned, all ages, sects, and degrees of men, women, and children, of whole Christendom (an horrible and most dreadful thing to think), have been at once drowned in abominable idolatry, of all other vices most detested of God, and most damnable to man." Accordingly, it is usual to identify this period with that time of apostasy which is predicted in Scripture, the Pope being the man of sin, and the Church being the mother of abominations, mentioned in the Apocalypse. Thus Bishop Newton says, "In the same proportion as the power of the [Roman] empire decreased, the authority of the Church increased, the latter at the expense and ruin of the former; till at length the Pope grew up above all, and 'the wicked one' was fully manifested and 'revealed,' or the 'lawless one,' as he may be called; for the Pope is declared again and again not to be bound by any law of God or man." "The tyrannical power, thus described by Daniel and St. Paul, and afterwards by St. John, is, both by ancients and moderns, generally denominated Antichrist, and the name is proper and expressive enough, as it may signify both the enemy of Christ, and the vicar of Christ."[2] "The mind of Europe was prostrated at the feet of a priest," says a dissenting writer. "The stoutest hearts quailed at his frown. Seated on the throne of blasphemy, he 'spake great words against the Most High,' and 'thought to change times and laws.' Many hated him, but all stood in awe of his power. Like Simon Magus he 'bewitched the people.' Like Nebuchadnezzar, 'whom he would he slew.'" I need not give you the trouble of listening to more of such language, which you may buy by the yard at the first publisher's shop you fall in with. Thus it is the Man paints the Lion. Go into the first Protestant church or chapel or public meeting which comes in your way, you will hear it from the pulpit or the platform. The Church (who can doubt it?) is a sorceress, intoxicating the nations with a goblet of blood.

However, all are not satisfied to learn by rote what they are to affirm on matters so important, and to feed all their life long on the traditions of the nursery. They examine for themselves, and then forthwith we have another side of the question in dispute. For instance, I say, hear what that eminent Protestant

[2] Dissert. 22.

historian, M. Guizot, who was lately Prime Minister of France, says of the Church in that period, in which she is reported by our popular writers to have been most darkened and corrupted. You will observe (what makes his remarks the stronger) that, being a Protestant, he does not believe the Church really to have been set up by Christ himself, as a Catholic does, but to have taken her present form in the middle age; and he contrasts, in the extract I am about to read, the pure Christianity of primitive times, with that later Christianity, as he considers it, which took an ecclesiastical shape.

"If the Church had not existed," he observes, "I know not what would have occurred during the decline of the Roman Empire. I confine myself to purely human considerations, I cast aside every element foreign to the natural consequence of natural facts, and I say that, if Christianity had only continued, as it was in the early ages,—a belief, a sentiment, an individual conviction,—it is probable it would have fallen amidst the dissolution of the empire, during the invasion of the barbarians. . . . I do not think I say too much when I affirm, that, at the close of the fourth and the commencement of the fifth century, *the Christian Church was the salvation of Christianity.*"[3]

In like manner, Dr. Waddington, the present Protestant Dean of Durham, in his Ecclesiastical History,[4] observes to the same purport: "At this crisis," viz., when the Western Empire was overthrown, and occupied by unbelieving barbarians, "at this crisis it is not too much to assert, that *the Church was the*

[3] Europ. Civ., p. 56, Beckwith. [4] Ch. xiii.

instrument of Heaven for the preservation of the Religion. Christianity itself, unless miraculously sustained, would have been swept away from the surface of the West, had it not been rescued by an established body of ministers, or had that body been less zealous or less influential." And then he goes on to mention six special benefits which the Church of the middle ages conferred on the world; viz., first, she provided for the exercise of charity; secondly, she inculcated the moral duties by means of her penitential discipline; thirdly, she performed the office of legislation in an admirable way; fourthly, she unceasingly strove to correct the vices of the existing social system, setting herself especially against the abomination of slavery; fifthly, she laboured anxiously in the prevention of crime and of war; and lastly, she has preserved to these ages the literature of the ancient world.

Now, without entering into the controversy about idolatry, sorcery, and blasphemy, which concerns matters of *opinion*, are these Protestant testimonies, which relate to matters of *fact*, compatible with such imputations? Can blasphemy and idolatry be the salvation of Christianity? Can sorcery be the promoter of charity, morality, and social improvement? Yet, in spite of the fact of these contrary views of the subject,—in spite of the nursery and schoolroom authors being against us, and the manly and original thinkers being in our favour,—you will hear it commonly spoken of as *notorious*, that the Church in the middle ages was a witch, a liar, a profligate, a seducer, and a bloodthirsty tyrant; and we, who are her faithful children, are superstitious and slavish, because we entertain some love and reverence for her, who, as a certain number of her opponents confess, was then, as she is now, the mother of peace, and humanity and order.

2. So much for the middle ages; next I will take an instance of modern times. If there be any set of men in the whole world who are railed against as the pattern of all that is evil, it is the Jesuit body. It is vain to ask their slanderers what they know of them; did they ever see a Jesuit? can they say whether there are many or few? what do they know of their teaching? "Oh! it is quite *notorious*," they reply: "you might as well deny the sun in heaven; it is notorious that the Jesuits are a crafty, intriguing, unscrupulous, desperate, murderous, and exceedingly able body of men; a secret society, ever plotting against liberty, and government, and progress, and thought, and the prosperity of England. Nay, it is awful; they disguise themselves in a thousand shapes, as men of fashion, farmers, soldiers, labourers, butchers, and pedlars; they prowl about with handsome stocks, and stylish waistcoats, and gold chains about their persons, or in fustian jackets, as the case may be; and they do not hesitate to shed the blood of any one whatever, prince or peasant, who stands in their way." Who can fathom the inanity of such statements?—which are made and therefore, I suppose, believed, not merely by the ignorant, but by educated men, who ought to know better, and will have to answer for their false witness. But all this is persisted in; and it is affirmed that they were found to be too bad even for Catholic countries, the governments of

which, it seems, in the course of the last century, forcibly obliged the Pope to put them down.

Now I conceive that just one good witness, one person who has the means of knowing how things really stand, is worth a tribe of these pamphleteers, and journalists, and novelists, and preachers, and orators. So I will turn to a most impartial witness, and a very competent one ; one who was born of Catholic parents, was educated a Catholic, lived in a Catholic country, was ordained a Catholic priest, and then, renouncing the Catholic religion, and coming to England, became the friend and *protégé* of the most distinguished Protestant Prelates of the present day, and the most bitter enemy of the faith which he had once professed —I mean the late Rev. Joseph Blanco White. Now hear what he says about the Jesuits in Spain, his native country, at the time of their suppression.

"The Jesuits,"[5] he says, "till the abolition of that order, had an almost unrivalled influence over the better classes of Spaniards. They had nearly monopolised the instruction of the Spanish youth, at which they toiled without pecuniary reward, and were equally zealous in promoting devotional feelings both among their pupils and the people at large. . . . . Wherever, as in France and Italy, literature was in high estimation, the Jesuits spared no trouble to raise among themselves men of eminence in that depart-

---

[5] I have omitted some clauses and sentences which either expressed the *opinions* of the author, as distinct from his testimony, or which at least are irrelevant to the matter in hand ; which is simply to show, not what a Protestant can speak *against* (which no one can doubt), but what he can say in *favour* of, this calumniated body : however, to prevent misrepresentation, the entire passage shall be given at the end of the Volume.

ment. In Spain their chief aim was to provide their houses with popular preachers, and zealous, yet prudent and gentle confessors. Pascal, and the Jansenist party, of which he was the organ, accused them of systematic laxity in their moral doctrines; but the charge, I believe, though plausible in theory, was perfectly groundless in practice. . . . . . The influence of the Jesuits on Spanish morals, from everything I have learned, was undoubtedly favourable. Their kindness attracted the youth from their schools to their Company; and . . . . they greatly contributed to the preservation of virtue in that slippery age, both by the ties of affection, and the gentle check of example. Their churches were crowded every Sunday with regular attendants, who came to confess and receive the sacrament. . . . . Their conduct was correct and their manners refined. They kept up a dignified intercourse with the middle and higher classes, and were always ready to help and instruct the poor, without descending to their level. . . . . . Whatever we may think of the political delinquencies of their leaders, their bitterest enemies have never ventured to charge the Order of Jesuits with moral irregularities." Does this answer to the popular notion of a Jesuit? Will Exeter Hall be content with the testimony of one who does not speak from hereditary prejudice, but from actual knowledge? Certainly not; and in consequence it ignores all statements of the kind; they are to be uttered, and they are to be lost; and the received slander is to keep its place as part and parcel of the old stock in trade, and in the number of the heirlooms of Protestantism, the properties of its stage, the family pictures of its old mansion, in the great controversy between the Lion of the tribe of Judah and the children of men.

3. Now I will go back to primitive times, which shall furnish me with a third instance of the subject I am illustrating. Protestants take it for granted, that the history of the monks is a sore point with us; that it is simply one of our difficulties; that it at once puts us on the defensive, and is, in consequence, a brilliant and effective weapon in controversy. They fancy that Catholics can do nothing when monks are mentioned, but evade, explain away, excuse, deny, urge difference of times, and at the utmost make them out not quite so bad as they are reported. They think monks are the very types and emblems of laziness, uselessness, ignorance, stupidity, fanaticism, and profligacy. They think it a paradox to say a word in their favour, and they have converted their name into a title of reproach. As a Jesuit means a knave, so a monk means a bigot. Here, again, things would show very differently, if Catholics had the painting; but I will be content with a Protestant artist, the very learned, and thoughtful, and celebrated German historian, who is lately dead, Dr. Neander. No one can accuse him of any tendencies towards Catholicism; nor does he set about to compose a panegyric. He is a deep-read student, a man of facts, as a German should be; and as a narrator of facts, in his Life of St. Chrysostom, he writes thus:—

"It was by no means intended that the monks should lead a life of listless contemplation; on the contrary, manual labour was enjoined on them as a duty by their rational adherents, by Chrysostom, as well as Augustine, although many fanatical mystics, and advocates of an inactive life" (who, by the way, were not Catholics, but heretics) "rejected, under the cloak of sanctity, all connexion of a laborious with a contemplative life. Cassian relates, that not only the monasteries of Egypt, but that the districts of Libya, when suffering from famine, and also the unfortunate men who languished in the prisons of cities, were supported by the labour of the monks. Augustine relates that the monks of Syria and Egypt were enabled, by their labour and savings, to send ships laden with provisions to distressed districts. The monks of the East were remarkable for their hospitality, although their cells and cloisters were infinitely poorer than those of their more recent brethren of the West. The most rigid monks, who lived only on salt and bread, placed before their guests other food, and at times consented to lay aside their accustomed severity, in order to persuade them to partake of the refreshments which were set before them. A monk on the Euphrates collected together many blind beggars, built dwellings for them, taught them to sing Christian hymns with him, and induced a multitude of men, who sought him from all classes, to contribute to their support.

"Besides the promotion of love and charity, there was another object which induced the lawgivers of monachism to enjoin labour as an especial duty. They wished to keep the passions in subjection, and to maintain a due balance between the spiritual and physical powers of human nature, because the latter, if unemployed and under no control, easily exercise a destructive influence over the former.

"Among the rules of Basil, we find the following decision respecting the trades which formed the occupation of the monks. Those should be preferred, which did not interfere with a peaceable and tranquil life; which occasioned but little trouble in the provision of proper materials for the work, and in the sale of it when completed; which required not much useless or injurious intercourse with men, and did not gratify irrational desires and luxury; while those who followed the trades of weavers and shoemakers were permitted to labour so far as was required by the necessities, but by no means to administer to the vanities of life. Agriculture, the art of building, the trades of a carpenter and a smith, were in themselves good, and not to be rejected; but it was to be feared that they might lead to a loss of repose, and cause the monks to be much separated from each other. Otherwise, agricultural occupation was particularly to be recommended; and it was by agriculture that the monks, at a later period, so much contributed to the civilization of the rude nations of the West.

"The most venerated of the monks were visited by men of every class. A weighty word, one of those pithy sentiments, uttered by some great monk, of which so many have been handed down to us, proceeding from the mouth of a man universally respected, and supported by the impression which his holy life and venerable appearance had created, when spoken at a right moment, oftentimes effected more than the long and repeated harangues of other men. The children were sent to the monks from the cities to receive their blessings; and on these occasions their minds were strewed with the seeds of Christian truth, which took deep root. Thus, Theodoret says of the Monk Peter: 'He often placed me on his knees and fed me with bread and grapes; for my mother, having had experience of his spiritual grace, sent me to him once every week to receive his blessing.'

"The duties of education were particularly recommended to the monks by Basil. They were enjoined to take upon themselves voluntarily the education of orphans; the education of other youths when entrusted to them by their parents. It was by no means necessary that these children should become monks; they were, if fitted for it, early instructed in some trade or art; and were afterwards at liberty to make a free choice of their vocation. The greatest care was bestowed on their religious and moral acquirements. Particular houses were appointed, in which they were to be brought up under the superintendence of one of the oldest and most experienced monks, known for his patience and benignity, that their faults might be corrected with paternal mildness and circumspect wisdom. Instead of the mythical tales, passages out of the Holy Scriptures, the history of the divine miracles, and maxims out of Solomon's Proverbs, were given them to learn by heart, that they might be taught in a manner at the same time instructive and entertaining.

"The monks of the East greatly contributed to the conversion of the heathen, both by their plain, sincere discourse, and by the veneration which their lives inspired: and their simple mode of living rendered it easy for them to establish themselves in any place."

Now, the enemies of monks may call this an *ex parte* statement if they will,—though as coming from a Protestant, one does not see with what justice it can undergo such an imputation. But this is not the point. I am not imposing this view of the Monastic Institute on any one; men may call Neander's representation *ex parte;* they may doubt it, if they will; I only say there *are* evidently two sides to the question, and therefore that the Protestant public, which is quite ignorant of more sides than one, and fancies none but a knave or a fool can doubt the received Protestant tradition on the subject of monks, is, for the very reason of its ignorance, first furiously positive that it is right, and next singularly likely to be wrong.

Audi alteram partem, hear both sides, is generally an Englishman's maxim; but there is one subject on which he has intractable prejudices, and resolutely repudiates any view but that which is familiar to him from his childhood. Rome is his Nazareth; "Can any good come out of Nazareth?" settles the question with him; happy, rather, if he could be brought to imitate the earnest inquirer in the Gospel, who, after urging this objection, went on nevertheless to obey the invitation which it elicited, "Come and see!"

3.

And here I might conclude my subject, which has proposed to itself nothing more than to suggest, to those whom it concerns, that they would have more reason to be confident in their view of the Catholic religion, if it ever had struck them that it needed some proof, if there ever had occurred to their minds at least the possibility of truth being maligned, and Christ being called Beelzebub; but I am tempted, before concluding, to go on to try whether something of a monster indictment, similarly frightful and similarly fantastical to that which is got up against Catholicism, might not be framed against some other institution or power, of parallel greatness and excellence, in its degree and place, to the communion of Rome. For this purpose I will take the British Constitution, which is so specially the possession, and so deservedly the glory, of our own people; and in taking it I need hardly say, I take it for the very reason that it is so rightfully the object of our wonder and veneration. I should be but a fool for my pains, if I laboured to prove it otherwise; it is one of the greatest of human works, as admirable in its own line, to take the productions of genius in very various departments, as the Pyramids, as the wall of China, as the paintings of Raffaelle, as the Apollo Belvidere, as the plays of Shakespeare, as the Newtonian theory, and as the exploits of Napoleon. It soars, in its majesty, far above the opinions of men, and will be a marvel, almost a portent, to the end of time; but for that very reason it is more to my purpose, when I would show you how even it, the British Constitution, would fare, when submitted to the intellect of Exeter Hall, and handled by practitioners, whose highest effort at dissection is to chop and to mangle.

I will suppose, then, a speaker, and an audience too, who never saw England, never saw a member of parliament, a policeman, a queen, or a London mob;

who never read the English history, nor studied any one of our philosophers, jurists, moralists, or poets; but who has dipped into Blackstone and several English writers, and has picked up facts at third or fourth hand, and has got together a crude farrago of ideas, words, and instances, a little-truth, a deal of falsehood, a deal of misrepresentation, a deal of nonsense, and a deal of invention. And most fortunately for my purpose, here is an account transmitted express by the private correspondent of a morning paper, of a great meeting held about a fortnight since at Moscow, under sanction of the Czar, on occasion of an attempt made by one or two Russian noblemen to spread British ideas in his capital. It seems the emperor thought it best, in the present state of men's minds, when secret societies are so rife, to put down the movement by argument rather than by a military force; and so he instructed the governor of Moscow to connive at the project of a great public meeting which should be opened to the small faction of Anglo-maniacs, or John-Bullists, as they are popularly termed, as well as to the mass of the population. As many as ten thousand men, as far as the writer could calculate, were gathered together in one of the largest *places* of the city; a number of spirited and impressive speeches were made, in all of which, however, was illustrated the fable of the "Lion and the Man," the man being the Russ, and the lion our old friend the British; but the most successful of all is said to have been the final harangue, by a member of a junior branch of the Potemkin family, once one of the imperial aides-de-camp, who has spent the last thirty years in the wars of the Caucasus. This distinguished veteran, who has acquired the title of Blood-sucker, from his extraordinary gallantry in combat with the Circassian tribes, spoke at great length ; and the express contains a portion of his highly inflammatory address, of which, and of certain consequences which followed it, the British minister is said already to have asked an explanation of the cabinet of St. Petersburg : I transcribe it as it may be supposed to stand in the morning print :

The Count began by observing that the events of every day, as it came, called on his countrymen more and more importunately to choose their side, and to make a firm stand against a perfidious power, which arrogantly proclaims that there is nothing like the British Constitution in the whole world, and that no country can prosper without it; which is yearly aggrandizing itself in East, West, and South, which is engaged in one enormous conspiracy against all States, and which was even aiming at modifying the old institutions of the North, and at dressing up the army, navy, legislature, and executive of his own country in the livery of Queen Victoria. "Insular in situation," he exclaimed, "and at the back gate of the world, what has John Bull to do with continental matters, or with the political traditions of our holy Russia?" And yet there were men in that very city who were so far the dupes of insidious propagandists and insolent traitors to their emperor, as to maintain that England had been a civilized country longer than Russia. On the contrary, he maintained, and he would shed the last drop of his blood in maintaining, that, as for its boasted Constitution, it was a crazy, old-fashioned piece of furniture, and an eyesore in the nineteenth century, and would not last a dozen years. He had the best information for saying so. He could understand those who had never crossed out of their island, listening to the songs about "Rule Britannia," and "*Rosbif*," and "Poor Jack," and the "Old English Gentleman;" he understood and he pitied them; but that Russians, that the conquerors of Napoleon, that the heirs of a paternal government, should bow the knee, and kiss the hand, and walk backwards, and perform other antics before the face of a limited monarch, this was the incomprehensible foolery which certain Russians had viewed with so much tenderness. He repeated, there were in that city educated men, who had openly professed a reverence for the atheistical tenets and fiendish maxims of John-Bullism.

Here the speaker was interrupted by one or two murmurs of dissent, and a foreigner, supposed to be a partner in a Scotch firm, was observed in the extremity of the square, making earnest attempts to obtain a hearing. He was put down, however, amid enthusiastic cheering, and the Count proceeded with a warmth of feeling which increased the effect of the terrible invective which followed. He said he had used the words "atheistical" and "fiendish" most advisedly, and he would give his reasons for doing so. What was to be said to any political power which claimed the attribute of Divinity? Was any term too strong for such a usurpation? Now, no one would deny Antichrist would be such a power; an Antichrist was contemplated, was predicted in Scripture, it was to come in the last times, it was to grow slowly, it was to manifest itself warily and craftily, and then to have a mouth speaking great things against the Divinity and against His attributes. This prediction was most literally and exactly fulfilled in the British Constitution. Antichrist was not only to usurp, but to profess to usurp the arms of heaven—he was to arrogate its titles. This was the special mark of the beast, and where was it fulfilled but in John-Bullism? "I hold in my hand," continued the speaker, "a book which I have obtained under very remarkable circumstances. It is not known to the British people, it is circulated only among the lawyers, merchants, and aristocracy, and its restrictive use is secured only by the most solemn oaths, the most fearful penalties, and the utmost vigilance of the police. I procured it after many years of anxious search by the activity of an agent, and the co-operation of an English bookseller, and it cost me an enormous sum to make it my own. It is called 'Blackstone's Commentaries on the Laws of England,' and I am happy to make known to the universe its odious and shocking mysteries, known to few Britons, and certainly not known to the deluded persons whose vagaries have been the occasion of this meeting. I am sanguine in thinking that when they come to know the real tenets of John Bull, they will at once disown his doctrines with horror, and break off all connexion with his adherents.

"Now, I should say, gentlemen, that this book, while it is confined to certain classes, is of those classes, on the other hand, of judges, and lawyers, and privy councillors, and justices of the peace, and police magistrates, and clergy, and country gentlemen, the guide, and I may say, the gospel. I open the book, gentlemen, and what are the first words which meet my eyes? '*The King can do no wrong.*' I beg you to attend, gentlemen, to this most significant assertion; one was accustomed to think that no child of man had the gift of impeccability; one had imagined that, simply speaking, impeccability was a divine attribute; but this British Bible, as I may call it, distinctly ascribes an absolute sinlessness to the King of Great Britain and Ireland. Observe, I am using no words of my own, I am still but quoting what meets my eyes in this remarkable document. The words run thus: 'It is an axiom of the law of the land that the *King himself can do no wrong.*' Was I wrong, then, in speaking of the atheistical maxims of John Bullism? But this is far from all: the writer goes on actually to ascribe to the Sovereign (I tremble while I pronounce the words) *absolute perfection;* for he speaks thus: 'The law ascribes to the King in his political capacity ABSOLUTE PERFECTION ; the *King can do no wrong!*'—(groans). One had thought that no human power could thus be described; but the British legislature, judicature, and jurisprudence, have had the unspeakable effrontery to impute to their crowned and sceptred idol, to their doll,"—here cries of "shame, shame," from the same individual who had distinguished himself in an earlier part of the speech—"to this doll, this puppet whom they have dressed up with a lion and a unicorn, the attribute of ABSOLUTE PERFECTION!" Here the individual who had several times interrupted the speaker sprung up, in spite of the efforts of persons about him to keep him down, and cried out, as far as his words could be collected, "You cowardly liar, our dear good little Queen," when he was immediately saluted with a cry of "Turn him out," and soon made his exit from the meeting.

Order being restored, the Count continued: "Gentlemen, I could wish you would have suffered this emissary of a foreign potentate (immense cheering), who is insidiously aiming at forming a political party among us, to have heard to the end that black catalogue of charges against his Sovereign, which as yet I have barely commenced. Gentlemen, I was saying that the Queen of England challenges the divine attribute of ABSOLUTE PERFECTION! but, as if this were not enough this Blackstone continues, 'The King, moreover, is not only incapable of *doing* wrong, but even of *thinking* wrong!! *he can never do an improper thing; in him is no* FOLLY *or* WEAKNESS!!!'" (Shudders and cheers from the vast assemblage, which lasted alternately some minutes.) At the same time a respectably dressed gentleman below the platform begged permission to look at the book; it was immediately handed to him; after looking at the passages, he was observed to inspect carefully the title-page and binding; he then returned it without a word.

The Count, in resuming his speech, observed that he courted and challenged investigation, he should be happy to answer any question, and he hoped soon to publish, by subscription, a translation of the work, from which he had been quoting. Then, resuming the subject where he had left it, he made some most forcible and impressive reflections on the miserable state of those multitudes, who, in spite of their skill in the mechanical arts, and their political energy, were in the leading-strings of so foul a superstition. The passage he had quoted was the first and mildest of a series of blasphemies so prodigious, that he really feared to proceed, not only from disgust at the necessity of uttering them, but lest he should be taxing the faith of his hearers beyond what appeared reasonable limits. Next, then, he drew attention to the point that the English Sovereign distinctly claimed, according to the same infamous work, to be the "*fount* of justice;" and, that there might be no mistake in the matter, the author declared, "that she *is never bound in justice to do anything.*" What, then, is her method of acting? Unwilling as he was to defile his lips with so profane a statement, he must tell them that this abominable writer coolly declared that the Queen, a woman, only did acts of reparation and restitution as a matter of *grace!* He was not a theologian, he had spent his life in the field, but he knew enough of his religion to be able to say that grace was a word especially proper to the appointment and decrees of Divine Sovereignty. All his hearers knew perfectly well that nature was one thing, grace another; and yet here was a poor child of clay claiming to be the fount, not only of justice, but of grace. She was making herself a first cause of not merely natural, but spiritual excellence, and doing nothing more or less than simply emancipating herself from her Maker. The Queen, it seemed, never obeyed the law on compulsion, according to Blackstone; that is, her Maker could not compel her. This was no mere deduction of his own, as directly would be seen. Let it be observed, the Apostle called the predicted **Antichrist** "the wicked one," or, as it might be more correctly translated, "the lawless," because he was to be the proud despiser of all law; now, wonderful to say, this was the very assumption of the British Parliament. "The Power of Parliament," said Sir Edward Coke, "is so transcendent and absolute, that it cannot be *confined* within any bounds!! It has sovereign and uncontrollable authority!!" Moreover, the Judges had declared that "it is so high and mighty in its nature, that it *may make law*, and THAT WHICH IS LAW IT MAY MAKE NO LAW!" Here verily was the mouth speaking great things; but there was more behind, which, but for the atrocious sentiments he had already admitted into his mouth, he really should not have the courage, the endurance to utter. It was sickening to the soul, and intellect, and feelings of a Russ, to form the words on his tongue, and the ideas in his imagination. He would say what must be said as quickly as he could, and without comment. The gallant speaker then delivered the following passage from Blackstone's volume, in a very distinct and articulate whisper: "Some have not scrupled to call its power—the OMNIPOTENCE of Parliament!" No one can conceive the thrilling effect of these words; they were heard all over the immense assemblage; every man turned pale; a dead silence followed; one might have heard a pin drop. A pause of some minutes followed.

The speaker continued, evidently labouring under intense emotion :—" Have you not heard enough, my dear compatriots, of this hideous system of John-Bullism? was I wrong in using the words fiendish and atheistical when I entered upon this subject? and need I proceed further with blasphemous details, which cannot really add to the monstrous bearing of the passages I have already read to you? If the Queen 'cannot do wrong,' if she 'cannot even think wrong,' if she is 'absolute perfection,' if she has 'no folly, no weakness,' if she is the 'fount of justice,' if she is 'the fount of grace,' if she is simply 'above law,' if she is 'omnipotent,' what wonder that the lawyers of John-Bullism should also call her 'sacred!' what wonder that they should speak of her as 'majesty!' what wonder that they should speak of her as a 'superior being!' Here again I am using the words of the book I hold in my hand. 'The people' (my blood runs cold while I repeat them) 'are led to consider their Sovereign *in the light of a* SUPERIOR BEING.' 'Every one is under him,' says Bracton, 'and he is under no one.' Accordingly, the lawbooks call him 'Vicarius Dei in terrâ,' 'the Vicar of God on earth;' a most astonishing fulfilment, you observe, of the prophecy, for Antichrist is a Greek word, which means 'Vicar of Christ.' What wonder, under these circumstances, that Queen Elizabeth, assuming the attribute of the Creator, once said to one of her Bishops: 'Proud Prelate, *I made you, and I can unmake you!*' What wonder that James the First had the brazen assurance to say, that 'As it is atheism and blasphemy in a creature to dispute the Deity, so it is presumption and sedition in a subject to dispute a King in the height of his power!' Moreover, his subjects called him the 'breath of their nostrils;' and my Lord Clarendon, the present Lord Lieutenant of Ireland, in his celebrated History of the Rebellion, declares that the same haughty monarch actually on one occasion called himself 'a god;' and in his great legal digest, commonly called the 'Constitutions of Clarendon,' he gives us the whole account of the King's banishing the Archbishop, St. Thomas of Canterbury, for refusing to do him homage. Lord Bacon, too, went nearly as far when he called him 'Deaster quidam,' 'some sort of little god.' Alexander Pope, too, calls Queen Anne a goddess: and Addison, with a servility only equalled by his profaneness, cries out, "Thee goddess, thee Britannia's isle adores.' Nay, even at this very time, when public attention has been drawn to the subject, Queen Victoria causes herself to be represented on her coins as the goddess of the seas, with a pagan trident in her hand.

"Gentlemen, can it surprise you to be told, after such an exposition of the blasphemies of England, that, astonishing to say, Queen Victoria is distinctly pointed out in the Book of Revelation as having the number of the beast! You may recollect that number is 666; now, she came to the throne in the year thirty-seven, at which date she was eighteen years old. Multiply then 37 by 18, and you have the very number 666, which is the mystical emblem of the lawless King!!!

"No wonder then, with such monstrous pretensions, and such awful auguries, that John-Bullism is, in act and deed, as savage and profligate, as in profession it is saintly and innocent. Its annals are marked with blood and corruption. The historian Hallam, though one of the ultra-bullist party, in his Constitutional History, admits that the English tribunals are 'disgraced by the brutal manners and iniquitous partiality of the bench.' 'The general behaviour of the bench,' he says elsewhere, 'has covered it with infamy.' Soon after, he tells us that the dominant faction inflicted on the High Church Clergy 'the disgrace and remorse of perjury.' The English Kings have been the curse and shame of human nature. Richard the First boasted that the evil spirit was the father of his family; of Henry the Second St. Bernard said, 'From the devil he came, and to the devil he will go;' William the Second was killed by the enemy of man, to whom he had sold himself, while hunting in one of his forests; Henry the First died of eating lampreys; John died of eating peaches; Clarence, a king's brother, was drowned in a butt of malmsey wine; Richard the Third put to death his Sovereign, his Sovereign's son, his two brothers, his wife, two nephews, and half-a-dozen friends. Henry the Eighth successively married and murdered no less than six hundred women. I quote the words of the 'Edinburgh Review,' that, according to Hollinshed, no less than 70,000 persons died under the hand of the executioner in his reign. Sir John Fortescue tells us that in his day there were more persons executed for robbery in England in one year, than in France in seven. Four hundred persons a year were executed in the reign of Queen Elizabeth. Even so late as the last century, in spite of the continued protests of foreign nations, in the course of seven years there were 428 capital convictions in London alone. Burning of children, too, is a favourite punishment with John Bull, as may be seen in this same Blackstone, who notices the burning of a girl of thirteen given by Sir

Matthew Hale. The valets always assassinate their masters; lovers uniformly strangle their sweethearts; the farmers and the farmers' wives universally beat their apprentices to death; and their lawyers in the inns of court strip and starve their servants, as has appeared from remarkable investigations in the law courts during the last year. Husbands sell their wives by public auction with a rope round their necks. An intelligent Frenchman, M. Pellet, who visited London in 1815, deposes that he saw a number of sculls on each side of the river Thames, and he was told they were found especially thick at the landing-places among the watermen. But why multiply instances, when the names of those two-legged tigers, Rush, Thistlewood, Thurtell, the Mannings, Colonel Kirk, Claverhouse, Simon de Monteforte, Strafford, the Duke of Cumberland, Warren Hastings, and Judge Jeffreys, are household words all over the earth? John-Bullism, through a space of 800 years, is *semper idem*, unchangeable in evil. One hundred and sixty offences are punishable with death. It is death to live with gipsies for a month; and Lord Hale mentions thirteen persons as having, in his day, suffered death thereon at one assize. It is death to steal a sheep, death to rob a warren, death to steal a letter, death to steal a handkerchief, death to cut down a cherry-tree. And, after all, the excesses of John-Bullism at home are mere child's play to the oceans of blood it has shed abroad. It has been the origin of all the wars which have desolated Europe; it has fomented national jealousy, and the antipathy of castes in every part of the world; it has plunged flourishing states into the abyss of revolution.

The Crusades, the Sicilian Vespers, the wars of the Reformation, the Thirty Years' War, the War of Succession, the Seven Years' War, the American War, the French Revolution, all are simply owing to John-Bull ideas; and, to take one definite instance, in the course of the last war, the deaths of two millions of the human race lie at his door; for the Whigs themselves, from first to last, and down to this day, admit and proclaim, without any hesitation or limitation, that that war was simply and entirely the work of John-Bullism, and needed not, and would not have been, but for its influence, and its alone.

"Such is that 'absolute perfection, without folly and without weakness,' which, revelling in the blood of man, is still seeking out her victims, and scenting blood all over the earth. It is that woman Jezebel, who fulfils the prophetic vision, and incurs the prophetic denunciation. And, strange to say, a prophet of her own has not scrupled to apply to her that very appellation. Dead to good and evil, the children of Jezebel glory in the name; and ten years have not passed since, by a sort of infatuation, one of the very highest Tories in the land, a minister, too, of the established religion, hailed the blood-stained Monarchy under the very title of the mystical sorceress. Jezebel surely is her name, and Jezebel is her nature; for drunk with the spiritual wine-cup of wrath, and given over to believe a lie, at length she has ascended to heights which savour rather of madness than of pride; she babbles absurdities, and she thirsts for impossibilities. Gentlemen, I am speaking the words of sober seriousness; I can prove what I say to the letter; the extravagance is not in me but in the object of my denunciation. Once more I appeal to the awful volume I hold in my hands. I appeal to it, I open it, I cast it from me. Listen, then, once again; it is a fact; Jezebel has declared her own *omnipresence*. 'A consequence of the royal prerogatives,' says the antichristian author, 'is the legal UBIQUITY of the King!' 'His Majesty is *always present* in all his courts: his judges are the *mirror* by which the King's image is reflected;' and further, 'From this *ubiquity*' (you see he is far from shrinking from the word), 'from this *ubiquity* it follows that the Sovereign can never be NONSUIT!!' Gentlemen, the sun would set before I told you one hundredth part of the enormity of this child of Moloch and Belial. Inebriated with the cup of insanity, and flung upon the stream of recklessness, she dashes down the cataract of nonsense, and whirls amid the pools of confusion. Like the Roman emperor, she actually has declared herself immortal! she has declared her eternity! Again, I am obliged to say it, these are no words of mine; the tremendous sentiment confronts me in black and crimson characters in this diabolical book. 'In the law,' says Blackstone, 'the Sovereign is said *never to die!*' Again, with still more hideous expressiveness, 'The law ascribes to the Sovereign an ABSOLUTE IMMORTALITY. THE KING NEVER DIES.'

"And now, gentlemen, your destiny is in your own hands. If you are willing to succumb to a power which has never been contented with what she was, but has been for centuries extending her conquests in both hemispheres, then the humble individual who has addressed you will submit to the necessary con-

sequence; will resume his military dress, and return to the Caucasus; but if, on the other hand, as I believe, you are resolved to resist unflinchingly this flood of satanical imposture and foul ambition, and force it back into the ocean; if, not from hatred to the English—far from it—from *love* to them (for a distinction must ever be drawn between the nation and its dominant John-Bullism); if, I say, from love to them as brothers, from a generous determination to fight their battles, from an intimate consciousness that they are in their secret hearts *Russians*, that they are champing the bit of their iron lot, and are longing for you as their deliverers; if, from these lofty notions as well as from a burning patriotism, you will form the high resolve to annihilate this dishonour of humanity; if you loathe its sophisms, ' De minimis non curat lex,' and ' Malitia supplet ætatem,' and ' Tres faciunt collegium,' and ' Impotentia excusat legem,' and ' Possession is nine parts of the law,' and ' The greater the truth, the greater the libel'—principles which sap the very foundations of morals; if you wage war to the knife with its blighting superstitions of primogeniture, gavelkind, mortmain, and contingent remainders; if you detest, abhor, and abjure the tortuous maxims and perfidious provisions of its *habeas corpus, quare impedit,* and *qui tam* (hear, hear); if you scorn the mummeries of its wigs, and bands, and coifs, and ermine (vehement cheering); if you trample and spit upon its accursed fee simple and fee tail, villanage, and free soccage, fiefs, heriots, seizins, feuds (a burst of cheers, the whole meeting in commotion); its shares, its premiums, its post-obits, its percentages, its tariffs, its broad and narrow gauge"
—Here the cheers became frantic, and drowned the

speaker's voice, and a most extraordinary scene of enthusiasm followed. One half of the meeting was seen embracing the other half; till, as if by the force of a sudden resolution, they all poured out of the square, and proceeded to break the windows of all the British residents. They then formed into procession, and directing their course to the great square before the Kremlin, they dragged through the mud, and then solemnly burnt, an effigy of John Bull which had been provided beforehand by the managing committee, a lion and unicorn, and a Queen Victoria. These being fully consumed, they dispersed quietly; and by ten o'clock at night the streets were profoundly still, and the silver moon looked down in untroubled lustre on the city of the Czars.

Now, my Brothers of the Oratory, I protest to you my full conviction that I have not caricatured this parallel at all. Were I, indeed, skilled in legal matters, I could have made it far more natural, plausible, and complete; but, as for its extravagance, I say deliberately, and have means of knowing what I say, having once been a Protestant, and being now a Catholic—knowing what is said and thought of Catholics, on the one hand, and, on the other, knowing what they really *are*—I deliberately assert that no absurdities contained in the above sketch can equal—nay, that no conceivable absurdities can surpass—the absurdities which are firmly believed of Catholics by sensible, kind-hearted, well-intentioned Protestants. Such is the consequence of having looked at things all on one side, and shutting the eyes to the other.

LECTURE II.

TRADITION THE SUSTAINING POWER OF THE PROTESTANT VIEW.

CONSIDERING, what is as undeniable a fact as that there is a country called France, or an ocean called the Atlantic, the actual extent, the renown, and the manifold influence of the Catholic Religion—considering that it surpasses in territory and in population any other Christian communion, nay, surpasses all others put together,—considering that it is the religion of two hundred millions of souls, that it is found in every quarter of the globe, that it penetrates into all classes of the social body, that it is received by entire nations, that it is so multiform in its institutions, and so exuberant in its developments, and so fresh in its resources, as any tolerable knowledge of it will be sure to bring home to our minds,—that it has been the creed of intellects the most profound and the most refined, and the source of works the most beneficial, the most arduous, and the most beautiful, —and, moreover, considering that, thus ubiquitous, thus commanding, thus philosophical, thus energetic, thus efficient, it has remained one and the same for centuries,—considering that all this must be owned by its most virulent enemies, explain it how they will;

surely it is a phenomenon the most astounding, that a nation like our own should so manage to hide this fact from their minds, to intercept their own vision of it, as habitually to scorn, and ridicule, and abhor the professors of that Religion, as being, from the nature of the case, ignorant, unreasoning, superstitious, base, and grovelling. It is familiar to an Englishman to wonder at and to pity the recluse and the devotee who surround themselves with a high enclosure, and shut out what is on the other side of it; but was there ever such an instance of self-sufficient, dense, and ridiculous bigotry, as that which rises up and walls in the minds of our fellow-countrymen from all knowledge of one of the most remarkable phenomena which the history of the world has seen? This broad fact of Catholicism—as real as the continent of America, or the Milky Way—which Englishmen cannot deny, they will not entertain; they shut their eyes, they thrust their heads into the sand, and try to get rid of a great vision, a great reality, under the name of Popery. They drop a thousand years from the world's chronicle, and having steeped them thoroughly in sin and idolatry would fain drown them in oblivion. Whether for philosophic remark or for historical research, they will not recognise what infidels recognise as well as Catholics—the vastness, the grandeur, the splendour, the loveliness of the manifestations of this time-honoured ecclesiastical confederation. Catholicism is for fifteen hundred years as much a fact, and as great a one (to put it on the lowest ground) as is the imperial sway of Great Britain for a hundred; how can it then be actually imbecile or extravagant to believe in it and to join it, even granting it were an error? But this island, as far as religion is concerned, really must be called, one large convent, or rather workhouse; the old pictures hang on the walls; the world-wide Church is chalked up on every side as a wivern or a griffin; no pure gleam of light finds its way in from without; the thick atmosphere refracts and distorts such straggling rays as gain admittance. Why, it is not even a *camera obscura;* cut off from Christendom though it be, at least it might have a true picture of that Christendom cast in miniature upon its floor; but in this inquisitive age, when the Alps are crested, and seas fathomed, and mines ransacked, and sands sifted, and rocks cracked into specimens, and beasts caught and catalogued, as little is known by Englishmen of the religious sentiments, the religious usages, the religious motives, the religious ideas of two hundred millions of Christians poured to and fro, among them and around them, as if, I will not say, they were Tartars or Patagonians, but as if they inhabited the moon. Verily, were the Catholic Church in the moon, England would gaze on her with more patience, and delineate her with more accuracy, than England does now.

This phenomenon is what I in part brought before you in my last Lecture: I said we were thought dupes and rogues, because we were not known: because our countrymen would not be at the pains, or could not stand the shock of realizing that there are two sides to every question, and that in this particular question, perhaps, they had taken the false side. And this evening I am proceeding to the inquiry *how* in a century of light, where we have re-written our grammars and revolutionized our chronology, all this can possibly come to pass; how it is that the old family picture of the Man and the Lion keeps its place, though all the rest of John Bull's furniture has been condemned and has been replaced. Alas! that he should be inspecting the silks and the china, and the jewellery of East and West, but refuse to bestow a like impartial examination on the various forms of Christianity!

I.

Now, if I must give the main and proximate cause of this remarkable state of mind, I must simply say that Englishmen go by that very mode of information in its worst shape, which they are so fond of imputing against Catholics; they go by *tradition*, immemorial, unauthenticated *tradition*. I have no wish to make a rhetorical point, or to dress up a polemical argument. I wish you to investigate the matter philosophically, and to come to results which, not you only, Brothers of the Oratory, who are Catholics, but all sensible men, will perceive to be just and true. I say, then, Englishmen entertain their present monstrous notions of us, mainly because those notions are received on information not authenticated, but immemorial. This it is that makes them entertain those notions; they talk much of free inquiry; but towards us they do not dream of practising it; they have been taught what they hold in the nursery, in the school-room, in the lecture-class, from the pulpit, from the newspaper, in society. Each man teaches the other: "How do *you* know it?" "Because *he* told me." "And how does *he* know it?" "Because *I* told *him*;" or, at very best advantage, "We both know it, because it was so said when we were young; because no one ever said the contrary; because I recollect what a noise, when I was young, the Catholic Relief Bill made; because my father and the old clergyman said so, and Lord Eldon, and George the Third; and there was Mr. Pitt obliged to give up office, and Lord George Gordon, long before that, made a riot, and the Catholic Chapels were burnt down all over the country." Well, these are your grounds for knowing it; and how did these energetic Protestants whom you have mentioned know it themselves? Why, they were told by others before them, and those others by others again a great time back; and there the telling and teaching is lost in fog; and this is mainly what has to be said for the anti-Catholic notions in question. Now this is to believe on *tradition*.

Take notice, my Brothers, I am not reprobating the proper use of tradition; it has its legitimate place and its true service. By tradition is meant, what has ever been held, as far as we know, though we do not know how it came to be held, and for that very reason think it true, because else it would not be held. Now, tradition is of great and legitimate use as an *initial* means of gaining notions about historical and other facts; it is the way in which things first come to us; it is natural and necessary to trust it; it is an informant we make use of daily. Life is not long enough for proving everything; we are obliged to take a great many things upon the credit of others. Moreover, tradition is really a ground in reason, an argument for believing, to a certain point; but then observe, we do not commonly think it right and safe, on the score of mere vague testimony, to keep our eyes and ears so very closely shut against every other evidence, every other means of proof, and to be so furiously certain and so energetically positive that we know all about the matter in question. No; we open our senses wide to what may be said on the other side. We make use of tradition, but we are not content with it; it is enough to begin with, not enough to finish upon.

Tradition, then, being information, not authenticated, but immemorial, is a *prima-facie* evidence of the facts which it witnesses. It is sufficient to make us take a thing for granted, in default of real proof; it is sufficient for our having an *opinion* about it; it is sufficient often to make us feel it to be *safest* to act in a certain way under circumstances; it is *not* sufficient in reason to make us *sure*, much less to make us angry with those who take a different view of the matter. It is not sufficient to warrant us to dispense with proof the other way, if it be offered to us. Supposing, for instance, there was a general belief or impression in England, running up beyond the memory of man, though unsupported by any distinct evidence, that the composer Tallis was the author of the Protestant Hundredth Psalm tune, or that Charles the Second was poisoned, or that Bishop Butler of Durham died a Catholic, I consider we certainly should have acquiesced in the tradition, taken it for granted, and made it our own, as long as it was our only means of forming an opinion on the respective points in question. We should have thought the fact to be such, while there was nothing to set against it. Nor would any other course have been reasonable. But, supposing, in contravention of these traditions, a manuscript of the Psalm tune in question was found in some German library, in the handwriting of Luther; or supposing a statement existed purporting to be drawn up by Charles's medical attendants, accounting for his death, and attributing it, with all appearance of truth, to some natural complaint; or, again, supposing his death was imputed to a very unlikely person, Bishop Ken, or Mr. Evelyn; or supposing Butler's chaplain had left an account of Butler's last hours, from which it was demonstrable that up to the last day of his life he was a Protestant; should we passionately reject, or superciliously make light of this separate evidence, because we were content with our tradition? or, if we were tempted to do so, could we possibly defend our conduct in reason, or recommend it to another? Surely, it would be as extravagant to refuse the presumptions or the evidence offered us in the second place, as to refuse the tradition in the first. Thus, a tradition being an anonymous informant, is of force only under the proviso that it cannot be plausibly disputed.

I am speaking of a single or solitary tradition; for if there be two or three distinct traditions, all saying the same thing, then it is a very different matter; then, as in the case of two or three independent witnesses in a judicial proceeding, there is at once a cumulation of evidence, and its joint effect is very great. Thus, supposing, besides the current belief in England, there was a local tradition, in some out of the way district in Ireland, to the effect that a certain family had gained its estates in reward for the share which its ancestor had in the assassination of Charles the Second, we should certainly consider it at least a singular coincidence; for it would be a second tradition, and if proved to be distinct and independent, would quite alter the influence of the first upon our minds, just as two witnesses at a trial produce an effect on judge and jury simply different from what either of them would produce by himself. And in this way a multiplication of traditions may make a wonderfully strong proof, strong enough even for a person to die for, rather than consent to deny the fact attested; and, therefore, strong enough in reason for him to be very positive upon, very much excited, very angry, and very determined. But when such strong feeling and pertinacity of purpose are created by a mere single and solitary tradition, I cannot call that state of mind conviction, but prejudice.

Yet this, I must maintain, is the sort of ground on which Protestants are so certain that the Catholic Church is a simple monster of iniquity. If you asked the first person you met why he believed that our religion was so baneful and odious, he would not say, "I have had good proofs of it;" or, "I *know Catholics* too well to doubt it;" or, "I am *well read in history*, and I can vouch for it;" or, "I have lived such a long time in *Catholic countries*, I ought to know;"—(of course, I do not mean that no one would make such a reply, but I mean that it would not be the reply of the mass of men; far from it). No; single out a man from the multitude, and he would say something of this sort: "I am *sure* it is;" he will look significant, and say, "You will find it a hard job to make me think otherwise;" or he will look wise and say, "I can make a pretty good guess how things go on among you;" or he will be angry, and cry out, "Those fellows, the priests, I would not believe them, though they swore themselves black in the face;" or he will speak loudly, and overbear and drown all remonstrance: "It is too notorious for proof; every one knows it; every book says it; it has been so ruled long ago. It is rather too much in the nineteenth century to be told to begin history again, and to have to reverse our elementary facts." That is, in other words, the multitude of men hate Catholicism mainly on tradition, there being few, indeed, who have made fact and argument the primary or the supplemental grounds of their aversion to it. And observe, they hate it on a single, isolated tradition, not a complex, conclusive tradition—not the united tradition of many places. It is true, indeed, that Holland, and Geneva, and Prussia, each has its own tradition against the Catholic Church; but our countrymen do in no sense believe, from any judgment they form on those united British and foreign traditions, but from the tradition of their own nation alone; which, though certainly it comprises millions of souls, nevertheless, is so intimately one by the continual intercourse and mutual communication of part with part, that it cannot with any fairness be considered to contain a number of separate testimonies, but only one. Yet this meagre evidence, I say, suffices to produce in the men of this generation an enthusiastic, undoubting and energetic persuasion that we torture heretics, immure nuns, sell licences to sin, and are plotting against kings and governments; all, I say, because this was said of Catholics when they were boys. It is the old heirloom, the family picture, which is at once their informant and their proof.

Nor is this phenomenon, remarkable as it is, without its parallel in former passages of the world's history. We have a notable instance in Holy Writ; to which I hope I may allude without risking a theological discussion. We read there of certain parties animated with extreme religious bitterness, simply on the incentive, and for the defence, of traditions which were absolutely worthless. The popular party in Judea, at the Christian era, were the dupes of a teaching, professing, indeed, the authority of their forefathers, or what they called "the tradition of the ancients;" but, in reality, nothing more or less than the "commandment and tradition of men;" of fallible men, nay, not only deceivable, but actually deceived men. This was the fatal flaw in their argument; the tradition might have been kept ever so accurately and religiously, it might with full certainty have been derived from the foregoing generation, and have existed beyond the furthest memory; but this proved nothing while it was traceable up to *man*, not to a divine informant, as its ultimate resolution or first origin. The stream cannot rise higher than its source; if the wellspring of the tradition be human, not divine, what profits its fidelity? Such as is the primary authority, so will be the continuous, the latest derivation. And this, accordingly, was the judgment pronounced in the instance to which I have alluded, on both the doctrine and its upholders. "In vain do they worship Me, teaching doctrines and commandments of *men*." As is the origin, so is the tradition; when the origin is true, the tradition will be true;

when the origin is false, the tradition will be false. There can most surely be true traditions, that is traditions from true sources; but such traditions though they really be true, do not profess to prove themselves; they come accompanied by other arguments; the true traditions of Divine Revelation are proved to be true by miracle, by prophecy, by the test of cumulative and collateral evidences, which directly warrant and verify them. Such were not the traditions of the Pharisee—they professed to speak for themselves, they bore witness to themselves they were their own evidence; and, as might have been expected, they were not trustworthy—they were mere frauds; they came, indeed, down the stream of time, but that was no recommendation, it only put the fraud up higher; it might make it venerable, it could not make it true.

Yet it is remarkable, I say, how positive and fanatical the Jewish people was in its maintenance of these lies. It was irritated, nay maddened, at hearing them denounced; rose up fiercely against their denouncers; and thought they did God service in putting them to death. It is plain, then, that a popular feeling is not necessarily logical because it is strong.

Now, of course, a great number of persons will not easily allow the fact, that the English animosity against Catholicism is founded on nothing more argumentative than tradition; but, whether I shall succeed in proving this point or not, I think I have at least shown already that tradition is, in itself, quite a *sufficient* explanation of the feeling. I am not assigning a trifling and inadequate cause to so great an effect. If the Jews could be induced to put to death the Founder of our Religion and His disciples on tradition, there is nothing ridiculous in saying that the British scorn and hatred of Catholicism may be created by tradition also. The great question is, the matter of fact, *is* tradition the cause? I say it is, and in saying so, observe, I am speaking of the multitude, not dwelling on exceptions, however numerous in themselves; for doubtless there is a certain number of men, men of thought and reading, who oppose Catholicism, not merely on tradition, but on better arguments; but, I repeat, I am speaking of the great mass of Protestants. Again, bear in mind, I am speaking of what really *is* the fact, not of what the mass of Protestants will *confess*. Of course, no man will admit, if he can help it, even to himself, that he is taking his views of the Catholic Church from Bishop Newton, or buckling on his sword against her preachers, merely because Lord George Gordon did the like; on the contrary, he will perhaps sharply retort, "I never heard of Bishop Newton or of Lord George Gordon—I don't know their names;" but the simple question which we have to determine is the real matter of fact, and not whether the persons who are the subjects of our investigation will themselves admit it. To this point then, viz., the matter of fact —*Do* Protestants go by tradition? on which I have said something already, I shall now proceed to direct your attention.

How, then, stands the matter of fact? Do the people of this country receive their notion of the Catholic Church in the way of argument and examination, as they would decide in favour of railroads over other modes of conveyance, or on plans of parish relief, or police regulations, and the like? or does it come to them mainly as a tradition which they have inherited, and which they will not question, though they have in their hands abundant reasons for questioning it? I answer, without a doubt, it comes to them as a tradition; the fact is patent and palpable: the tradition is before our eyes, unmistakable; it is huge, vast, various, engrossing; it has a monopoly of the English mind, it brooks no rival, and it takes summary measures with rebellion.

2.

When King Henry began a new religion, when Elizabeth brought it into shape, when her successors completed and confirmed it, they were all of them too wise, and too much in earnest, not to clench their work. They provided for its continuance after them. They, or at least the influences which ruled them, knew well enough that Protestantism, left to itself, could not stand. It had not that internal consistency in its make, which would support it against outward foes, or secure it against internal disorders. And the event has justified their foresight; whether you look at Lutheranism or Calvinism, you find neither of those forms of religion has been able to resist the action of thought and reason upon it during a course of years; both have changed and come to nought. Luther began his religion in Germany, Calvin in Geneva; Calvinism is now all but extinct in Geneva, and Lutheranism in Germany. It could not be otherwise; such an issue was predicted by Catholics as well as instinctively felt by the Reformers, at the time that Protestantism started. Give it rope enough, and any one could prophesy its end, so its patrons determined that rope it should not have, but that private judgment should come to a close with their own use of it. There was enough of private judgment in the world, they thought, when they had done with it themselves. So they forcibly shut-to the door which they had opened, and imposed on the populations they had reformed an artificial tradition of their own, instead of the liberty of inquiry and disputation. They worked their own particular persuasion into the political framework of things, and made it a constitutional or national principle; in other words, they established it.

Now, you may say that Catholicism has often been established also. True, but Catholicism does not *depend* on its establishment for its existence, nor does its tradition live upon its establishment; it can do without establishment, and often dispenses with it to an advantage. A Catholic nation, as a matter of course, establishes Catholicism because it *is* a Catholic nation; but in such a case Catholicism and its tradition come first, and establishment comes second; the establishment is the spontaneous act of the people; it is a national movement, the Catholic people does it, and not the Catholic Church. It is but the accident of a particular state of things, the result of the fervour of the people; it is the will of the masses; but, I repeat, it is not necessary for Catholicism. Not necessary, I maintain, and Ireland is my proof of it; there Catholicism has been, not only not established; it has been persecuted for three hundred years, and at this moment it is more vigorous than ever; whereas, I defy you to bring any instance of a nation remaining Lutheran or Calvinist for even a hundred years, under similarly unpromising circumstances. Where is the country in the whole world, where Protestantism has thriven under persecutions, as Catholicism has thriven in Ireland? You might, indeed, allege in explanation of the fact, that persecution binds a body together; but I do not think that even persecution would, for any course of years, bind Protestants together in one body; for the very principle of private judgment is a principle of disunion, and that principle goes on acting in weal and in woe, in triumph and in disappointment, and its history gives instances of this. But I am speaking, not of what is supposable under certain circumstances, but of what has been the fact; and I say, looking at the subject historically, Protestantism cannot last without an establishment, though Catholicism can; and next, I say, that that establishment of Protestantism is not the work of the people, is not a development of their faith, is not carried by acclamation, but is an act of calculating heads, of State policy, of kingcraft; the work of certain princes, statesmen, bishops, in order, if possible to make that national which as yet is not national, and which, without that patronage, never would be national; and, therefore, in the case of Protestantism, it is not a matter of the greater or less expediency, sometimes advisable, sometimes not, but is always necessary, always imperative, if Protestantism is to be kept alive. Establishmentism is the very life of Protestantism; or, in other words, Protestantism comes in upon the nation, Protestantism is maintained not in the way of reason and truth, not by appeals to facts, but by tradition, and by a compulsory tradition; and this, in other words, is an establishment.

Now, this establishment of Protestantism was comparatively an easy undertaking in England, without the population knowing much what Protestantism meant, and I will tell you why: there are certain peculiarities of the English character, which were singularly favourable to the royal purpose. As I have just said, the legitimate instruments for deciding on the truth of a religion are these two, fact and reason, or in other words, the way of history and the way of science; and to both the one and the other of these, the English mind is naturally indisposed. Theologians proceed in the way of reasoning; they view Catholic truth as a whole, as one great system of which part grows out of part, and doctrine corresponds to doctrine. This system they carry out into its fulness, and define in its details, by patient processes of reason; and they learn to prove and defend it by means of frequent disputations and logical developments. Now, all such abstract investigations and controversial exercises are distasteful to an Englishman; they suit the Germans, and still more the French, the Italians, and the Spaniards; but as to ourselves, we break away from them as dry, uncertain, theoretical, and unreal. The other means of attaining religious truth is the way of history; when, namely, from the review of past times and foreign countries, the student determines what was really taught by the Apostles in the beginning. Now, an Englishman, as is notorious, takes comparatively little interest in the manners, customs, opinions, or doings of foreign countries. Surrounded by the sea, he is occupied with himself; his attention is concentrated on himself; and he looks abroad only with reference to himself. We are a home people; we like a house to ourselves, and we call it our castle; we look at what is immediately before us; we are eminently practical; we care little for the past; we resign ourselves to existing circumstances; we are neither eclectics nor antiquarians; we live in the present. Foreign politics excite us very little; the Minister of Foreign Affairs may order about our fleets, or sign protocols, at his good pleasure, provided he does nothing to cripple trade, or to raise the price of wheat or cotton. Much less do we care to know how they worship, or what they believe, in Germany or in Spain; rather, we are apt to despise their whole apparatus of religion, whatever it is, as odd and outlandish; and as to past times, English divines have attempted as little for ecclesiastical history as they have attempted for theological science.

Now you see how admirably this temper of Englishmen fits in with the exigencies of Protestantism; for two of the very characteristics of Protestantism are, its want of past history, and its want of fixed teaching. I do not say that no Protestants have investigated or argued; that no Protestants have made appeals to primitive Christianity; such an assertion would be absurd; it was a rule of the game, as it may be called, that they should do so; they were obliged to say what it was that they held, and to prove it they were obliged to recur to ecclesiastical history; certainly; but they have done so because they could not help it; they did so for the moment;

they did so for a purpose; they did so as an *argumentum ad hominem*; but they did so as little as they could, and they soon left off doing so. Now especially the Latitudinarian party professes to ignore doctrine, and the Evangelical to ignore history. In truth, philosophy and history do not come natural to Protestantism; it cannot bear either; it does not reason out any point; it does not survey steadily any course of facts. It dips into reason, it dips into history; but it breathes more freely when it emerges again. Observe, then;—the very exercises of the intellect, by which religious truth is attained, are just those which the Englishman is too impatient, and Protestantism too shallow, to abide; the natural disposition of the one most happily jumps with the needs of the other. And this was the first singular advantage of Protestantism in England: Catholics reasoned profoundly upon doctrine, Catholics investigated rigidly the religious state of other times and places: in vain,—they had not found the way to gain the Englishman; whereas their antagonists had found a weapon of their own, far more to the purpose of the contest than argument or fact.

That weapon is, what is so characteristic of our people, loyalty to the Sovereign. If there is one passion more than another which advantageously distinguishes the Englishman, it is that of personal attachment. He lives in the present, in contrast to the absent and the past. He ignores foreigners at a distance! but when they come to him, if they come recommended by their antecedents, and make an appeal to his eyes and his ears, he almost worships them. We all recollect with what enthusiasm the populace received Marshal Soult on his visit to London a few years ago; it was a warm and hearty feeling, elicited by the sight of a brave enemy and a skilful commander, and it took his own countrymen altogether by surprise. The reception given to Louis Philippe, who was far from popular among us, was of a similarly hospitable character; nay, Napoleon himself, who had been the object of our bitterest hatred, on his appearance as a prisoner off the British coast, was visited by numbers with an interest, respect, and almost sympathy, which I consider (*mutatis mutandis*) would not all have been shown towards Wellington or Blucher, had they been prisoners in France. Again, I suppose the political principles of the Emperor Nicholas are as cordially hated in England as his religious principles are in disrepute in Rome; yet even he, on his successive visits to the two places, encountered a far less flattering reception from the Roman populace than from the people of England. Who so unpopular, thirty years ago, as that remarkable man, Lord Londonderry? yet, when he appeared at George the Fourth's coronation, the sight of his noble figure and bearing drew shouts of applause from the multitude, who had thought they hated him. George himself, worthless as he seems to have been, for how many years had he been an object of popular admiration! till his wife, a more urgent candidate for the eye of pity and sympathy, supplanted him. Charles the Second, the most profligate of monarchs, lived in the hearts of his people till the day of his death. It is the way with Englishmen. A saint in rags would be despised; in broadcloth, or in silk, he would be thought something more than ordinary.

St. Francis of Assisi, bareheaded and barefooted, would be hooted; St. Francis Xavier, dressed up like a mandarin, with an umbrella over his head, would inspire wonder and delight. A Turk, a Parsee, a Chinese, a Bonze—nay, I will say, a chimpanzee, a hippopotamus—has only to show himself in order to be the cynosure of innumerable eyes, and the idol of his hour. Nay, even more,—I will say a bold thing, —but I am not at all sure, that, except at seasons of excitement like the present, the Pope himself, however he may be abused behind his back, would not be received with cheers, and run after by admiring crowds, if he visited this country, independent of the shadow of Peter which attends him, winning favour and attracting hearts, when he showed himself in real flesh and blood, by the majesty of his presence and the prestige of his name. Such, I say, is the Englishman; with a heart for many objects, with an innate veneration for merit, talents, rank, wealth, science, not in the abstract, however, but as embodied in a visible form; and it is the consciousness of this characteristic which renders statesmen at this moment, of whatever cast of politics, so afraid of the appearance of cardinals and a hierarchy in the midst of the people they have to govern.

3.

These antagonist peculiarities of the English character which I have been describing, lay clear and distinct before the sagacious intellects which were the ruling spirits of the English Reformation. They had to deal with a people who would be sure to revolt from the unnatural speculations of Calvin, and who would see nothing attractive in the dreamy and sensual doctrines of Luther. The emptiness of a ceremonial, and the affectation of a priesthood, were no bribe to its business-like habits and its ingrained love of the tangible. Definite dogma, intelligible articles of faith, formularies which would construe, a consistent ritual, an historical ancestry, would have been thrown away on those who were not sensitive of the connexion of faith and reason. Another way was to be pursued with our countrymen to make Protestantism live; and that was to embody it in the person of its Sovereign. English Protestantism is the religion of the throne: it is represented, realised, taught, transmitted in the succession of monarchs and an hereditary aristocracy. It is religion grafted upon loyalty; and its strength is not in argument, not in fact, not in the unanswerable controversialist, not in an apostolical succession, not in sanction of Scripture—but in a royal road to faith, in backing up a King whom men see, against a Pope whom they do not see. The devolution of its crown is the tradition of its creed; and to doubt its truth is to be disloyal towards its Sovereign. Kings are an Englishman's saints and doctors; he likes somebody or something at which he can cry "huzzah," and throw up his hat. Bluff King Hal, glorious Bess, the Royal Martyr, the Merry Monarch, the pious and immortal William, the good King George, royal personages very different from each other,—nevertheless, as being royal, none of them comes amiss, but they are all of them the objects of his devotion, and the resolution of his Christianity.

It was plain, then, what had to be done in order

to perpetuate Protestantism in a country such as this. Convoke the legislature, pass some sweeping ecclesiastical enactments, exalt the Crown above the Law and the Gospel, down with Cross and up with the lion and the dog, toss all priests out of the country as traitors; let Protestantism be the passport to office and authority, force the King to be a Protestant, make his Court Protestant, bind Houses of Parliament to be Protestant, clap a Protestant oath upon judges, barristers-at-law, officers in army and navy, members of the universities, national clergy; establish this stringent Tradition in every function and department of the State, surround it with the lustre of rank, wealth, station, name, and talent; and this people, so impatient of inquiry, so careless of abstract truth, so apathetic to historical fact, so contemptuous of foreign ideas, will *ex animo* swear to the truth of a religion which indulges their natural turn of mind, and involves no severe thought or tedious application. The Sovereign is the source and the centre, as of civil, so of ecclesiastical arrangements; truth shall be synonymous with order and good government;—what can be simpler than such a teaching? Puritans may struggle against it, and temporarily prevail; sceptics may ridicule it, object, expose and refute; readers of the Fathers may try to soften and embellish it with the colours of antiquity; but strong in the constitution of the law, and congenial to the heart of the people, the royal tradition will be a match for all its rivals, and in the long run will extinguish the very hope of competition.

So counselled the Achitophels of the day; it was devised, it was done. Then was the inauguration of the great picture of the Lion and the Man. The Virgin Queen rose in her strength; she held her court, she showed herself to her people; she gathered round her peer and squire, alderman and burgess, army and navy, lawyer and divine, student and artisan. She made an appeal to the chivalrous and the loyal, and forthwith all that was noble, powerful, dignified, splendid, and intellectual, touched the hilt of their swords, and spread their garments in the way for her to tread upon. And first of all she addressed herself to the Law; and that not only because it was the proper foundation of a national structure, but also inasmuch as, from the nature of the case, it was her surest and most faithful ally. The Law is a science, and therefore takes for granted afterwards whatever it has once determined; hence it followed, that once Protestant, it would be always Protestant; it could be depended on; let Protestantism be recognised as a principle of the Constitution, and every decision, to the end of time, would but illustrate Protestant doctrines and consolidate Protestant interests. In the eye of the Law precedent is the measure of truth, and order the proof of reasonableness, and acceptableness the test of orthodoxy. It moves foward by a majestic tradition, faithful to its principles, regardless of theory and speculation, and therefore eminently fitted to be the vehicle of English Protestantism such as we have described it, and to co-operate with the monarchical principle in its establishment. Moreover, a number of delicate questions which had been contested in previous centuries, and had hitherto been involved in contradictory precedents, now received once for all a Protestant solution. There had been prolonged disputes between the Pontificate and the Regale, the dispute about Investitures, of Rufus with St. Anselm, of Henry the Second with St. Thomas, of Henry of Winchester with St. Edmund; and the eighth Harry had settled it in his own way, when, on Cardinal Fisher's refusing to acknowledge his spiritual power, he had, without hesitation, proceeded to cut off his head; but the Law, with its Protestant bias, could now give dignity and form to what, up to this time, to say the least, were *ex parte* proceedings. It was decided, once for all, what was the rule and what the exception; the courts gave judgment that the saints were to be all in the wrong, the kings were to be all in the right; whatever the Crown had claimed was to be its due, whatever the Pope claimed was to be a usurpation. What could be more simple and conclusive? the most sacred power in the order of nature, "whose voice is the harmony of the world," to whom "all things in earth do homage," the hereditary wisdom and the collective intelligence of a mighty nation in Parliament assembled, the venerable Judges of the land were retained in the interests of a party, their ripe experience, their profound thought, their subtle penetration, their well regulated prudence, were committed for good and all to the politics of a crisis.

So much for the Law; but this was only one of those great functions of the nation which became the instrument of the Protestant Tradition. Elizabeth had an influence on her side, over and above, and even greater than the authority of the Law. She was the queen of fashion and of opinion. The principles of Protestantism rapidly became the standard generally, to which genius, taste, philosophy, learning, and investigation were constrained and bribed to submit. They are her legacy to the nation, and have been taken for granted ever since as starting-points in all discussion and all undertakings. In every circle, and in every rank of the community, in the court, in public meetings, in private society, in literary assemblages, in the family party, it is always assumed that Catholicism is absurd. No one can take part in the business of the great world, no one can speak and debate, no one can present himself before his constituents, no one can write a book, without the necessity of professing that Protestant ideas are self-evident, and that the religion of Alfred, St. Edward, Stephen Langton, and Friar Bacon, is a bygone dream. No one can be a Catholic without apologising for it. And what is in vogue in the upper classes is ever, as we know, ambitiously aped in the inferior. The religious observances of the court become a reigning fashion throughout the social fabric, as certainly as its language or its mode of dress; and, as an aspirant for distinction advances from a lower grade of society to an upper, he necessarily abandons his vulgar sect, whatever it is, for the national Protestantism. All other ways of thought are as frightful as the fashions of last year; the present is the true and the divine; the past is dark because its sun has set, and ignorant because it is dumb, and living dogs are worth more than dead lions. As to Catholicism, the utmost liberality which can be extended towards it, is to call it pretty poetry, bearable in a tragedy, intolerable in fact; the utmost charity towards its professors is to confess that they may be better than their creed,—perhaps believe it, and are only dupes,—perhaps doubt it, and are only cowards. Protestantism sets the tone in all things; and to have the patronage of the wealthy, the esteem of the cultivated, and the applause of the many, Catholics must get its phrases by heart.

It is the profession of a gentleman; Catholicism, of underbred persons, of the vulgar-minded, the uncouth, and the ill-connected. We all can understand how the man of fashion, the profligate, the spendthrift, have their own circles, to which none but men of their own stamp and their own opinions are admitted; how to hate religion and religious men, to scoff at principle, and to laugh at heaven and hell, and to do all this with decorum and good breeding, are the necessary title for admittance; and how, in consequence, men at length begin to believe what they so incessantly hear said, and what they so incessantly say by rote themselves,—begin to suspect that, after all, virtue, as it is called, is nothing else than hypocrisy grafted on licentiousness; and that purity and simplicity and earnestness and probity are but the dreams of the young and the theoretical:—it is by a similar policy, and by a similar process, that the fathers and patrons of the English Reformation have given a substance, a momentum, and a permanence to their tradition, and have fastened on us Catholics, first the imputation, then the repute of ignorance, bigotry, and superstition.

And now I will mention a distinct vehicle of the Protestant tradition in England, which was an instance of good fortune, greater than its originators could possibly have anticipated or contrived. Protestantism became, not only the tradition of law and of good society, but the tradition of literature also. There is no English literature before the age of Elizabeth; but with the latter years of her reign begins that succession of great authors which continues to flow on down to this day. So it was, that about the commencement of the sixteenth century learning revived; on the taking of Constantinople by the Turks, the men of letters of the imperial city, and, what was of more consequence, its libraries, became the property of the West. Schools were opened for the cultivation of studies which had made Greece as renowned among the nations in the gifts of intellect as Judea has been in the gifts of grace. The various perfections of the Greek language, the treasures of Greek thought, the life and taste of Greek art, after the sleep of ages, burst upon the European mind. It was like the warmth, the cheerfulness, and the hues of spring succeeding to the pure and sublime, but fantastic forms of winter frost-work. The barbarism, the sternness, the untowardness of the high and noble medieval school, eyed with astonishment the radiance, and melted beneath the glow of a genius unrivalled in the intellectual firmament. A world of ideas, transcendent in beauty and endless in fertility, flooded the imagination of the scholar and the poet. The fine arts underwent a classical development, and the vernacular tongues caught the refinement and the elegance of the age of Pericles and Alexander. The revival began in Catholic Italy; it advanced into Catholic France; at length it showed itself in Protestant England. A voice came forth from the grave of the old world, as articulate and keen as that of a living teacher; and it thrilled into the heart of the people to whom it came, and it taught them to respond to it in their own tongue,—and that teaching was coincident in this country with the first preaching of Protestantism. It was surely a most lucky accident for the young religion, that, while the English language was coming to the birth with its special attributes of nerve, simplicity, and vigour, at its very first breathings Protestantism was at hand to form it upon its own theological *patois*, and to educate it as the mouth-piece of its own tradition. So, however, it was to be; and soon,

> As in this bad world below
> Noblest things find vilest using,"

the new religion employed the new language for its purposes, in a great undertaking, the translation of its own Bible; a work which, by the purity of its diction, and the strength and harmony of its style, has deservedly become the very model of good English, and the standard of the language to all future times. The same age, which saw this great literary achievement, gave birth to some of the greatest masters of thought and composition in distinct departments of authorship. Shakespeare, Spenser, Sidney, Raleigh, Bacon, and Hooker are its own; and they were, withal, more or less the panegyrists of Elizabeth and her Religion, and moreover, at least the majority of them, adherents of her creed, because already clients of her throne. The Mother of the Reformation is, in the verses of Shakespeare, "a fair vestal throned by the west;" in the poem of Spenser she is the Faery Queen, Gloriana, and the fair huntress, Belphebe, while the militant Christian is rescued from the seductions of Popery, Duessa, by Una, the True Church, or Protestant Religion. The works of these celebrated men have been but the beginning of a long series of creations of the highest order of literary merit, of which Protestantism is the intellectual basis, and Protestant institutions the informing object. What was wanting to lead the national mind a willing captive to the pretensions of Protestantism, beyond the fascination of genius so manifold and so various? What need of controversy to refute the claims of Catholicism, what need of closeness of reasoning, or research into facts, when under a Queen's smile this vast and continuous Tradition had been unrolled before the eyes of men, luminous with the most dazzling colours, and musical with the most subduing strains? Certainly the lion's artists, even had they had the fairest play, could have set up no rival exhibition as original and as brilliant as this.

Nor was it court poets alone, as time went on, who swelled the torrent of the Protestant Tradition. Milton from the middle class, and Bunyan from among the populace, exerted an influence superior to Shakespeare himself, whose great mind did not condescend to the direct inculcation of a private or a sectarian creed. Their phrases, their sentiments, are the household words of the nation, they have become its interpreters of Scripture, and, I may say, its prophets,—such is the magical eloquence of their compositions; so much so, that I really shall not be far from the mark in saying of them, and this is true of Shakespeare also, that the ordinary run of men find it very difficult to determine, in respect to the proverbs, instances, maxims, and half sentences, which are in the nation's mouth, which, and how much, is from the Bible, and how much from the authors I have mentioned. There is a saying, "Give me the framing of a nation's proverbs, and others may frame its laws;" and its proverbs are the produce of its literature. What, indeed, could possibly stand against the rush of vehemence of such a Tradition, which has grown fuller and fuller, and more and more impetuous, with every successive quarter of a century! Clarendon and the statesmen, Locke and the philosophers, Addison and the essayists, Hume, Robertson, and the historians, Cowper and the minor poets, the reviews and magazines of the present century, all proceed upon the hypothesis, which they think too self-evident for proof, that Protestantism is synonymous with good sense, and Catholicism with weakness of mind, fanaticism, or some unaccountable persuasion or fancy. Verse and prose, grave and gay, the scientific and the practical, history and fable, all is animated spontaneously, or imperiously subdued, by the spirit of Henry and Elizabeth. I say, "imperiously subdued," because the Tradition of Protestantism is strong enough, not only to recommend, but to force its reception on each successive generation of authors. It compels when it cannot persuade. There is Alexander Pope, a Catholic, and who would discover it from the run of his poems? There is Samuel Johnson, born a Protestant, yearning for the Catholic Church, and bursting out into fitful defences of portions of her doctrine and discipline, yet professing to the last that very Protestantism which could neither command his affections, nor cure his infirmities. And, in our own time, there was Walter Scott, ashamed of his own Catholic tendencies and cowering before the jealous frown of the tyrant

Tradition. There was Wordsworth, obliged to do penance for Catholic sonnets by anti-Catholic complements to them. Scott, forsooth, must plead antiquarianism in extenuation of his prevarication; Wordsworth must plead Pantheism; and Burke again, must plead political necessity. Liberalism, scepticism, infidelity, these must be the venial errors, under plea of which a writer escapes reprobation for the enormity of feeling tenderly towards the Religion of his fathers, and of his neighbours around him. That Religion labours under a proscription of three centuries, and it is outlawed by immemorial custom.

No wonder, then, that Protestantism, being the religion of our literature, has become the Tradition of civil intercourse and political life; no wonder that its assumptions are among the elements of knowledge, unchangeable as the moods of logic, or the idioms of language, or the injunctions of good taste, or the proprieties of good manners. Elizabeth's reign is "golden," Mary is "bloody," the Church of England is "pure and apostolical," the Reformers are "judicious," the Prayer Book is "incomparable," or "beautiful," the Thirty-nine Articles are "moderate." "Pope" and "pagan" go together, and "the Pope, the Devil, and the Pretender." The anti-Catholic rancour is carried into your marts of commerce; London is burned down, and forthwith your greatest architect is instructed to set up a tall pillar to perpetuate the lie, that the Papists were the incendiaries. Take your controversy with you when you sit down to cards and let the taunting name of Pope Joan be the title of your game. Run a horse the coming year, and among your Sorcerers, Lamplighters, Malibrans, and Priams, you will find Crucifix a striking, perhaps a lucky name for your beast; it is but the emblem of an extinct superstition. Dress up for some fancy ball, or morris-dance, and let the Grand Turk jump about on one side of you, and the Pope with cross, and beads, and triple crown, upon the other. Go to the stage of the Mountebank, and teach him, when he displays his sleight-of-hand, to give effect to his tricks by the most sacred words of the Catholic ritual. Into your very vocabulary let Protestantism enter; let priest, and mass, and masspriest, and mass-house have an offensive savour on your palate; let monk be a word of reproach; let Jesuitism and Jesuitical, in their first intention, stand for what is dishonourable and vile. What chance has a Catholic against so multitudinous, so elementary a Tradition. Here is the Tradition of the Court, and of the Law, and of Society, and of Literature, strong in themselves, and acting on each other, and acting on a willing people, and the willing people acting on them, till the whole edifice stands self-supported, reminding one of some vast arch (as at times may be seen), from which the supports have crumbled away by age, but which endures still, and supports the huge mass of brickwork which lies above it, by the simple cohesion of parts which that same age has effected. My Brothers of the Oratory, you see what I meant when I spoke of the Tradition of the Pharisees, and said that it might be powerful in influence, though it was argumentatively weak; you see why it is that the fair form of Catholicism, as it exists in the east, west, and south, never crosses the retina of a Protestant's imagination:—it is the incubus of this Tradition, which cumbers the land, and opposes an impregnable barrier between us and each individual Protestant whom we happen to address. Whoever he is, he thinks he knows all about our religion before speaking to us,—nay, perhaps much better than we know it ourselves. And now, if I said no more, I have said abundantly sufficient for the point I have had in view; and yet there is one portion of the subject still behind, which is almost more to my purpose than anything which I have hitherto mentioned.

4.

Protestantism is also the Tradition of the Anglican Clergy; and in speaking of them with reference to it, as I am going to speak, Brothers of the Oratory, do not suppose me to be forgetful either of their private worth or their social uses. As the other functions of the Constitution subserve the temporal welfare of the community, so does the established clergy minister to it with a special fidelity. But here I am all along speaking of Kings, Lords, Commons, Law, Literature, and so also of the Clergy, not simply as parts of the body politic, but as organs of Protestantism; and, as I have pointed out the office which other political ranks and departments fulfil in its propagation, so am I now to speak of the duties of the Religious Establishment. I say, then, that its especial duty as a religious body, is not to inculcate any particular theological system, but to watch over the anti-Catholic Tradition, to preserve it from rust and decay, to keep it bright and keen, and ready for action on any emergency or peril. It is the way with human nature to start with vigour, and then to flag; years tell upon the toughest frames; time introduces changes; prejudices are worn away; asperities are softened; views opened; errors are corrected; opponents are better understood; the mind wearies of warfare. The Protestant Tradition, left to itself, would in the course of time languish and decline; laws would become obsolete, the etiquette and usages of society would alter, literature would be enlivened with new views, and the old Truth might return with the freshness of novelty. It is almost the mission of the established clergy, by word and writing, to guard against this tendency of the public mind. In this specially consists its teaching; I repeat, not in the shreds of Catholic doctrine which it professes, not in proofs of the divinity of any creed whatever, not in separating opinion from faith, not in instructing in the details of morals, but mainly in furbishing up the old-fashioned weapons of centuries back; in cataloguing and classing the texts which are to batter us, and the objections which are to explode among us, and the insinuations and the slanders which are to mow us down. The Establishment is the keeper in ordinary of those national types and blocks from which Popery is ever to be printed off,—of the traditional view of every Catholic doctrine, the traditional account of every ecclesiastical event, the traditional lives of popes and bishops, abbots and monks, saints and confessors,—the traditional fictions, sophisms, calumnies, mockeries, sarcasms, and invectives with which Catholics are to be assailed.

This, I say, is the special charge laid upon the Establishment. Unitarians, Sabellians, Utilitarians,

Wesleyans, Calvinists, Swedenborgians, Irvingites, Freethinkers, all these it can tolerate in its very bosom; no form of opinion comes amiss; but Rome it cannot abide. It agrees to differ with its own children on a thousand points, one is sacred—that her Majesty the Queen is "The Mother and Mistress of all Churches;" on one dogma it is infallible, on one it may securely insist without fear of being unseasonable or excessive—that "the Bishop of Rome hath no jurisdiction in this realm." Here is sunshine amid the darkness, sense amid confusion, an intelligible strain amid a Babel of sounds; whatever befalls, here is sure footing; it is, "No peace with Rome," "Down with the Pope," and "The Church in danger." Never has the Establishment failed in the use of these important and effective watchwords; many are its shortcomings, but it is without reproach in the execution of this its special charge. Heresy, and scepticism, and infidelity, and fanaticism, may challenge it in vain; but fling upon the gale the faintest whisper of Catholicism, and it recognises by instinct the presence of its connatural foe. Forthwith, as during the last year, the atmosphere is tremulous with agitation, and discharges its vibrations far and wide. A movement is in birth which has no natural crisis or resolution. Spontaneously the bells of the steeples begin to sound. Not by an act of volition, but by a sort of mechanical impulse, bishop and dean, archdeacon and canon, rector and curate, one after another, each on his high tower, off they set, swinging and booming, tolling and chiming, with nervous intenseness, and thickening emotion, and deepening volume, the old ding-dong which has scared town and country this weary time; tolling and chiming away, jingling and clamouring and ringing the changes on their poor half-dozen notes, all about "the Popish aggression," "insolent and insidious," "insidious and insolent," "insolent and atrocious," "atrocious and insolent," "atrocious, insolent, and ungrateful," "ungrateful, insolent, and atrocious," "foul and offensive," "pestilent and horrid," "subtle and unholy," "audacious and revolting," "contemptible and shameless," "malignant," "frightful," "mad," "meretricious,"—bobs (I think the ringers call them), bobs, and bobs-royal, and triple-bob-majors, and grandsires,—to the extent of their compass and the full ring of their metal, in honour of Queen Bess, and to the confusion of the Holy Father and the Princes of the Church.[1]

So it is now; so it was twenty years ago; nay, so it has been in all years as they came, even the least controversial. If there was no call for a contest, at least there was the opportunity of a triumph. Who could want matter for a sermon, if ever his thoughts would not flow, whether for convenient digression, or effective peroration? Did a preacher wish for an illustration of heathen superstition or Jewish bigotry, or an instance of hypocrisy, ignorance, or spiritual pride? the Catholics were at hand. The deliverance from Egypt, the golden calf, the fall of Dagon, the sin of Solomon, the cruelties of Jezebel, the worship of Baal, the destruction of the brazen serpent, the finding of the Law, the captivity in Babylon, Nebucho-

[1] The foregoing lecture in 1851 was, by an accidental coincidence, written simultaneously with an able pamphlet by Serjeant Bellasis, *apropos* of the conduct of the Anglican clergy of the day.

donosor's image, Pharisees, Sadducees, Herodians, and Zealots, mint, anise, and cummin, brazen pots and vessels, all in their respective places and ways, would give opportunity to a few grave words of allusion to the " monstrous errors," or the " childish absurdities " of the " Romish faith." Does any one wish an example of pride? there stands Wolsey ; of barbarity? there is the Duke of Alva ; of rebellion ? there is Becket ; of ambition ? there is Hildebrand ; of profligacy ? there is Cæsar Borgia ; of superstition? there is Louis the Eleventh ; of fanaticism ? there are the Crusaders. Saints and sinners, monks and laymen, the devout and the worldly, provided they be but Catholics, are heaped together in one indiscriminate mass, to be drawn forth for inspection and exposure according to the need.

The consequence is natural ;—tell a person of ordinary intelligence, Churchman or Dissenter, that the vulgar allegations against us are but slanders,— simple lies, or exaggerations, or misrepresentations ; or, as far as they are true, admitting of defence or justification, and not to the point ; and he will laugh in your face at your simplicity, or lift up hands and eyes at your unparalleled effrontery. The utmost concession he will make is to allow the possibility of incidental and immaterial error in the accusations which are brought against us ; but the substance of the traditional view he believes, as firmly as he does the Gospel, and, if you reject it and protest against it, he will say it is just what is to be expected of a Catholic, to lie and to circumvent. To tell him, at his time of life, that Catholics do not rate sin at a fixed price, that they may not get absolution for a sin in prospect, that priests can live in purity, that nuns do not murder each other, that the laity do not make images their God, that Catholics would not burn Protestants if they could! Why, all this is as perfectly clear to him as the sun at noonday; he is ready to leave the matter to the first person he happens to meet; every one will tell us just the same; only let us try; he never knew there was any doubt at all about it; he *is* surprised, for he thought we granted it. When he was young, he has heard it said again and again; to his certain knowledge it has uniformly been said the last forty, fifty, sixty years, and no one ever denied it; it is so in all the books he ever looked into; what is the world coming to? What is true, if this is not? So, Catholics are to be whitewashed! What next?

And so he proceeds in detail;— the Papists not worship the Virgin Mary! why, they call her "Deipara," which means "equal to God."

The Pope not the man of sin! why, it is a fact that the Romanists distinctly maintain that "the Pope is God, and God is the Pope."

The Pope's teaching not a doctrine of devils! here is a plain proof of it; Cardinal Bellarmine expressly "maintains that, if the Pope commanded us to practise vice or shun virtue, we are obliged to do so, under pain of eternal damnation."

Not a Pope Joan! why, she was "John the Eighth, her real name was Gilberta, she took the name of John English, delivered public lectures at Rome, and was at length unanimously elected Pope."

What! Councils infallible! open your eyes, my brother, and judge for yourself: "fifteen hundred public women followed the train of the Fathers of Constance."

Jesuits! here are at least twenty thousand in England; and, horrible to say, a number of them in each of the Protestant Universities, and doubtless a great many at Oscott.

Beauty and sanctity of the Popish festivals! do you not know that the Purification "is the very feast that was celebrated by the ancient Pagan Romans in honour of the goddess Proserpina?"

The Papists not corrupters of the Scriptures! look into their Bibles, and you will find they read the prophecy in Genesis, "*She* shall crush thy head, and thou shalt lie in wait for *her* heel."

Popery preach Christ! no; "Popery," as has been well said, "is the religion of priestcraft; from the beginning to the end it is nothing but priest, priest, priest."[1]

I shall both weary and offend you, my Brothers, if I proceed. Even absurdity becomes tiresome after a time, and slanders cast on holy things and persons, when dwelt on, are too painful for a Catholic's ears; yet it was necessary for my subject to give instances of the popular views of us and of our creed, as they are formed under the operation of the Tradition of Elizabeth.

Here I am reminded of another sort of Tradition, started by a very different monarch, which in the event was handled very differently. It is often told how Charles the Second once sent a grave message to the Royal Society. That scientific body was founded in

---

[1] *Vide* Stephen's Spirit of the Church of Rome; Edgar's Variations; Cramp's Text-Book of Popery, &c.; the books I happen to have at hand.

his reign, and the witty king, as became his well-known character, could not help practising a jest upon it. He proposed a question for its deliberation; he asked it, as I daresay you have often heard, to tell him how it was that a live fish weighed less heavily in water than after it was dead. The Society, as it was in duty bound, applied itself to solve the phenomenon, and various were the theories to which it gave occasion. At last it occurred to its members to determine the fact, before deciding on any of them; when, on making the experiment, to their astonishment they found that the hypothesis was a mere invention of their royal master's, because the dead fish was not heavier in water than the living.

Well would it be if Englishmen in like manner, instead of taking their knowledge of us at (what may be called) royal hand, would judge about us for themselves, before they hunted for our likeness in the book of Daniel, St. Paul's Epistles, and the Apocalypse. They then would be the first to smile at their own extravagances; but, alas! as yet, there are no such signs of such ordinary prudence. Sensible in other matters, they lose all self-command when the name of Catholicism is sounded in their ears. They trust the voice of Henry or Elizabeth, with its thousand echoes, more than their own eyes, and their own experience; and they are zealous in echoing it themselves to the generation which is to follow them. Each in his turn, as his reason opens, is indoctrinated in the popular misconception. At this very time, in consequence of the clamour which has been raised against us, children in the streets, of four and five years old, are learning and using against us terms of abuse, which will be *their* tradition all through their lives, till they are grey-headed, and have, in turn, to teach it to their grandchildren. They totter out, and lift their tiny hands, and raise their thin voices, in protest against those whom they are just able to understand are very wicked and very dangerous ; and they run away in terror when they catch our eye. Nor will the growth of reason set them right ; the longer they live, and the more they converse with men, the more will they hate us. The Maker of all, and only He, can shiver in pieces this vast enchanted palace in which our lot is cast ; may He do it in His time !

LECTURE III.

FABLE THE BASIS OF THE PROTESTANT VIEW.

It was my aim, Brothers of the Oratory, in my preceding Lecture, to investigate, as far as time and place allowed, how it was that the one-sided view of the great religious controversy, which commenced between Rome and England three centuries since, has been so successfully maintained in this country. Many things have changed among us during that long period; but the hatred and the jealousy entertained by the population towards the Catholic Faith, and the scorn and pity which are felt at the sight of its adherents, have not passed away, have not been mitigated. In that long period, society has undergone various alterations; public opinion has received a development new in the history of the world, and many remarkable revolutions in national principle have followed. The received views on the causes and the punishment of crime, on the end of government, on the mutual relations of town and country, on international interests, and on many other great political questions, have sustained, to say the least, great modifications; sciences, unknown before, bearing upon the economy of social life, have come into being; medicine has been the subject of new doctrines, which have had their influence on various civil and municipal arrangements; how is it, then, that the feeling against Catholicism has remained substantially what it was in the days of Charles the Second or of George the Third? How is it that Protestantism has retained its ascendency, and that Catholic arguments and Catholic principles are at once misconstrued and ignored? And what increases the wonder is, that externally to our own island it has happened otherwise; there is scarcely a country besides ours where Catholicism is not at least respected, even if it is not studied; and what is more observable still, scarcely a country besides ours, originally Protestant, in which Protestantism even exists at present,—if by Protestantism is understood the religion of Luther and Calvin. The phenomenon, great in itself, becomes greater by its thus seeming to be all but peculiar to the British population.

And this latter consideration is important also, as it anticipates a solution of the difficulty which the Protestant, were he able, would eagerly adopt. He would be eager to reply, if he could, that the Protestant spirit has survived in the land amid so many changes in political and social science, because certain political theories were false, but Protestantism is true; but if this is the case, why has it not kept its ground and made its way in other countries also? What cause can be assigned for its decay and almost extinction in those other countries, in Germany, Holland, Switzerland and New England, diverse from each other in situation, in government, in language, and in character, where once it flourished? Evidently it must be a cause peculiar to England; those foreign countries must have something in common with each other which they have not in common with us. Now what is peculiar to our country is an established Tradition of Protestantism; what those other countries have in common with each other is the absence of such Tradition. Fact and argument have had fair play in other countries; they have not had fair play here; the religious establishment has forbidden them fair play. But fact and argument are the tests of truth and error; Protestantism, then, has had an adventitious advantage in this country, in consequence of which it has not been tried,—as, in the course of years, otherwise it would have been tried, and as it has been tried elsewhere—on its own merits. Instead, then, of concluding that it is true, because it has remained here during three centuries substantially the same, I should rather conclude that it is false because it has not been able during that period to remain the same abroad. To the standing, compulsory Tradition existing here, I ascribe its continuance here; to fact and reason operating freely elsewhere, I ascribe its disappearance elsewhere.

This view of the subject is confirmed to us, when we consider, on the one hand, the character of our countrymen, and on the other, the character of those instruments and methods by which the Tradition of Protestantism is perpetuated among them. It has been perpetuated, directly or indirectly, by the sanction of an oath, imposed on all those several sources of authority, and influence, from which principles, doctrines, and opinions are accustomed to flow. There is an established Tradition of law, and of the clergy, and of the court, and of the universities, and of literature, and of good society; and all these act upon a people peculiarly susceptible of the claims of personal merit, of embodied authority, of constituted order, of rank, and of reputation in the world, and little sensitive in comparison of abstract argument, logical sequence, moral fitness, historical results, or foreign transactions.

This was the point at which I stopped last week; now I shall continue my investigation, and I shall introduce what I have to say by means of an objection.

I.

It may be objected, then, to the conclusions at which I have arrived, that I on my part have simply ignored the fact of the innumerable multitude of independent testimonies which every one of the divines, the scholars, the lawyers, the men of letters, the statesmen, the men of the world, who have made the last three centuries glorious in Britain, has borne in his turn, in favour of Protestantism and to the disadvantage of the Catholic religion.

Bacon and Hooker, Taylor and Chillingworth, Hampden, Clarendon, and Falkland, Russell, Somers and Walpole, Hobbes and Locke, Swift and Addison, Hume and Robertson, Warburton and Horsley, Pitt and Fox, Walter Scott and Hallam, and a multitude of other illustrious names, nay, the whole host of educated men, are all separate authorities; each speaks for himself; they do not copy, the one from the other: there are among them men of extensive reading, profound philosophy, intimate knowledge of the world; they are all men of intelligence, and at least able to give an opinion. It is absurd to say otherwise. This simple consideration, it may be said, overthrows from its very foundation the argument drawn out in my last week's Lecture, about the traditional character of Protestantism in England. Indeed, my argument turns against myself; for I incidentally allowed on that occasion that a number of distinct testimonies, conspiring together into one view or representation, was a real and sound reason, nay, among the strongest of conceivable reasons, in its behalf; now, this is just the state of the case as regards the argument for Protestantism, as drawn from the common consent of the English court, clergy, bar, literature, and general society.

This is what will be said; and I reply as follows:—I do not deny that there are great names on the side of Protestantism, which require to be considered by themselves;—minds, which certainly are superior to the influences of party, the prejudices of education, the suggestions of self-interest, the seductions of place and position, and the tyranny of public opinion. And again, there are Protestant arguments, clear and broad, which remain, whether Protestantism is received, or whether it is not. I allow all this: but now I am considering, not the Protestantism of the few, but of the many: those great men, and those philosophical arguments, whatever be their weight, have no influence with the many. Crowds do not assemble in Exeter Hall, mobs do not burn the Pope, from reverence for Lord Bacon, Locke, or Butler, or for anything those gifted men have recorded. I am treating of the unpopularity of Catholicism, now and here, as it exists in the year 1851, and in London, or in Edinburgh, or in Birmingham, or in Bristol, or in Manchester, or in Glasgow; among the gentlemen and yeomen of Yorkshire, Devonshire, and Kent; in the Inns of Court, and in the schools and colleges of the land; and I say this Tradition does not flow from the mouth of the half-dozen wise, or philosophic, or learned men who can be summoned in its support, but is a tradition of nursery stories, school stories, public-house stories, club-house stories, drawing-room stories, platform stories, pulpit stories;—a tradition of newspapers, magazines, reviews, pamphlets, romances, novels, poems, and light literature of all kind, literature of the day;—a tradition of selections from the English classics, bits of poetry, passages of history, sermons, chance essays, extracts from books of travel, anonymous anecdotes, lectures on prophecy, statements and arguments of polemical writers, made up into small octavos for class-books, and into pretty miniatures for presents;—a tradition floating in the air; which we found in being when we first came to years of reason; which has been borne in upon us by all we saw, heard, or read, in high life, in parliament, in law courts, in general society; which our fathers told us had ever been in their day; a tradition, therefore, truly universal and immemorial, and good as far as a tradition can be good, but after all, not more than a tradition is worth: I mean, requiring some ultimate authority to make it trustworthy. Trace up, then, the tradition to its very first startings, its roots and its sources, if you are to form a judgment whether it is more than a tradition. It may be a good tradition, and yet after all good for nothing. What profit, though ninety-nine links of a chain be sound, if the topmost is broken? Now I do not hesitate to assert, that this Protestant Tradition, on which English faith hangs, is wanting just in the first link. Fierce as are its advocates, and high as is its sanction, yet, whenever we can pursue it through the mist of immemorial reception in which it commonly vanishes, and can arrive at its beginnings, forthwith we find a flaw in the argument. Either facts are not forthcoming, or they are not sufficient for the purpose : sometimes they turn out to be imaginations or inventions, sometimes exaggerations, sometimes misconceptions ; something or other comes to light which blunts their efficiency, and throws suspicion on the rest. Testimonies which were quoted as independent turn out to be the same, or to be contradictory of each other, or to be too improbable to be true, or to have no good authority at all: so that our enemies find they cannot do better, after all, than fall back on the general reception of the Tradition itself, as a reason for receiving the Tradition ; and they find it prudent to convict us of all manner of crimes, on the simple ground of our being notoriously accused of them.

Hard measure, scanty justice! It is a principle of English law, that no one should bring a charge against another without being under the obligation of supporting it. Where should we be, any one of us—who would be safe—if any person who chose might, at any moment he would, impute to us what he pleased, bring us into court, call no witnesses, and obtain our conviction on his simple assertion ? Why, at very least, an accuser is bound to make oath of the truth of what he says ; and that is but the first step of an investigation, not the termination of the process. And he must swear to a fact, not to an opinion, not to a surmise, not to what he has heard others say, but to what he has witnessed or knows. Nay, even though there be reasons for being sure of the guilt of the accused, it is a maxim of our law not to make him criminate himself, but to aim at convicting him by other means and by other men. It seems a plain dictate of common equity, that an accuser should have something to say for himself, before he can put the accused on his defence.

This righteous rule is simply set aside in the treatment of Catholics and their religion. Instead of the *onus probandi*, as it is called, the burden of proof, lying with the accuser, it is simply thrown upon the accused. Any one may get up of a sudden, and may say what he will to our prejudice, without producing any warrant at all for the truth of his charge. He is not called upon to establish his respectability, or to state his opportunities or methods of knowing; he need not give presumptive proof of his allegation; he need not give his authorities; he need only accuse; and upon this the Protestant public turns round to the poor Catholic, and asks what he has to say in his defence, as if he had yet anything to defend. There is a saying, that "a fool can ask more questions than a hundred wise men can answer;" and a bigot or a fanatic may be quite as successful. If a man presented himself this moment and said to me, "You robbed a person in the street of his pocket-book some ten years ago," what could I possibly say, except simply, "I did not"? How could I prove it was false, even if I took on myself to do so till I was informed of the town, or the year, or the occasion, or the person on whom the pretended offence was committed? Well, supposing my accuser went on to particulars, and said that I committed the crime in Birmingham, in the month of June, in the year 1840, and in the instance of a person of the name of Smith. This, of course would be something, but no one would say even then that it was enough; that is, supposing I had to reply to him on the spot. At the very moment I might not be able to say where I was on the specified day, and so I could only repeat as emphatically as I was able, that the charge was utterly untrue.

Next, supposing me to ask his reasons for advancing it;—how he knew it was I? did he see me? or was he told by an eye-witness? and supposing he were to decline to give me any information whatever, but contented himself with saying "that I was shuffling and evasive, for the thing was quite notorious." And next, supposing I suddenly recollected that, up to the year 1845, I had never once been in Birmingham in the course of my life; yet, on my stating this, the accuser were to cry out that I should not escape, in spite of my attempt to throw dust in his eyes; for he had a score of witnesses to prove the fact, and that, as to the exact year it was a mere point of detail, on which any one might be mistaken. And supposing, on this unsupported allegation, a magistrate, without witness brought, or oath administered, or plausibility in the narrative, in spite of the accuser's character, which was none of the best, in spite of the vagueness of his testimony, were to send me to prison,—I conceive public opinion would say I was shamefully treated.

But further, supposing when I was safely lodged in prison, some anonymous writer, in some third-rate newspaper, were boldly to assert that all priests were in the practice of stealing pocket-books from passengers in the streets; and in proof thereof were to appeal first to the notorious case of a priest in Birmingham who had been convicted of the offence, and then to the case of a second priest which was given in detail in some manuscript or other, contained somewhere or other in the royal library of Munich, and occurring some time or other between the seventh and the seventeenth centuries; and, supposing upon this anonymous article or letter, petitions were got up and signed numerously, and despatched to the Imperial Parliament, with the object of sending all priests to the treadmill for a period not exceeding six months, as reputed thieves, whenever they were found walking in the public thoroughfares;—would this answer an Englishman's ideas of fairness or of humanity?

Now I put it to the experience—I put it to the conscience of the Protestant world,—whether such is not the justice which it deals out to Catholics as a matter of course. No evidence against us is too little; no infliction too great. Statement without proof, though inadmissible in every other case, is all fair when we are concerned. A Protestant is at liberty to bring a charge against us, and challenge us to refute, not any proof he brings, for he brings none, but his simple assumption or assertion. And perhaps we accept his challenge, and then we find we have to deal with matters so vague or so minute, so general or so particular, that we are at our wit's end to know how to grapple with them. For instance, "Every twentieth man you meet is a Jesuit in disguise;" or, "Nunneries are, for the most part, prisons." How is it possible to meet such sweeping charges? The utmost we can do, in the nature of things, is to show that this particular man, or that, is not a Jesuit; or that this or that particular nunnery is not a prison; but who said he was?—who said it was? What our Protestant accuser asserted was, that every *twentieth* man was a Jesuit, and *most* nunneries were prisons. How is this refuted by clearing this or that person or nunnery of the charge? Thus, if the accuser is not to be called on to give proofs of what he says, we are simply helpless, and must sit down meekly under the imputation.

At another time, however, a definite fact is stated, and we are referred to the authority on which it is put forward. What is the authority? Albertus Magnus, perhaps, or Gerson, or Baronius, with a silence about volume and page: their works consisting of five, ten, fifteen, twenty, or thirty folios, printed in double columns. How are we possibly to find the needle in this stack of hay? Or, by a refinement of unfairness, perhaps a wrong volume or page is carelessly given; and when we cannot find there the statement which our opponent has made, we are left in an unpleasant doubt whether our ill success is to be ascribed to our eyes or to his pen.

Sometimes, again, the crime charged on us is brought out with such startling vividness and circumstantial finish as to seem to carry its own evidence with it, and to dispense, in the eyes of the public, with the references which in fairness should attend it. The scene is laid in some fortress of the savage Apennine, or in secluded Languedoc, or in remote Poland, or the high table-land of Mexico; or it is a legend about some priest of a small village of Calabria, called Buonavalle, in the fourteenth century; or about a monk of the monastery of S. Spirito, in S. Fillippo d'Argiro, in the time of Charlemagne. Or the story runs, that Don Felix Malatesta de Guadalope, a Benedictine monk of Andalusia, and father confessor to the Prince of the Asturias, who died in 1821, left behind him his confessions in manuscript, which were carried off by the French, with other valuable documents, from his convent, which they pillaged in their retreat from the field of Salamanca ; and that, in these confessions, he frankly avows that he had killed three of his monastic brothers of whom he was jealous, had poisoned half-a-dozen women, and sent off in boxes and hampers to Cadiz and Barcelona thirty-five infants ; moreover, that he felt no misgivings about these abominable deeds, because, as he observes with great *naïveté*, he had every day, for many years, burnt a candle to the Blessed Virgin ; had cursed periodically all heretics, especially the royal family of England ; had burnt a student of Coimbra for asserting the earth went round the sun ; had worn about him, day and night, a relic of St. Diego; and had provided that five hundred masses should be said for the repose of his soul within eight days after his decease.

Tales such as this, the like of which it is very easy to point out in print, are suitably contrived to answer the purpose which brings them into being. A Catholic who, in default of testimony offered in their behalf, volunteers to refute them on their internal evidence, and sets about (so to say) cross-examining them, finds himself at once in an untold labyrinth of embarrassments. First he inquires, *is* there a village in Calabria of the name of Buonavalle ? *is* there a convent of S. Spirito in the Sicilian town specified ? did it *exist* in the time of Charlemagne ? who were the successive confessors of the Prince of the Asturias during the first twenty years of this century? what has Andalusia to do with Salamanca? when was the last *Auto da fé* in Spain? did the French pillage any convent whatever in the neighbourhood of Salamanca about the year 1812?—questions sufficient for a school examination. He goes to his maps, gazetteers, guidebooks, travels, histories;—soon a perplexity arises about the dates : are his editions *recent* enough for his purpose? do their historical notices go *far enough back ?* Well, after a great deal of trouble, after writing about to friends, consulting libraries, and comparing statements, let us suppose him to prove most conclusively the utter absurdity of the slanderous story, and to bring out a lucid, powerful, and unanswerable reply ; who cares for it by that time? who cares for the story itself? it has done its work ; time stops for no man ; it has created or deepened the impression in the minds of its hearers that a monk commits murder or adultery as readily as he eats his dinner. Men forget the process by which they receive it, but there it is, clear and indelible. Or supposing they recollect the particular slander ever so well, still they have no taste or stomach for entering into a long controversy about it ; their mind is already made up ; they have formed their views ; the author they have trusted may, indeed, have been inaccurate in some of his details ; it can be nothing more. Who can fairly impose on them the perplexity and whirl of going through a bout of controversy, where "one says," and "the other says," and "*he* says that *he* says that *he* does not say or ought not to say what he does say or ought to say?" It demands an effort and strain of attention which they have no sort of purpose of bestowing. The Catholic cannot get a fair hearing; his book remains awhile in the shop windows, and then is taken down again. So true is this, from the nature of the human mind, that even though my present audience is well disposed, not hostile, to Catholicism, I should scarcely venture, in these Lectures, to enter into any minute investigation of this or that popular calumny, from my conviction that I should be detailing matters which, except in the case of the very few, would engross without interesting, and weary without making an impression.

Yet I think I may be able still, or at least I will try, without taxing your patience to the utmost, to bring before you two or three actual specimens of the mode in which the accusation against Catholics is conducted; which may serve to give you some insight into the value of the Tradition which king, lords and commons, are so zealous in upholding. The mighty Tradition flows on, replenished and refreshed continually by rivulets which, issuing from new fountainheads, make their way, in faithful and unfailing succession, into the main stream. I am going to put my finger on three of these small fountain-heads of the Tradition,—which, as I have already complained, are not commonly accessible;—they shall not be springs of a vulgar quality, but they shall represent the intelligence, the respectability, and the strong sense of English society. The first shall be a specimen of the Tradition of Literature, the second of the Tradition of Wealth, and the third of the Tradition of Gentlemen.

2.

1. The first, which has to do with names well known in the aristocracy of talent and learning, will be somewhat tedious, do what I will; and I shall introduce it with a story. It is related by the learned Dr. Bentley, in his controversy with Boyle, about a century and a half ago, on some point of historical criticism. In the course of that controversy, his opponent happened to spell wrongly the name of a Greek town; and when he was set right, he made answer that it was the custom of our English writers so to spell it, and he proceeded to quote as many as five of them in proof of his assertion. On this Bentley observes, "An admirable reason, and worthy to be his own; as if the most palpable error, that shall happen to obtain and meet with reception, must therefore never be mended." After this, the "slashing" critic goes on to allude to the instance of an unlearned English priest, truly or not I know not, "who for thirty years together" (perhaps it was on taking the first ablution in the Mass) "had always said, 'Quod ore mumpsimus,' instead of 'Quod ore sumpsimus,'" and when, says Bentley, "a learned man told him of his blunder, 'I'll not change,' says he, 'my old Mumpsimus for your new Sumpsimus.'" Now, this happily applies to the subject which I am going to illustrate, as you will presently see.

I need not remind you how much is said among Protestants of the gross ignorance and superstition of the middle age: indeed, we Catholics of the present date are considered its legitimate and veritable heirs. On this subject, one of the best read, most dispassionate and deservedly esteemed writers of the present day, who, if any one, might be supposed in historical matters an original authority, in his " View of the State of Europe during the Middle Ages," writes as follows :—

"In the very best view that can be taken of monasteries," he says, after allowing that many might be above reproach, "their existence is deeply injurious to the general morals of a nation. They withdraw men of pure conduct and conscientious principle from the exercise of social duties, and leave the common mass of human vice more unmixed. Such men are always inclined to form schemes of ascetic perfection, which can only be fulfilled in retirement; but, in the strict rules of monastic life, and under the influence of a grovelling superstition, their virtue lost all its usefulness. They fell implicitly into the snares of crafty priests, who made submission to the Church, not only the condition, but the measure of all praise." Now comes the passage to which I am directing your attention. Observe, he is going on to his *proof* of what he has asserted. "He is a good Christian, says Eligius, a saint of the seventh century, who comes frequently to church, who presents an oblation that it may be offered to God on the altar; who does not taste the fruits of his land till he has consecrated a part of them to God; who can repeat the Creed or the Lord's Prayer. Redeem your souls from punishment, while it is in your power; offer presents and tithes to churches, light candles in holy places, as much as you can afford, come more frequently to church, implore the protection of the saints; for, if you observe these things, you may come with security at the day of judgment to say, 'Give unto us, O Lord, for we have given unto Thee!'" The author then continues, "With such *a definition of the Christian character*, it is not surprising that any *fraud and injustice* became honourable, when it contributed to the riches of the clergy and the glory of their order."[1]

Now, observe first, he quotes St. Eligius, or Eloi, in order to show that Catholics were at that time taught that true Christianity consisted, not in the absence of fraud and injustice, or again, of immorality, hatred, or strife—but in merely coming to church, paying tithes, burning candles, and praying to the saints. But, observe next, he does not quote from St. Eligius' own work, or refer to it on his own authority, but, well-read man as he is, notwithstanding, he is content to rely on the authority of two other writers, and (what many well-read men would have omitted to do) he candidly confesses it. He refers to Dr. Robertson, the Scotch historian, and the celebrated German historian and critic, Mosheim. I do not see, then, that much blame attaches to this writer for publishing what you will see presently is a most slanderous representation, beyond, indeed, his taking for granted the Protestant Tradition, his exercising faith in it as true, his not doubting the fidelity of the two authors in question, and, therefore, in a word, his saying " Mumpsimus " and passing it on.

Next we come to Dr. Robertson, the historian of Scotland, Charles the Fifth, and America, the friend of Hume, Adam Smith, Gibbon, and a host of literati of the latter part of last century. In his history of the reign of the Emperor Charles the Fifth, who lived at

[1] Hallam's Middle Ages, vol. iii. p. 353.

the time of the Reformation, after observing that "the Christian religion degenerated, during those ages of darkness, into an illiberal superstition;" that "the barbarous nations, instead of aspiring to *sanctity and virtue*, imagined that they satisfied every obligation of duty by a scrupulous *observance of external ceremonies*,"—Dr. Robertson annotates as follows:— "*All the religious maxims and practices* of the dark ages are a proof of this. I shall produce *one remarkable testimony* in confirmation of it, from an author canonised by the Church of Rome, St. Eloy, or Eligius." And then he proceeds to quote, nearly in the same words as Mr. Hallam, though omitting some clauses and adding others, a translation from the passage which Mosheim sets down in his history, as if the original text of the saint's. And then he adds the remark of Dr. Maclaine, Mosheim's English translator, whom he is pleased to call "learned and judicious," and whose remark he calls a "very proper reflection." This remark is as follows:—"We see here," says Maclaine, "a large and ample description of the character of a good Christian, in which there is not *the least* mention of the love of God, resignation to His will, obedience to His laws, or of justice, benevolence, and charity towards men." Here, then, we trace our "Mumpsimus" a step higher, from Hallam, to Robertson, from Robertson to the "learned and judicious" Maclaine.

Robertson and Maclaine were Scotchmen; but the Tradition was not idle the while in the south either. There was a certain learned Mr. White, well known, somewhat later than Robertson, in the University of Oxford. He was Professor of Arabic in that seat of learning, and happened one year to preach a set of lectures, which added most considerably to his reputation. I should not have noticed the circumstances attending them, did they not throw light on the measure of authority due to the divines, scholars, historians, statesmen, lawyers, and polite writers, who are the doctors of the Protestant Tradition. The lectures in question, which are delivered at Oxford yearly, on some theological subject, are in the appointment of the governors of the place; who, feeling the responsibility attached to this exercise of patronage, anxiously look about for the safest, or the most brilliant, or the most rising, or the most distinguished of their members, to whom to commit the guardianship of Protestantism, and the fair fame of the University. Some such person Mr. White was considered; and, on his appointment, he selected for his lectures a subject of great interest—the rise and genius of Mahomet and his religion. Of learning he had enough; eloquence, perhaps, he wanted; yet what must have surprised his audience, when the time came for his exhibition, was the special elegance, splendour, and vivacity, which showed themselves in his style. His periods, far from savouring of the austereness of an oriental linguist, displayed the imagery, the antithesis, the flow and the harmony of a finished rhetorician. The historian Gibbon, no mean judge of composition, goes out of his way, to speak of his lectures as "a volume of controversy" more "elegant and ingenious" than any Mohammedan pulpit was likely to have produced, had Oxford become Mohammedan, instead of Protestant; and is pleased to observe that the writer "sustains the part of a lively and eloquent advocate" while he "sometimes rises to the merit of an historian and a philosopher." Such were the lectures delivered, and such was the reputation in consequence obtained by the Arabic Professor: however, after a time, it came to light that a great portion of the volume, at least many of its finest passages, were the writing of another. Indeed he was obliged to confess that he employed in the work, and actually paid for it, a country curate in Devonshire (who, I think, had once been a dissenting preacher), whom he supplied with the raw material of thought, and who returned it back to him in a dress suitable to the audience to whom it was to be presented. This was the man, who was getting credit for what was not his own, who, in treating of Mahomet, must make a diversion from his course—which never comes amiss in a Protestant volume—in order to bring a charge of incapability and pretence against the Catholic Church; and what should he unluckily choose for the instrument of his attack but the identical passage of St. Eligius, and on that same authority of Mosheim, which we have already seen used by Hallam, Robertson, and Maclaine. Mr. White writes thus:—

"*No representation can convey stronger ideas of the melancholy state of religion* in the seventh century, than the description of the character of a good Christian, as drawn at that period by St. Eligius, or Eloi, Bishop of Noyon." And then he quotes the extract already cited, from the pages of Mosheim.

And now we are approaching the fountain-head of the Tradition, but first I must just allude to one other author of name, who bears the same testimony to "Mumpsimus," and simply on the same authority.

This is an elegant writer, a divine and an Archdeacon of the Established Church, Jortin, who in the year 1773, published " Remarks on Ecclesiastical History." In the table of contents prefixed to the third volume, we are referred to " Eligius' *system* of Religion : " and turning to the page set against that descriptive title, we are told, " In this seventh century, . . monkery flourished prodigiously, and the monks and Popes were in the firmest union. As to true religion, here is the *sum and substance* of it, as it is *drawn up* for us by Eligius, one of the principal saints of that age." And then follows the cut and dried passage as given by Mosheim.

Now, at last, let us proceed to the first father of Mumpsimus, the Lutheran Mosheim himself. His words run thus in his Ecclesiastical History: "During this century (the seventh) true religion lay buried under a senseless mass of superstitions, and was unable to raise her head. The earlier Christians . . taught that Christ had made expiation for the sins of men by His death and His blood; the latter " (those of the seventh century) " seemed to inculcate that the gates of heaven would be closed against none who should enrich the clergy or the Church with their donations. The former were studious to maintain a holy simplicity, and to follow a pure and chaste piety, the latter place the *substance* of religion *in external rites and bodily exercises*." And then, in order to illustrate this contrast, which he has drawn out, between the spirituality of the first Christians and the formality of the Papists, he quotes the famous passage which has been the matter of our investigation.

Brothers of the Oratory, take your last look at

the Protestant Tradition, ere it melts away into thin air from before your eyes. It carries with it a goodly succession of names, Mosheim, Jortin, Maclaine, Robertson, White, and Hallam. It extends from 1755 to the year 1833. But in this latter year, when it was now seventy-eight years old, it met with an accident, attended with fatal consequences. Some one for the first time, instead of blindly following the traditional statement, thought it worth while first to consult St. Eligius himself. His work is in every good library; but to no one had it occurred to take it down from the shelf, till the present Protestant Dean of Durham, Dr. Waddington, who was engaged in publishing an Ecclesiastical History at the date I have named. At first, indeed, he relied on his Protestant masters; and taking Mosheim for his guide, and quoting St. Eligius from Mosheim's volume, he observes that, as a saint was "a person of influence in his day, we may venture to record what, in his opinion, was the *sum and substance* of true religion." Then follows the old extract. This is at the 153rd page of Dr. Waddington's work; but, by the time he got to page 298, he had turned to the original, and the truth came out. He found that the received Protestant extract was only a small portion, nay, only sentences picked out here and there, of a very long sermon,—other sentences, of which, close by, and in the very midst of those actually quoted, contained all those very matters, the supposed absence of which was the very charge brought against St. Eligius, by Mosheim, Maclaine, Robertson, Jortin, White, and Hallam. They, forsooth, pure Protestants, had been so shocked and scandalized, that there was nothing of moral virtue in the saint's idea of a Christian, nothing of love of God or of man; nothing of justice, of truth, of knowledge, of honesty; whereas, in matter of fact, there turned out to be an abundance of these good things, drawn out in sentences of their own, though certainly not in the other sentences which those authors had extracted. I will quote what Dr. Waddington says, on his discovery of his mistake:—

He says that " the sense, and even the words " of the passage which he had cited, " had been previously retailed both by Robertson and Jortin, and the original quoted by Mosheim;" but that he had since "been led to look more particularly into the life of Eligius, as it is published in the 'Spicilegium Dacherii?'" Then he continues, "he"—that is himself, the Author—"was pleased to discover many excellent precepts and pious exhortations scattered among the strange matter"—so he speaks as a Protestant—"with which it abounds. But at the same time it was with great sorrow and some shame, that he ascertained the *treachery* of his historical conductor," that is, Mosheim. "The expressions cited by Mosheim," he continues, "and cited, too, with a direct reference to the 'Spicilegium,'" in which the Sermon is contained, "were forcibly brought together *by a very unpardonable mutilation* of his authority. They are to be found, indeed, in a Sermon preached by the Bishop, but found in the *society of so many good and Christian maxims*, that it had been charitable entirely to overlook them, as it was certainly unfair to weed them out and heap them together, without notice of the rich harvest that surrounds them."

He then proceeds to quote some of those exhortations of the Saint to which he alludes, and which Mosheim had omitted. For instance :—" Wherefore, my brethren, love your friends *in* God, and love your enemies *for* God, for he who loveth his neighbour hath fulfilled the law. . . . He is a good Christian who believes not in charms or inventions of the devil, but places the whole of his hope in Christ alone; who receives the stranger with joy, as though he were receiving Christ himself, . . . who gives alms to the poor in proportion to his possessions, . . . who has no deceitful balances or deceitful measures, . . . who both lives chastely himself, and teaches his neighbours and his children to live chastely, and in the fear of God. . . . Behold, ye have heard, my brethren, what sort of people good Christians are . . . to the end that ye be true Christians, always ponder the precepts of Christ in your mind, and also fulfil them in your practice. . . . Keep peace and charity, recall the contentious to concord, avoid lies, tremble at perjury, bear no false witness, commit no theft, . . . observe the Lord's day, . . . do as you would be done by, . . . visit the infirm, . . . seek out those who are in prison." So the holy Bishop proceeds; and *then* he adds, "If you observe *these things*, you may appear boldly at God's tribunal in the day of judgment, and say, Give, Lord, as we have given." Scattered about in the midst of these exhortations, are the few sentences, excellent also, in spite of Dr. Waddington, though they are not the whole of Christianity, which the Protestant writers have actually quoted.

Such is the Sermon upon which Dr. Maclaine

makes this (as Dr. Robertson thinks) "very proper reflection:" "We see here a large and ample description of the character of a good Christian, in which there is not *the least* mention of the love of God, resignation to His will, obedience to His laws, or justice, benevolence, or charity towards men." But as Mosheim and his followers have their opinion of St. Eligius, so, in turn, has Dr. Waddington his opinion of Mosheim. "The impression," he says, "which" Mosheim, by "stringing together" certain sentences "without any notice of the context, conveys to his readers, is *wholly false*; and the *calumny* thus indirectly cast upon his author is not the less reprehensible, because it falls on one of the obscurest saints in the Roman calendar. If the very essence of history be truth, and if any deliberate violation of that be sinful in the profane annalist, still less can it deserve pardon or mercy in the historian of the Church of Christ."

This, as I have said, took place in 1833: two years later the exposure was repeated, in a brilliant paper inserted by Dr. Maitland in an Ecclesiastical Magazine; the Editor, moreover, drawing the special attention of his readers to his correspondent's remarks.[2]

However, after all—after surveying the whole course of the exposure—I could not help expressing to myself my intense misgivings that the efforts of Dr. Waddington and Dr. Maitland to do justice to the saint would be in vain. I knew enough of the Protestant mind, to be aware how little the falsehood of any one of its traditions is an effectual reason for

---

[2] I do not add Dr. Lingard, as being a Catholic authority.

its relinquishing it; and I find too truly that I was not mistaken in my anticipation. Mumpsimus still reigns. In a new edition of Mosheim's history, published in 1841, the editor, a recent successor of Mr. White in the Oxford lectures, reprints those precious legacies, the text of Mosheim, the "very proper reflection" of Maclaine, and the garbled quotation from St. Eligius, for the benefit of the rising generation of divines, without a word of remark, or anything whatever to show that a falsehood had been recklessly uttered, a falsehood blindly perpetuated, a falsehood luminously exposed.

3.

2. I have given you, my Brothers, a specimen of the Tradition of Literature; now I proceed to the Tradition of Wealth, Respectability, Virtue, and Enlightened Religion ; for all these, in a country like ours, are supposed to go together, the Tradition of our merchants, traders, and men of business, and of all who have anything to lose, and are, therefore, conscientiously attached to the Constitution. And I shall select, as the organ of their Tradition, a writer whom they will at once acknowledge to be an unexceptionable representative of their ideas. If there be a periodical of the day which lays claim to knowledge of this globe, and of all that is in it, which is catholic in its range of subjects, its minute curiosity, and its world-wide correspondence, which has dealings with all the religions of the earth, and ought to have the largeness and liberality of view which such manifold intercourse is calculated to create,

it is the *Times* newspaper. No men avow so steady a devotion to the great moral precepts embodied in the Decalogue, as its conductors, or profess so fine a sense of honour and duty, or are so deeply conscious of their own influence on the community, and of the responsibilities which it involves, or are so alive to the truth of the maxim, that, in the general run of things, honesty is the best policy. What noble, manly, disinterested sentiments do they utter! what upright intention, strong sense, and sturdy resolution, are the staple of their compositions! what indignation do they manifest at the sight of vice or baseness! what detestation of trickery! what solemn resolve to uphold the oppressed! what generous sympathy with innocence calumniated! what rising of heart against tyranny! what gravity of reprobation! how, when Catholic and Protestant are in fierce political antagonism, they can mourn over breaches of charity in which they protest the while they had no share! with what lively sensibility and withering scorn do they encounter the accusation, made against them by rivals every half-dozen years, of venality or tergiversation! If anywhere is to be found the sternness of those who are severe because they are pure—who may securely cast stones, for none can cast at them—who, like the Cherub in the poem, are "faithful found among the faithless"—you would say that here at length you had found the incorruptible and infallible, the guides in a bad world, who, amid the illusions of reason and the sophistries of passion, see the path of duty on all questions whatever, with a luminousness, a keenness, and a certainty special to themselves. When, then, I would illustrate the value of the Anti-Catholic Tradition, as existing among the money-making classes of the community, I cannot fix upon a more suitable sample than the statements of these accomplished writers. Accordingly I refer to their columns; and towards the end of a leading article, in the course of the last month or six weeks, I find the following sentence:—"It is the practice, as our readers are aware, in Roman Catholic countries, for the clergy to post up a list of *all the crimes* to which human frailty can be tempted, placing opposite to them the *exact sum* of money for which their perpetration will be indulged."[3] And what makes this statement the more emphatic, is the circumstance that, within two or three sentences afterwards,—ever mindful, as I have said, of the Tables of the Law,—the writer takes occasion to refer to the divine prohibition, "Thou shalt not bear false witness against thy neighbour."

Such is a specimen of the Tradition, marvellous to say, as it exists among the classes who are well-to-do in the world. You see, they are so clear on the point, that, for all their mercantile sense of the value of character, their disgust at false intelligence, their severity with fraud, and their sensitiveness at libel, they have no hesitation in handing down to the next generation this atrocious imputation, that the Catholic Church proclaims that she is commissioned by the Moral Governor of the world to bestow on her children permission to perpetrate any sin whatever, for which they have a fancy, on condition of their paying her a price in money for that perpetration, in proportion to the heinousness of the offence.

June, 1851.

Now this accusation is not only so grave in itself, but, miserable to say, is so industriously circulated, that, before using it for the purpose for which I have introduced it, in order to remove all suspicion against us, I am induced to go out of my way to enunciate, as briefly and as clearly as I can, what the Catholic Church really does teach upon the subject.[4] The charge in question then rests on a confusion between the *forgiveness of sins* and *admission to Church communion*, two ideas perfectly distinct from each other, both in themselves and in Catholic theology. Every scandalous sin contains in it, as we consider, two separate offences, the offence against God, and the offence against the Church; just as Protestants would allow that murder is at once a sin against God and our neighbour, a sin in the eyes of God, and a crime in the eyes of the law. And, as human society has the arbitrary power of assigning punishments to offences against itself, heavy or light, or of overlooking the offence altogether, or of remitting the penalty when imposed, so has the Church. And as the magistrate often inflicts a fine, under sanction of the law, instead of committing to prison, so does the Church allow of the commutation of her own punishments, which are called censures, into alms to the poor, into offerings for some religious object, or even into the mere paying the expenses of the process, that is, the costs of the suit. And as the connivance or free pardon of the magistrate is no pardon in the sight of Heaven of the adulterer or the burglar, nor is

---

[4] The subject of indulgences does not enter into the charge as contained in the extract from the *Times;* but I purpose to add a word about it before the end of the Volume.

supposed to be such, so neither does the offender receive, nor is he promised, any forgiveness of his sin, either by the Church's taking off the censure (whether in consequence of an almsgiving or otherwise), or by her forbearing, which is the common case, to inflict censure altogether. It is true, the Church has the power of forgiving sins also, which I shall speak of directly; but this is by a different instrument, and by a totally different process, as every Catholic knows.

I repeat, the Catholic who perpetrates any great and public sin offends his Maker, and offends his ecclesiastical Society; the injury against his Maker is punished by an *ipso facto* separation from His favour; the injury against his Society, when it is visited at all, is visited by excommunication or other spiritual infliction. The successor of St. Peter has the power committed to him of pardoning both offences, the offence against God and the offence against the Church; he is the ultimate source of all jurisdiction whether external or internal, but he commonly restores such a sinner to the visible society of Christians, by an act of his own or of the metropolitan or ordinary, and he reconciles him to God by the agency of the priesthood. Repentance is required on the part of the offender for both restorations; but the *sin* is forgiven, and its punishment remitted only in one of them,—viz., in the Sacrament of *Penance;* and in this Sacrament, in which is the only real pardon, no money is, or ever can be paid. The Sacrament cannot be bought; such an act would be a horrible crime; you know this, my Brothers, as I know it myself; we witness to each other that such is the received teaching among us. It is utterly false then to assert that it has ever been held in the Catholic Church that "the perpetration of crime could be indulged" for any sum of money. Neither for sins committed, nor sins to come, has money ever been taken as an equivalent, for one no more than for the other. On the other hand, it is quite true that the injury done to the Church, when it happens to have been visited with a censure (which is not a common case), has certainly sometimes been compensated by the performance of some good work and in the number of such works, almsdeeds and religious offerings are included. I repeat, the Church as little dreams of forgiving the sinner by removing the censure and readmitting him to public communion, as the magistrate by letting a culprit out of prison.

And in matter of fact, the two acts, the external reconciliation and the inward absolution, are not necessarily connected together. The Church is composed of bad as well as good, according to the Parable, which prophesied that the net should gather of every kind; a man then may be readmitted to visible fellowship on a general profession of repentance, yet when he proceeds to the Sacrament of Penance, may be unable to satisfy the priest that his repentance is sincere, and thus may fail of absolution. Then he would be in a case, alas! so commonly found in the Church, and ever to be found—viz., allowed to attend mass, to hear sermons, to take part in rites, offices, and processions, and regarded as a Christian, yet debarred from the use of the Sacraments, deprived of Penance and of Holy Eucharist, getting no benefit from Indulgences, meriting nothing for his salvation, but on the contrary being separate from his God, and lying under His wrath, and a dead branch, though he has offered his alms, and is visibly connected with the trunk. On the other hand, it is quite conceivable in idea, that the spiritual reconciliation, that is, the forgiveness of sin, might be bestowed without the external or ecclesiastical restoration. Something like this took place, I think, in the case of the Emperor Napoleon, who up to the time of his death, lay under the censures of the Church, and was excommunicate, yet in his last days expressed a desire to be reconciled to God. To the ecclesiastical society whom he had offended, he was not publicly reconciled; but it is never too late to be saved; he confessed, he received the priest's reconciliation to the Church and to God; and if his repentance was true, he departed with an absolute certainty of Heaven, though he had not received that pontifical restoration to the visible body to which offerings and alms have sometimes been attached.[5]

However, in spite of the clear and broad distinction I have been laying down, it is the Tradition of Protestantism, immutable and precise, as expressed in the words of its eminent Teacher and Doctor I have quoted, that the Catholic Church professes to forgive sins past and to come, on the payment of a price. So it has come down to us, so it will flow on; and the mighty flood of falsehood is continually fed and

---

[5] I think I recollect an *absolutio post mortem*, when La Belle Poule was sent out for his remains. I do not forget the passage in the Council, *Pie admodum, ne hac ipsâ occasione quis pereat*, &c. Sess. 14, de Pœn. c. 7. *Vide* Ferrari's Biblioth. v. Absol. art. 1. 55—57.

kept to the full by fresh and fresh testimonies, separate and independent, till scepticism is overcome and opposition is hopeless. And now I am going to give you an account of one of these original authorities, as they are considered, who has lately presented himself to the world in the person of a zealous Protestant clergyman, who once visited Belgium, and on occasion of the late outcry about "Popish Aggression" was moved to give his brethren the benefit of his ocular testimony in behalf of one of the most flagrant abuses and abominations of "that corrupt Church."

His account, given at a public meeting, was to the following effect:—That in the year 1835, when on a visit to Brussels, he was led to inspect the door of the Cathedral, St. Gudule's; and that there he saw fastened up a catalogue of sins, with a specification of the prices of which remission of each might severally be obtained. No circumstance, it would appear, called for his giving this information to the world for the long space of sixteen years; and it is a pity, for the Protestant cause, that another sixteen did not pass before circumstances suggested his doing so. Why did he not consign it to some safe volume of controversy, weighty enough for England, too heavy for the Channel, instead of committing it to the wings of the wind and the mercy of reporters? Then tranquilly and leisurely would the solemn tale have ventured out upon platforms and into pulpits, when contemporaries were gone, and would have taken its place beside my own Don Felix of Andalusia and similar worthies of Exeter Hall. But the fates willed otherwise; the accessory was to join the main stream at once, and to its surprise to be tumbled violently into its bed. The noise drew attention; curiosity was excited; the windings of the infant rill were prematurely tracked to its source; so we can now put our finger on the first welling of its waters, and we can ascertain the composition of a Protestant tradition.

On the news of this portentous statement getting to Brussels, it excited a commotion which it could not rouse among the Catholics of England. We are familiarised to calumny, and have learned resignation ; the good Belgians were surprised and indignant at what they had thought no sane man would have ventured to advance. Forthwith a declaration was put forth by the persons especially interested in the Cathedral, categorically denying the charge. It is signed by the Dean of Brussels, who is also curé of the Cathedral, by his four assistant clergymen, by the churchwardens, by the judge of the high court of justice, and two other judges, and by others. They observe that they had privately asked the accuser to withdraw his statement, and on his refusal they made the following terse Declaration :—

"The undersigned look upon it as a duty to come forward and protest against the allegations of the" clergyman in question. "They declare, upon their honour, that such a notice as the one spoken of by the said clergyman has never disgraced the entrance, either of the church of St. Gudule, or of any other church of Brussels, or of the whole country. They further declare, that they have never even suspected for one instant that permission to sin could, for any possible motive, be granted, nor that any one could ever obtain remission of his sins for money. Such a doctrine they repudiate with indignation, as it is, and always has been, repudiated by the whole of the Catholic Church." This declaration is dated, "Brussels, April 2, 1851."

One thing alone was wanting to complete the refutation of the slander; and that was, to account how its author was betrayed into so extraordinary a misrepresentation. No one will accuse a respectable person of wilful and deliberate falsehood; did his eyes or his memory deceive him? or did he really see something on the door, which he wrongly translated and interpreted by his prejudices? That the latter is the true explanation of the phenomenon, is probable from a piece of information with which a Brussels journal supplies us. I dare say you know that in cathedrals and large churches abroad chairs are used for worship instead of benches; and they are generally farmed by the beadles or others attached to the church, who let them out to all comers at the price of a small copper coin every time they are used. Now, it so happens that on the right-hand door of the transept of this church of St. Gudule there really is affixed a black board, on which there is a catalogue in the French language of the price to be paid, not for sins, but for the use of these chairs. The inscription translated runs as follows:—" A chair without cushion, one cent (about a farthing); a chair with cushions, two cents. On great festival days; a chair without cushion, two cents; a chair with cushion, four cents." This board, it may be supposed, our anti-Catholic witness mistook for that abominable sin-table, the description of which so deservedly shocked the zealous Protestants of Faversham.

Such is the ultimate resolution, as detected in a particular instance, of that uniform and incontestable Protestant Tradition, that we sell sin for money. The exposure happened in March and April; but Protestantism is infallible, and the judgment of its doctors irreversible; accordingly, in the following June, the newspaper I have mentioned thought it necessary to show that the Tradition was not injured by the blow; so out came the Tradition again, "though brayed in a mortar," not at all the worse for the accident, in that emphatic statement which I quoted when I opened the subject, and which I now quote again that I am closing it. "It is the practice," the writer pronounces *ex cathedrâ*, "*as our readers are aware*, in Roman Catholic countries to post up a list of all the crimes to which human frailty can be tempted, placing opposite to them the exact sum of money for which their perpetration will be indulged."

4.

3. Two of my instances are despatched, and now I come to my third. There is something so tiresome in passing abruptly from one subject to another, that I need your indulgence, my Brothers, in making this third beginning; yet it has been difficult to avoid it, when my very object is to show what extensive subject-matters and what different classes of the community are acted on by the Protestant Tradition. Now I am proceeding to the Legislature of the Nation, and will give an instance of its operation in a respectable political party.

In this case, its fountain springs up, as it were, under our very feet, and we shall have no difficulty at all in judging of its quality. Its history is as follows:—

Coaches, omnibuses, carriages, and cars, day after day drive up and down the Hagley Road; passengers lounge to and fro on the foot-path; and close alongside of it are discovered one day the nascent foundations and rudiments of a considerable building. On inquiring, it is found to be intended for a Catholic, nay, even for a monastic establishment. This leads to a good deal of talk, especially when the bricks begin to show above the surface. Meantime the unsuspecting architect is taking his measurements, and ascertains that the ground is far from lying level; and then, since there is a prejudice among Catholics in favour of horizontal floors, he comes to the conclusion that the bricks of the basement must rise above the surface higher at one end of the building than at the other; in fact, that whether he will or no, there must be some construction of the nature of a vault or cellar at the extremity in question, a circumstance not at all inconvenient, considering it also happens to be the kitchen end of the building. Accordingly, he turns his necessity into a gain, and by the excavation of a few feet of earth, he forms a number of chambers convenient for various purposes, partly beneath, partly above the line of the ground. While he is thus intent on his work, loungers, gossipers, alarmists are busy at theirs too. They go round the building, they peep into the underground brickwork, and are curious about the drains;[6] they moralise

---

[6] It is undeniable, though the gentleman who has brought the matter before the public has accidentally omitted to mention it, that the Protestant feeling has also been excited by the breadth of the drain, which is considered excessive, and moreover *crosses the road*. There exists some nervousness on the subject in the neighbourhood, as I have been seriously given to understand. There is a remarkable passage, too, in

about Popery and its spread; at length they trespass upon the enclosure, they dive into the half-finished shell, and they take their fill of seeing what is to be seen, and imagining what is not. Every house is built on an idea; you do not build a mansion like a public office, or a palace like a prison, or a factory like a shooting box, or a church like a barn. Religious houses, in like manner, have their own idea; they have certain indispensable peculiarities of form and internal arrangement. Doubtless, there was much in the very idea of an Oratory perplexing to the Protestant intellect, and inconsistent with Protestant notions of comfort and utility. Why should so large a room be here? why so small a room there? why a passage so long and wide? and why so long a wall without a window? the very size of the house needs explanation. Judgments which had employed themselves on the high subject of a Catholic hierarchy and its need, found no difficulty in dogmatising on bedrooms and closets. There was much to suggest matter of suspicion, and to predispose the trespasser to doubt whether he had yet got to the bottom of the subject. At length one question flashed upon his

the scientific report, which our accuser brings forward, and which has never been answered or perhaps construed: "One of the compartments was larger than the rest, and *was evidently to be covered in without the building over it.*" This is not the first time a dwelling of mine has been the object of a mysterious interest. When our cottages at Littlemore were in course of preparation, they were visited on horseback and on foot by many of the most distinguished residents of the University of Oxford. Heads of houses and canons did not scruple to investigate the building within and without, and some of them went so far as to inspect and theorise upon the most retired portions of the premises. Perhaps some thirty years hence, in some "History of my own Times," speculations may be found on the subject, in aid of the Protestant Tradition.

mind: what can such a house have to do with cellars? cellars and monks, what can be their mutual relation? monks—to what possible use can they put pits, and holes, and corners, and outhouses, and sheds? A sensation was created; it brought other visitors; it spread; it became an impression, a belief; the truth lay bare; a tradition was born; a fact was elicited which henceforth had many witnesses. *Those cellars were cells.* How obvious when once stated! and every one who entered the building, every one who passed by, became, I say, in some sort, ocular vouchers for what had often been read of in books, but for many generations had happily been unknown to England, for the incarcerations, the torturings, the starvings, the immurings, the murderings proper to a monastic establishment.

Now I am tempted to stop for a while in order to *improve* (as the evangelical pulpits call it) this most memorable discovery. I will therefore briefly consider it under the heads of—1. THE ACCUSATION; 2. ITS GROUNDS; 3. THE ACCUSERS; and, 4. THE ACCUSED.

First.—THE ACCUSATION.—It is this,—that the Catholics, building the house in question, were in the practice of committing *murder.* This was so strictly the charge, that, had the platform selected for making it been other than we know it to have been, I suppose the speaker might have been indicted for libel. His words were these:—"It was not usual for a coroner to hold an *inquest,* unless where a rumour had got abroad that there was a *necessity* for one; and how was a rumour to come *from the underground cells of the convents?* Yes, he repeated, underground cells: and he would tell them something about such places.

At this moment, in the parish of Edgbaston, within the borough of Birmingham, there was a large convent, of some kind or other, being erected, and the whole of the underground was fitted up with cells; *and what were those cells for?*"

Secondly.—THE GROUNDS OF THE ACCUSATION.—they are simple; behold them: 1. That the house is built level; 2. and that the plot of earth on which it is built is higher at one end than at the other.

Thirdly.—THE ACCUSERS.—This, too, throws light upon the character of Protestant traditions. Not weak and ignorant people only, not people at a distance—but educated men, gentlemen well connected, high in position, men of business, men of character, members of the legislature, men familiar with the locality, men who know the accused by name,—such are the men who deliberately, reiteratedly, in spite of being set right, charge certain persons with pitiless, savage practices; with beating and imprisoning, with starving, with murdering their dependents.

Fourthly.—THE ACCUSED.—I feel ashamed, my Brothers, of bringing my own matters before you, when far better persons have suffered worse imputations; but bear with me. *I* then am the accused. A gentleman of blameless character, a county member, with whose near relatives I have been on terms of almost fraternal intimacy for a quarter of a century, who knows me by repute far more familiarly (I suppose) than anyone in this room knows me, putting aside my personal friends; he it is who charges me, and others like me, with delighting in blood, with enjoying the shrieks and groans of agony and despair, with presiding at a banquet of dislocated limbs, quivering muscles, and wild countenances. Oh, what a world is this! Could he look into our eyes and say it? Would he have the heart to say it, if he recollected of whom he said it? For who are we? Have we lived in a corner? have we come to light suddenly out of the earth? We have been nourished, for the greater part of our lives, in the bosom of the great schools and universities of Protestant England: we have been the foster sons of the Edwards and Henries, the Wykehams and Wolseys, of whom Englishmen are wont to make much; we have grown up amid hundreds of contemporaries, scattered at present all over the country, in those special ranks of society which are the very walk of a member of the legislature. Our names are better known to the educated classes of the country than those of any others who are not public men. Moreover, if there be men in the whole world who may be said to live *in publico*, it is the members of a College at one of our Universities; living, not in private houses, not in families, but in one or two apartments which are open to all the world, at all hours, with nothing, I may say, their own; with college servants, a common table,—nay, their chairs and their bedding, and their cups and saucers, down to their coal-scuttle and their carpet brooms,—a sort of common property, and the right of their neighbours. Such is that manner of life,—in which nothing, I may say, can be hid; where no trait of character or peculiarity of conduct but comes to broad day—such is the life I myself led for above a quarter of a century, under the eyes of numbers who are familiarly known to my accusers; such is almost the life which we all have led ever since we have been in Birmingham, with our house open to all comers, and ourselves accessible, I may almost say at any hour; and this being so, considering the *charge*, and the *evidence*, and the *accuser*, and the *accused*, could we Catholics desire a more apposite illustration of the formation and the value of a Protestant Tradition?

I set it down for the benefit of time to come; "though for no other cause," as a great author says, "yet for this: that posterity may know we have not loosely, through silence, permitted things to pass away as in a dream, there shall be for men's information extant thus much." One commonly forgets such things, from the trouble and inconvenience of having to remember them; let one specimen last, of many which have been suffered to perish, of the birth of an anti-Catholic tradition. The nascent fable has indeed failed, as the tale about the Belgian sin-table has failed, but it might have thriven: it has been lost by bad nursing; it ought to have been cherished awhile in those underground receptacles where first it drew breath, till it could comfortably bear the light; till its limbs were grown, and its voice was strong, and we on whom it bore had run our course, and gone to our account; and then it might have raised its head without fear and without reproach, and might have magisterially asserted what there was none to deny. But men are all the creatures of circumstances; they are hurried on to a ruin which they may see, but cannot evade: so has it been with the Edgbaston Tradition. It was spoken on the house-tops when it should have been whispered in closets, and it expired in the effort. Yet it might have been allotted, let us never forget, a happier destiny. It might have smouldered and spread through a portion of our Birmingham population; it might have rested obscurely on their memories, and now and then risen upon their tongues; there might have been flitting notions, misgivings, rumours, voices, that the horrors of the Inquisition were from time to time renewed in our subterranean chambers; and fifty years hence, if some sudden frenzy of the hour roused the Anti-Catholic jealousy still lingering in the town, a mob might have swarmed about our innocent dwelling, to rescue certain legs of mutton and pats of butter from imprisonment, and to hold an inquest over a dozen packing-cases, some old hampers, a knife-board, and a range of empty blacking bottles.

Thus I close my third instance of the sort of evidence commonly adducible for the great Protestant Tradition; not the least significant circumstance about them all being this, that though in the case of all three that evidence is utterly disproved, yet in not one of the three is the charge founded on it withdrawn. In spite of Dr. Waddington, Dr. Maitland, and Mr. Rose, the editors of Mosheim still print and publish his slander on St. Eligius; in defiance of the Brussels protest, and the chair tariff of St. Gudule, the Kent clergyman and the *Times* still bravely maintain our traffic in sins; in violence to the common sense of mankind, the rack and the pulley are still affirmed to be busy in the dungeons of Edgbaston;—for Protestantism must be maintained as the Religion of Englishmen, and part and parcel of the Law of the land.

And now, in conclusion, I will but state my conviction, which I am sure to have confirmed by every intelligent person who takes the trouble to examine the subject, that such slanders as I have instanced are the real foundation on which the anti-Catholic feeling mainly rests in England, and without which it could not long be maintained. Doubtless there are arguments of a different calibre, whatever their worth, which weigh against Catholics with half a-dozen members of a University, with the speculative Church-restorer, with the dilettante divine, with the fastidious scholar, and with some others of a higher character of mind; whether St. Justin Martyr said this or that; whether images should be dressed in muslin, or hewn out of stone; what is the result of criticism on passages in the prophets;—questions such as these, and others of a more serious cast, may be conclusive for or against the Church in the study or in the lecture-room, but they have no influence with the many. As to those charges which do weigh with the people at large, the more they can be examined, the more, I am convinced, will they be found to be untrue. It is by wholesale, retail, systematic, unscrupulous lying, for I can use no gentler term, that the many rivulets are made to flow for the feeding the great Protestant Tradition,—the Tradition of the Court, the Tradition of the Law, the Tradition of the Legislature, the Tradition of the Establishment, the Tradition of Literature, the Tradition of Domestic Circles, the Tradition of the Populace.

LECTURE IV.

TRUE TESTIMONY INSUFFICIENT FOR THE PROTESTANT VIEW.

I.

I CAN fancy, my Brothers, that some of you may have been startled at a statement I made at the close of my Lecture of last week. I then said, that the more fully the imputations which were cast upon us were examined, the more unfounded they would turn out to be; so that the great Tradition on which we are persecuted is little short of one vast pretence or fiction. On this you may be led to ask me whether I mean to deny all and everything which can be advanced to the disadvantage of the Catholic Church, and whether I recommend you to do the same? but this was not my meaning. Some things which are charged against us are doubtless true, and we see no harm in them, though Protestants do; other charges are true, yet, as we think, only go to form ingenious objections; others again are true, and relate to what is really sinful and detestable, as we allow as fully as Protestants can urge: but all these real facts, whatever their worth taken altogether, do not go any way towards proving true the Protestant Traditionary View of us; they are vague and unsatisfactory, and, to apply a common phrase, they beat about the bush. If you would have some direct downright proof that Catholicism is what Protestants make it to be, something which will come up to the mark, you must lie; else you will not get beyond feeble suspicions, which may be right, but may be wrong. Hence Protestants are obliged to cut their ninth commandment out of their Decalogue. "Thou shalt not bear false witness against thy neighbour" must go, must disappear; their position requires the sacrifice. The substance, the force, the edge of their Tradition is slander. As soon as ever they disabuse their minds of what is false, and grasp only what is true,—I do not say they at once become Catholics; I do not say they lose their dislike to our religion, or their misgivings about its working;—but I say this, either they become tolerant towards us, and cease to hate us personally,—or, at least, supposing they cannot shake off old associations, and are prejudiced and hostile as before, still they find they have not the means of communicating their own feelings to others. To Protestantism False Witness is the principle of propagation. There are indeed able men who can make a striking case out of anything or nothing, as great painters give a meaning and a unity to the commonest bush, and pond, and paling and stile: genius can do without facts, as well as create them; but few possess the gift. Taking things as they are, and judging of them by the long run, one may securely say, that the anti-Catholic Tradition could not be kept alive, would die of exhaustion, without a continual supply of fable.

I repeat, not everything which is said to our disadvantage is without foundation in fact; but it is not the true that tells against us in the controversy, but the false. The Tradition requires bold painting; its prominent outline, its glaring colouring, needs to be a falsehood. So was it at the time of the Reformation; the multitude would never have been converted by exact reasoning and by facts which could be proved; so its upholders were clever enough to call the Pope Antichrist, and they let the startling accusation sink into men's minds. Nothing else would have succeeded; and they pursue the same tactics now. No inferior charge, I say, would have gained for them the battle; else, why should they have had recourse to it? Few persons tell atrocious falsehoods for the sake of telling them. If truth had been sufficient to put down Catholicism, the Reformers would not have had recourse to fiction. Errors indeed creep in by chance, whatever be the point of inquiry or dispute; but I am not accusing Protestants merely of incidental or of attendant error, but I mean that falsehood is the very staple of the views which they have been taught to entertain of us.

I allow there are true charges which can be brought against us; certainly, not only do I not deny it, but I hardly could deny it without heresy. I say distinctly, did I take upon me to deny everything which could be said against us, I should be proving too much, I should startle the Catholic theologian as well as Protestants; for what would it be but implying that the Church contains none within her pale but the just and holy? This was the heresy of the Novatians and Donatists of old time; it was the heresy of our Lollards, and others, such as Luther, who maintained that bad men are not members of the Church, that none but the predestinate are her members. But this no Catholic asserts, every Catholic denies. Every Catholic has ever denied it, back to the very time of the Apostles and their Divine Master; and He and they deny it. Christ denies it, St. Paul denies it, the Catholic Church denies it; our Lord expressly said that the Church was to be like a net, which gathered of every kind, not only of the good, but of the bad too. Such was *His* Church; it does not prove then that we are *not* His Church, because we are *like* His Church; rather our being *like* the Primitive Christian body, is a reason for concluding that we are *one* with it. We cannot make His Church better than He made her; we must be content with her as He made her, or not pretend to follow Him. He said, "Many are called, few are chosen;" men come into the Church, and then they fall. They are not indeed sinning at the very time when they are brought into His family, at the time they are new born; but as children grow up, and converts live on, the time too frequently comes, when they fall under the power of one kind of temptation or other, and fall from grace, either for a while or for good. Thus, not indeed by the divine wish and intention, but by the divine permission, and man's perverseness, there is a vast load of moral evil existing in the Church; an enemy has sown weeds there, and those weeds remain among the wheat till the harvest. And this evil in the Church is not found only in the laity, but among the clergy too; there have been bad priests, bad bishops, bad monks, bad nuns, and bad Popes. If this, then, is the charge made against us, that we do not all live up to our calling, but that there are Catholics, lay and clerical, who may be proved to be worldly, revengeful, licentious, slothful, cruel, nay, may be unbelievers, we grant it at once. We not only grant it, but we zealously maintain it. "In a great house," says St. Paul, "there are not only vessels of gold and silver, but also of wood and of earth; and some indeed unto honour, but some unto dishonour." There are, alas, plenty of children of the Church, who by their bad lives insult and disgrace their Mother.

The Church, it is true, has been promised many great things, but she has not been promised the souls of all her children. She is promised truth in religious teaching; she is promised duration to the end of the world; she is made the means of grace; she is unchangeable in Creed and in constitution; she will ever cover the earth; but her children are not infallible separately, any more than they are immortal; not indefectible, any more than they are ubiquitous. Therefore, if Protestants wish to form arguments which really would tell against us, they must show, not that individuals are immoral or profane, but that the Church teaches, or enjoins, or recommends, what is immoral or profane; rewards, encourages, or at least does not warn and discountenance, the sinner; or promulgates rules, and enforces practices, which directly lead to sin;—and this indeed they try to do, but they find the task not near so pleasant as the short and easy method of adopting strong, round, thorough-going statements, which are not true.

We do not then feel as a difficulty, on the contrary we teach as a doctrine, that there are scandals in the Church. "It must needs be, that scandals come; nevertheless, woe to that man by whom the scandal cometh." There are, to all appearance, multitudes of Catholics who have passed out of the world unrepentant, and are lost; there are multitudes living in sin, and out of grace; priests may and do fall, in this or that country, at this or that time, though they are exceptions to the rule; or there may be parties or knots of ecclesiastics, who take a low view of their duty, or adopt dangerous doctrines; or they may be covetous, or unfeeling, as other men, and use their power tyrannically, or for selfish, secular ends. There may be a declension and deterioration of the priesthood of a whole country. There may be secret unbelievers, both among clergy and laity; or individuals who are tending in their imaginations and their reasonings to grievous error or heresy. There may be great disorders in some particular monastery or nunnery; or a love of ease and slothful habits, and a mere formality in devotion, in particular orders of Religious, at particular seasons. There may be self-indulgence, pride, ambition, political profligacy, in certain bishops in particular states of society, as for instance, when the Church has been long established and abounds in wealth. And there may have been Popes before now, who to the letter have fulfilled the awful description of the unfaithful servant and steward, who began to "strike the men servants and maid servants, and to eat and drink and be drunken." All this may be granted; but before the admission can avail as an argument against the Catholic Church, one thing has to be examined, whether on the whole her influence and her action is on the side of what is wrong, or rather (as is the case) simply powerful on the side of good; one thing has to be proved, that the scandals within her pale have been caused by her principles, her teaching, her injunctions, or, which pretty nearly comes to the same thing, that they do not also exist, and as grievously (Catholics would say, they exist far more grievously), external to her.

2.

Now here is the flaw in the argument. For instance, it is plausibly objected that disorders not only sometimes do, but must occur, where priests are bound to celibacy. Even the candid Protestant will be apt to urge against us, " You must not argue from the case of the few, from persons of high principle and high education ; but taking the run of men, you must allow that the vow will not be kept by numbers of those who have got themselves to take it." Now I will not reply, as I might well do, by pointing out the caution which the Church observes in the selection of her priests ; how it is her rule to train them carefully for many years beforehand with this one thought in view, that priests they are to be ; how she tries them during their training ; how she takes one and rejects another, not with any reflection on those who are rejected, but simply because she finds they are not called to this particular state of life ; how, when she has selected a man, a hundred provisions and checks in detail are thrown around his person, which are to be his safeguard in his arduous calling ; lastly, how, when he is once called to his high ministry, he has, unless he be wonderfully wanting to himself, the power of divine grace abundantly poured upon him, without which all human means are useless, but which can do, and constantly does, miracles, as the experience, not of priest merely, but of every one who has been converted from a life of sin, will abundantly testify ;—I might enlarge on considerations such as these, but I put them aside, because I wish to address myself to the question of fact.

When, then, we come to the matter of fact, whether celibacy *has been* and *is*, in comparison of the marriage vow, so dangerous to a clerical body, I answer that I am very sceptical indeed that in matter of fact a married clergy *is* adorned, in any special and singular way, with the grace of purity; and this is just the very thing which Protestants take for granted. What is the use of speaking against our discipline, till they have proved their own to be better? Now I deny that they succeed with their rule of matrimony, better than we do with our rule of celibacy; and I deny it on no private grounds, or secret means of information, or knowledge of past years. I have lived in one place all my days, and know very few married clergymen, and those of such excellence and consistency of life, that I should feel it to be as absurd to suspect any of them of the slightest impropriety in their conduct, as to suspect the Catholic priests with whom I am well acquainted; and this is saying a great deal. When I speak of a married ministry, I speak of it, not from any knowledge I possess more than another: but I must avow that the public prints and the conversation of the world, by means of many shocking instances, which of course are only specimens of many others, heavier or lighter, which do *not* come before the world, bring home to me the fact, that a Protestant rector or a dissenting preacher is not necessarily kept from the sins I am speaking of, because he happens to be married: and when he offends, whether in a grave way or less seriously, still in all cases he has by matrimony but exchanged a bad sin for a worse, and has become an adulterer instead of being a seducer. Matrimony only does this for him, that his purity is at once less protected and less suspected. I am very sceptical, then, of the universal correctness of Protestant ministers, whether in the Establishment or in Dissent. I repeat, I know perfectly well, that there are a great number of high-minded men among the married Anglican clergy who would as soon think of murder, as of trespassing by the faintest act of indecorum upon the reverence which is due from them to others; nor am I denying, what, though of course I cannot assert it on any knowledge of mine, yet I wish to assert with all my heart, that the majority of Wesleyan and dissenting ministers lead lives beyond all reproach; but still allowing all this, the terrible instances of human frailty of which one reads and hears in the Protestant clergy, are quite enough to show that the married state is no sort of testimonial for moral correctness, no safeguard whether against scandalous offences, or (much less) against minor forms of the same general sin. Purity is not a virtue which comes merely as a matter of course to the married any more than to the single, though of course there is a great difference between man and man; and though it is impossible to bring the matter fairly to an issue, yet for that very reason I have as much right to my opinion as another to his, when I state my deliberate conviction that there are, to say the least, as many offences against the marriage vow among Protestant ministers, as there are against the vow of celibacy among Catholic priests. I may go very much further than this in my own view of the matter, and think, as I do, that the priest's vow is generally the occasion of virtues which a married clergy does not contemplate even in idea; but I am on the defensive, and only insist on so much as is necessary for my purpose.

But if matrimony does not prevent cases of immorality among Protestant ministers, it is not celibacy which causes them among Catholic priests. It is not what the Catholic Church imposes, but what human nature prompts, which leads any portion of her ecclesiastics into sin. Human nature will break out, like some wild and raging element, under any system; it bursts out under the Protestant system; it bursts out under the Catholic; passion will carry away the married clergyman as well as the unmarried priest. On the other hand, there are numbers to whom there would be, not greater, but less, trial in the vow of celibacy than in the vow of marriage, as so many persons prefer Teetotalism to the engagement to observe Temperance.

Till, then, you can prove that celibacy causes what matrimony certainly does not prevent, you do nothing at all. This is the language of common sense. It is the world, the flesh, and the devil, not celibacy, which is the ruin of those who fall. Slothful priests, why, where was there any religion whatever, established and endowed, in which bishops, canons, and wealthy rectors were not exposed to the temptation of pride and sensuality? The wealth is in fault, not the rules of the Church. Preachers have denounced the evil, and ecclesiastical authorities have repressed it, far more vigorously within the Catholic pale, than in the English Establishment, or the Wesleyan Connexion. Covetous priests! shame on them! but has covetousness been more rife in cardinals or abbots than in the Protestant Bench, English or Irish? Party spirit, and political faction! has not party, religious and political, burnt as fiercely in high-church rectors and radical preachers, as in Catholic ecclesiastics? And so again, to take an extreme case,—be there a few infidels among the multitudes of the Catholic clergy: yet among the Anglican are there really none, are there few, who disbelieve their own Baptismal Service, repudiate their own Absolution of the Sick, and condemn the very form of words under which they themselves were ordained? Again, are there not numbers who doubt about every part of their system, about their Church, its authority, its truth, its articles, its creeds ; deny its Protestantism, yet without being sure of its Catholicity, and therefore never dare commit themselves to a plain assertion, as not knowing whither it will carry them? Once more, are there not in the Establishment those who hold that all systems of doctrine whatever are founded in a mistake, and who deny, or are fast denying, that there is any revealed truth in the world at all? Yet none of these parties, whatever they doubt, or deny, or disbelieve, see their way to leave the position in which they find themselves at present, or to sacrifice their wealth or credit to their opinions. Why, then, do you throw in my teeth that Wolsey was proud, or Torquemada cruel, or Bonner trimming, or this abbot sensual, or that convent in disorder; that this priest ought never to have been a priest, and that nun was forced into religion by her father; as if there were none of these evils in Protestant England, as if there were no pride in the House of Lords now, no time-serving in the House of Commons, no servility in fashionable preachers, no selfishness in the old, no profligacy in the young, no tyranny or cajolery in matchmaking, no cruelty in Union workhouses, no immorality in factories? If grievous sin is found in holy places, the Church cannot hinder it, while man is man: prove that she encourages it, prove that she does not repress it, prove that her action, be it greater or less, is not, as far as it goes, beneficial:— then, and not till then, will you have established a point against her.

For myself, my Brothers of the Oratory, I never should have been surprised, if, in the course of the last nine months of persecution some scandal in this or that part of our English Church had been brought to light and circulated through the country to our great prejudice. Not that I speak from any knowledge or suspicion of my own, but merely judging antecedently and on the chance of things. And, had such a case in fact been producible, it would, in the judgment of dispassionate minds, have gone for nothing at all, unless there is to be no covetous Judas, no heretical Nicolas, no ambitious Diotrephes, no world-loving Demas, in the Church of these latter days. Fraud in a priest, disorder in a convent, would have proved, not more, perhaps less, against Catholicism, than corruption in Parliament, peculation in the public offices, or bribery at elections tells against the British Constitution. Providentially no such calamity has occurred: but oh, what would not our enemies have paid for only one real and live sin in holy places to mock us withal! O light to the eyes, and joy to the heart, and music to the ear! O sweet tidings to writers of pamphlets, newspapers, and magazines; to preachers and declaimers, who have now a weary while been longing, and panting, and praying for some good fat scandal, one, only just one, well-supported instance of tyranny, or barbarity, or fraud, or immorality, to batten upon and revel in! What price would they have thought too great for so dear a fact, as that of one of our bishops or one of our religious houses had been guilty of some covetous aim, or some unworthy manœuvre! Their fierce and unblushing effort to fix such charges where they were impossible, shows how many eyes were fastened on us all over the country, and how deep and fervent was the aspiration that at least some among us might turn out to be a brute or a villain. To and fro the Spirit of false witness sped. She dropped upon the floor of the Parliament House in the form of a gentleman of Warwickshire, and told how a nun had escaped thereabouts from a convent window, which in consequence had ever since been crossed with iron bars: but it turned out that the window had been attempted by thieves, and the bars had been put up to protect the Blessed Sacrament from them. Then she flitted to Nottingham, and, in the guise of a town newspaper's correspondent, repeated the tale with the concordant witness, as she gave out, of a whole neighbourhood, who had seen the poor captive atop of the wall, and then wandering about the fields like a mad thing: but the Editor in London discovered the untruth, and unsaid in his own paper the slander he had incautiously admitted. Next she forced her way into a nunnery near London, and she assured the Protestant world that then and there an infant had suddenly appeared among the sisterhood; but the two newspapers who were the organs of her malice had to retract the calumny in open court, and to ask pardon to escape a prosecution.

Tales, I say, such as these showed the *animus* of the fabricators: but what, after all, would they have really gained had their imputations been ever so true? Though one bad priest be found here or there, or one convent be in disorder, or there be this or that abuse of spiritual power, or a school of ecclesiastics give birth to a heresy, or a diocese be neglected, nay, though a whole hierarchy be in declension or decay, this would not suffice for the argument of Protestantism. And Protestantism itself plainly confesses it. Yes, the Protestant Tradition must be fed with facts more wholesale, more stimulating, than any I have enumerated, if it is to keep its hold on the multitude. Isolated instances of crime, or widespread tepidity, or imperfections in administration, or antiquated legislation, such imputations are but milk-and-water ingredients in a theme so thrilling as that of Holy Church being a sorceress and the child of perdition. Facts that are only possible, and that only sometimes occur, do but irritate, by suggesting suspicions which they are not sufficient to substantiate. Even falsehood, that is decent and respectable, is unequal to the occasion. Mosheim and Robertson, Jortin and White, raise hopes to disappoint them. The popular demand is for the prodigious, the enormous, the abominable, the diabolical, the impossible. It must be shown that all priests are monsters of hypocrisy, that all nunneries are dens of infamy, that all bishops are the embodied plenitude of savageness and perfidy. Or at least we must have a cornucopia of mummery, blasphemy, and licentiousness,—of knives, and ropes, and faggots, and fetters, and pulleys and racks,—if the great Protestant Tradition is to be kept alive in the hearts of the population. The great point in view is to burn into their imagination, by a keen and peremptory process, a sentiment of undying hostility to Catholicism; and nothing will suffice for this enterprise but imposture, in its purest derivation from him whom Scripture emphatically calls the father of lies, and whose ordinary names, when translated, are the accuser and the slanderer.

This I shall prove as well as assert; and I shall do so in the following way. You know, my Brothers of the Oratory, that from time to time persons come before the Protestant public, with pretensions of all others the most favourable for proving its charges against us, as having once belonged to our Communion, and having left it from conviction. If, then, Protestants would know what sort of men we really are whom they are reprobating, if they wish to determine our internal state, and build their argument on a true foundation, and accommodate their judgment of us to facts, here is the best of opportunities for their purpose. The single point to ascertain is, the trustworthiness of the informants; that being proved, the testimony they give is definite; but if it is disproved, the evidence is worthless.

Now I am going to mention to you the names of two persons, utterly unlike each other in all things except in their both coming forward as converts from Catholicism; both putting on paper their personal experience of the religion they had left; both addressing themselves especially to the exposure of the rule of celibacy, whether in the priesthood or in convents; and, moreover, both on their first appearance meeting with great encouragement from Protestants, and obtaining an extensive patronage for the statements they respectively put forward. One was a man, the other a woman; the one a gentleman, a person of very superior education and great abilities, who lived among us, and might be interrogated and cross-examined at any time; the woman, on the other hand, had no education, no character, no principle, and, as the event made manifest, deserved no credit whatever. Whatever the one said was true, as often as he spoke to facts he had witnessed, and was not putting out opinions or generalising on evidence; whatever the other said was, or was likely to be, false. Thus the two were contrasted: yet the truth spoken against us by the man of character is forgotten, and the falsehood spoken against us by the unworthy woman lives. If this can be shown, do you need a clearer proof that falsehood, not truth, is the essence of the Protestant Tradition.

3.

The Rev. Joseph Blanco White, who is one of the two persons I speak of, was a man of great talent, various erudition, and many most attractive points of character. Twenty-five years ago, when he was about my present age, I became acquainted with him at Oxford, and I lived for some years on terms of familiarity with him. I admired him for the simplicity and openness of his character, the warmth of his affections, the range of his information, his power of conversation, and an intellect refined, elegant, and accomplished. I loved him from witnessing the constant sufferings, bodily and mental, of which he was the prey, and for his expatriation on account of his religion. At that time, not having the slightest doubt that Catholicism was an error, I found in his relinquishment of great ecclesiastical preferment in his native country for the sake of principle, simply a claim on my admiration and sympathy. He was certainly most bitter-minded and prejudiced against everything in and connected with the Catholic Church; it was nearly the only subject on which he could not brook opposition; but this did not interfere with the confidence I placed in his honour and truth; for though he might give expression to a host of opinions in which it was impossible to acquiesce, and was most precipitate and unfair in his inferences and inductions, and might be credulous in the case of alleged facts for which others were the authority, yet, as to his personal testimony, viewed as distinct from his judgments and suspicions, it never for an instant came into my mind to doubt it. He had become an infidel before he left Spain. While at Oxford he was a believer in Christianity: after leaving it he fell into infidelity again; and he died, I may say, without any fixed belief at all, either in a God or in the soul's immortality.

About the period of my acquaintance with him, he wrote various works against the Catholic Church, which in a great measure are repetitions of each other, throwing the same mass of testimonies, such as they are, into different shapes, according to the occasion.

And since his death, many years after the time I speak of, his Life has been published, repeating what is substantially the same evidence. Among these publications one was written for the lower classes; it was entitled, "The Poor Man's Preservative Against Popery;" and, if I mistake not, was put upon the catalogue of Books and Tracts of the great Church of England Society, the Society for Promoting Christian Knowledge. No work could be sent into the world with greater advantages; published under the patronage of all the dignitaries of the Establishment, put into the hands of the whole body of the clergy for distribution, at a low price, written in an animated style, addressed to the traditionary hatred of the Catholic Church existing among us, which is an introduction to any book, whatever its intrinsic value; and laden with a freight of accusation against her, which, as far as their matter was concerned, and the writer's testimony extended, were true as well as grave.

When I began collecting materials for this Lecture, not being able to lay my hand upon the publication at home, I sent for a copy to the Christian Knowledge depôt in this town, and to my surprise, I was told it was no longer in print. I repeated the application at the Society's office in London, and received the same reply. Now certainly there are reasons why a Society connected with the National Church should wish to withdraw the work of a writer, who ended, not only with hating the Papacy, but with despising the Establishment; yet considering its facts were so trustworthy, and its evidence so important, the Society hardly would have withdrawn it, if there had been any good reason for continuing it in print. Such a reason certainly *would* have been its popularity; I cannot conceive how persons, with the strong feelings against the Catholic religion entertained by the members of that Society, having given their solemn approbation, not only to the principle of a certain attack upon it, but to the attack itself, and being confident that the facts related were true, could allow themselves in conscience to withdraw it, on account of subsequent religious changes in the writer, supposing it actually to enjoy a sufficient popularity, and to be doing good service against Catholicism; and therefore I conclude, since it *was* withdrawn, that in spite of the forced circulation which the Society gave it, it had *not* made any great impression on the mass of men, or even interested the Established clergy in its favour. But anyhow, it never at any time was known, in matter of fact, as far as I can make out, to the population at large,—for instance, to the masses of a town such as this,—whatever consideration it may have enjoyed in the circles of the Establishment. Here, then, is a solemn testimony delivered against Catholics of which the basis of facts is true, which nevertheless has no popularity to show, is sustained at first by a forced sale, and then is abandoned by its very patrons; and now let us consider the character of the facts of which it consists.

They are such as the writer himself was very far from thinking a light imputation on the Church he had abandoned. He considered he had inflicted on Catholicism a most formidable blow, in giving his simple evidence against it; and it must be allowed that some of his facts are of a very grave nature. He was the subject and the witness of a most melancholy phenomenon, an Apostasy from the Catholic Faith. About a hundred and fifty years ago a school of infidelity arose in Protestant England ; the notorious Voltaire came over here from France, and on his return took back with him its arguments, and propagated them among his own countrymen. The evil spread; at length it attacked the French Catholic clergy, and during the last century there was a portion of them, I do not say a large portion, but an influential, who fraternised with the infidel, still holding their places and preferments in the Church. At the end of the century, about the time of the first sanguinary French Revolution, the pestilence spread into Spain ; a knot of the Spanish clergy became infidels, and as a consequence, abandoned themselves to a licentious life. Blanco White was one of these, and amid the political troubles in his country during the first years of this century, he managed to escape to England, where he died in the year 1841.

Now there was one circumstance which gave a particularly shocking character to the infidelity of these Spanish ecclesiastics, while it made it more intense. In France the infidel party was not afraid to profess itself infidel ; and such members of the clerical body as were abandoned enough to join it, did so openly; frequented its brilliant meetings and lived shamelessly, like men of fashion and votaries of sin. It was otherwise in Spain ; the people would not have borne this ; public opinion was all on the side of the Catholic religion ; such as doubted or disbelieved were obliged to keep it to themselves, and thus if they were ecclesiastics, to become the most awful of hypocrites. There *can* be hypocrites in the Church, as there may be hypocrites in any religion; but here you see *what* a hypocrite is in the Catholic Church, as seen in fact; not a person who takes up a religious profession in order to gratify some bad end, but, for the most part, one who has learned to disbelieve what he professes, after he has begun to profess it.[1] However, such a person is, on any explanation, an object of horror; and in Spain it was increased by the impatience, irritation, and fever of mind, which the constraint they lay under occasioned to these unhappy men. Their feelings, shut up within their breasts, became fierce and sullen; oppressed by the weight of the popular sentiment, they turned round in revenge upon its object, and they hated Catholicism the more, because their countrymen were Catholics.[2] They became a sort of secret society, spoke to each other only in private, held intercourse by signs, and plunged into licentiousness, even as a relief to the miserable conflicts which raged within them.

Earth could not show, imagination could not picture, Satan could not create, a more horrible spectacle. You will say, how was it possible? how could men who had, I will not merely say given themselves to God, but who had tasted the joy and the reward of such devotion, how could they have the heart thus to change? Why, the perpetrators of the most heinous

---

[1] *E.g.*, Mr. Blanco White says of one of the Spanish ecclesiastics whom he introduces, "He was . . . one of those, who, having *originally* taken their posts in the foremost ranks of asceticism, *with the most sincere desire of improvement for himself and others*, are afterwards involved in guilt by strong temptation, and reduced to secret moral degradation, *by want of courage to throw off the mask of sanctity.*" Life, vol. i. p. 121.

[2] I think I have heard him say that he had lost his knowledge of the Spanish tongue, not having the heart to keep it up.

crimes, men who have sold themselves to the world, and have gained their full price from it, even they look back with tears to those days of innocence and peace which once were theirs, and which are irrecoverably gone. Napoleon said that the day of his first communion was the happiest day of his life. Such men, too, actually part company with the presence of religion; they go forward on their own course, and leave it behind them in the distance. Their regret is directed to what not merely is past, but is away. But these priests were in the very bosom of the Church; they served her altars, they were in the centre of her blessings; how could they forget Jerusalem who dwelt within her? how could they be so thankless towards her sweetness and her brightness, and so cruel towards themselves? how could one who had realised that the Strong and Mighty, that the Gracious, was present on the Altar, who had worshipped there that Saviour's tender Heart, and rejoiced in the assurance of His love, how could he go on year after year (horrible!) performing the same rites, holding his Lord in his hands, dispensing Him to His people, yet thinking it all an idle empty show, a vain superstition, a detestable idolatry, a blasphemous fraud, and cursing the while the necessity which compelled his taking part in it? Why, in the case of one who ever had known the power of religion, it is incomprehensible; but, as regards the melancholy instance we are contemplating, it would really seem if you may take his own recollection of his early self in evidence of the fact, that he never had discovered what religion was. Most children are open to religious feelings, Catholic children of course more than others; some indeed, might complain that, as they advance to boyhood, religion becomes irksome and wearisome to them, but I doubt whether this is true of Catholic youth, till they begin to sin. True, alas, it is, that the nearer and more urgent excitement of guilty thoughts does render the satisfactions and consolations of Paradise insipid and uninviting; but even then their reason tells them that the fault is with themselves, not with religion; and that after all heaven is not only better, but pleasanter, sweeter, more glorious, more satisfying than anything on earth. Yet, from some strange, mysterious cause, this common law was not fulfilled in this hapless Spanish boy; he never found comfort in religion, not in childhood more than in manhood, or in old age. In his very first years, as in his last, it was a yoke and nothing more; a task without a recompense.

Thus he tells us, he "entertains a most painful recollection" of the "perpetual round of devotional practices" in which he was compelled to live. He "absolutely dreaded the approach of Sunday. Early on the morning of that formidable day, when he was only eight years old, he was made to go with his father to the Dominican convent,"[3] always for Mass, and every other week for confession. He did not get his breakfast for two hours, then he had to stand or kneel in the Cathedral, I suppose at High Mass, for two hours longer. Well, the second two hours probably was, as he says, a considerable trial for him. Again, from three to five he was in another church, I suppose for Vespers and Benediction. Then his father and he took a walk, and in the evening his father visited the sick in an hospital, and took his son with him. Per-

[3] P. 11.

haps his father's treatment of him, if we are to trust his recollection and impression of it, might be injudicious; he was lively, curious, and clever, and his father, who was a truly good, pious man, it may be, did not recollect that the habits of the old are not suitable in all respects to children. Mr. Blanco White complains, moreover, that he had no companions to play with, and no books to read; still, it is very strange indeed, that he never took pleasure in Mass and Benediction; he calls his Sunday employments a "cruel discipline;"[4] he describes his hearing Mass as "looking on while the priest went through it;"[5] speaking of a season of recreation granted to him, he mentions his religious duties as the drawbacks "on the accession of daily pleasures" he had obtained. However, "Mass, though a nuisance, was over in half an hour; confession, a more serious annoyance, was only a weekly task;"[6] and, as if to prove what I alluded to above, that no fascination of sin had at this time thrown religion into the shade, he adds, "My life was too happy in innocent amusement to be exposed to anything that might be the subject of painful accusation." No; it was some radical defect of mind. In like manner, saying office was to him never anything else than a "most burdensome practice."[7] "Another devotional task, scarcely less burdensome," was—what, my Brothers, do you think? "Mental Prayer," or "Meditation;" of which he gives a detailed and true description. He adds, "Soon after I was ordained a priest . . . . I myself was several times the leader of this mystical farce."[8] In his boyhood and youth he had to read half an hour, and to meditate on his knees another half. This for

[4] P. 12.   [5] P. 26.   [6] P. 32.   [7] P. 27.   [8] P. 29.

such a boy, might be excessive; but hear how he comments upon it: "To feel indignant, at this distance of time, may be absurd; but it is with difficulty that I can check myself when I remember what I have suffered in the cause of religion. Alas! my sufferings from that source are still more bitter in my old age."[9]

That a person, then who never knew what Catholicism had to give, should abandon it, does not seem very surprising; the only wonder is how he ever came to be a priest. If we take his own account of himself it is evident he had no vocation at all: he explains the matter, however, very simply, as far as his own share in it is concerned, by telling us that he chose the ecclesiastical state in order to avoid what he felt to be more irksome, a counting-house. "I had proposed to be sent to the navy, because at that time the Spanish midshipman received a scientific education. I could not indeed endure the idea of being doomed to a life of ignorance. This was easily perceived, and (probably with the approbation of the divines consulted on this subject) no alternative was left me. I was told I must return to the odious counting-house, from which I had taken refuge in the Church. I yielded, and in yielding mistook the happiness of drying up my mother's tears for a reviving taste for the clerical profession."[1]

4.

No wonder, under such circumstances, that Mr. Blanco White became an unbeliever; no wonder that

---

[9] P. 29. He goes on to say that he prefers to the vague word "religion" the use of "true Christianity," but this he gave up at last.

[1] P. 52.

his friends and associates became unbelievers too, if their history resembled his. It was the case of active inquisitive minds, unfurnished with that clear view of divine things which divine grace imparts and prayer obtains. The only question which concerns us here is, Were there many such ecclesiastics in the Spanish Church? If so, it certainly would be a very grave fact; if not so, it is most melancholy certainly, but not an argument, as I can see, against Catholicism, for there are bad men in every place and every system. Now it is just here that his testimony fails; there is nothing that I can find in his works to prove that the dreadful disease which he describes had spread even so widely as in France. In the first place, he only witnesses to a small part of Spain. He seems to have only been in three Spanish cities in his life: Seville, Madrid, and Cadiz;[2] and of these, while Seville is the only one of which he had a right to speak, the metropolis and a seaport are just two of the places, where, if there was laxity, you would expect it to be found. Again, Spain is not, like England, the seat of one people, an open country, with easy communication from sea to sea. On the contrary, you have populations so different, that you may call them foreign to each other; separated, moreover, not only morally, but by the mountain barriers which intersect the country in every direction; one part does not know another, one part is not like another, and therefore Mr. Blanco White's evidence is only good as far as it extends. You cannot infer the state of the northern dioceses from a southern; of Valentia, by what you

---

[2] On one occasion he ran down to Salamanca from Madrid, apparently for a day or two.

are told of Seville. Inspect then his narrative itself, and see what it results in. It amounts to this—that in the first years of this century there were a few priests at Seville who had studied Jansenistic theology, and largely imported French philosophy, and that they ended in becoming infidels, and some of them unblushing hypocrites. I cannot find mention of any except at Seville: and how many there? You may count them. First, "I became acquainted with a member of the upper clergy, a man of great reading, and secretly a most decided disbeliever in all religion." Secondly, "Through him I was introduced to another dignitary, a man much older than either of us, who had for many years held an office of great influence in the diocese, but who now lived in a very retired way. He was also a violent anti-Christian, as I subsequently found."[3] Thirdly, an intimate friend of his own, who was promoted from Seville to a canonry of Cordova, and who had been chaplain to the Archbishop of Seville.[4] Fourthly, himself. I am not able to number more, as given on his own personal knowledge,[5] though he certainly thought many others existed;[6] but this is

[3] P. 114.

[4] P. 17. I consider this to be the person mentioned in the "Evidences," p. 132, whom accordingly I have not set down as a separate instance.

[5] On his visit to Salamanca, he saw Melendez, a Deist (p. 128), who had been one of the judges of the Supreme Court at Madrid; a poet, too; whether an Ecclesiastic does not appear.

[6] Life, p. 117. "*Many other* members of the clergy." If he had a definite *knowledge* of others, or more than suspicion, I cannot understand his not giving us the number, or the rank, or the diocese, in short, something categorical, instead of an indirect allusion. The question, then, simply is, what his suspicions are worth. "Among my numerous acquaintance in the Spanish clergy, I have never met with any one, *possessed of bold talents*, who has not, sooner or later, changed from the

ever the case with men who do wrong; they quiet the voice within them by the imagination that all others are pretty much what they are themselves. I do not then trust his inferences.

And so again, as he fell into immoral practices himself, so did he impute the same to the mass of the Spanish clergy, whom he considered as "falling and rising, struggling and falling again,"[7] in a continual course; but here too, from the nature of the case, he could not speak of many on his personal knowledge. Nor was it to be supposed that a priest, who was

most sincere piety to a state of unbelief." (Doblado's Letters, v.) I observe—1. He had experience only of one diocese. 2. He evidently, by the very form of his words, does not speak of what he *knew*, when he says, "who *has* not *sooner or later*." 3. Observe, "possessed of *bold talents*." In like manner, he would, I think, have said, that when he was at Oxford, every one, "of bold talents," agreed with Archbishop Whately, then resident in the University (and my friend as well as his); but every one knows how small Dr. Whately's party was. I do not notice a passage in the "Poor Man's Preservative" (Dial. i. pp. 32, 33), for he is speaking of laity, and what he says of the clergy is very vague. After all, though I have a right to ask for proof, it is not necessary for my *argument* to deny, that the infidel party might have been as large in Spain even as in France; though in fact it seems to have been no larger than the small band of Apostates boasted of by the "Priests' Protection Society" in Dublin.

[7] Evid. p. 132. Again he says, "hundreds *might* be found" who live "a life of systematic vice" (p. 135). How very vague is "hundreds!" and "hundreds" out of 60,000 seculars, and 125,000 ecclesiastics in all, as I shall mention presently in the text. (Ibid. p. 133). He speaks vaguely of the "crowd" of priests; and he says the best of them, and he knew the best from confession, "mingled vice and superstition, grossness of feeling, and pride of office, in their character." I suspect that coarseness with him was one great evidence of vice; he despised uneducated persons. "I am surprised," he says of Tavora, Bishop of the Canary Islands (p. 129), "that a man of his *taste and information* accepted the Bishopric of a *semi-barbarous* portion of the Spanish dominions:" and this, though he attributes it "to his desire of improving the moral and intellectual state of those islands."

both disbelieving what he professed, and was breaking what he had vowed, should possess friends very different from himself. He formed the eighth of a group of ecclesiastics whom he much admired. One of these, as we have seen, was an infidel, but apparently only one; none of them, however, were blameless in their moral conduct. Besides these friends of his, he mentions a priest of a religious congregation, who had been his own confessor, in which capacity "he had no fault to find with him, nor could he discover the least indication of his not acting up to the principles he professed,"[8] who, however (as he was *told* by a young atheist merchant who knew the priest's "secret courses" well, and, "as he had afterwards sufficient

---

[8] This conscientiousness in his *duty* is remarkable in this priest, even if his account of him ought to be believed (for it stands on different grounds from those cases which he *knew*). Of himself, too, he says, his resolution was to do his *duty* to his charge, though an unbeliever. "I will not put myself forward in the Church. I will not affect zeal: whatever trust is put in me, as a confessor, I will conscientiously prove myself worthy of. I will urge people to observe every moral duty. I will give them the best advice in their difficulties, and comfort them in their distress. Such were the resolutions I made, and which, indeed, I *always* (sic) kept, in regard to the confidence reposed in my priestly office. In that respect I may positively and confidently assert, that I never availed myself of the privileges of my priesthood for anything immoral" (Life, vol. i. p. 112). This being the case, his *intention* in consecrating and administering the sacraments was valid, even though he was an unbeliever. I think my memory cannot play me false in saying, that in answer to a question once put to him, he declared emphatically that the bad priests never made use of the confessional for immoral purposes: he said, "They daren't. It would raise the people." Moreover, as time went on, he himself *withdrew altogether* from clerical duty. He speaks of another of the party, who having "for many years held an office of great influence in the diocese, now lived *in a very retired way*" (p. 114). I say all this in order to show what little bearing the unbelief of this small knot of priests had upon the Catholic population among whom they lived.

ground to be convinced," if such a vague statement is a sufficient testimony to the fact), "sinned and did penance by rotation."[9] Another, too, is mentioned laden with similar guilt, with whom he had been intimate, but whom he describes as deficient in mere natural principle: this man got involved in money matters and died of vexation.[1]

Ten, or, if it were, twenty bad ecclesiastics form a most melancholy catalogue certainly, but are not more, after all, than Protestants have scraped together and made apostates of, out of the zealous Catholic clergy of Ireland; and, as no one dreams of taking such melancholy cases as specimens of the Irish Church, neither are Mr. Blanco White's friends specimens of the Spanish. He says, indeed, "hundreds might be found," still not on his personal knowledge; and I for one cannot receive his second-hand information. However, in any case you must recollect first, that it was a time apparently of great religious declension, when Spain had imitated France, and a judgment was on the point of coming down upon the country. The Jesuits, the flower of the priesthood, whom as he says himself, "their bitterest enemies have never ventured to charge with moral irregularities," had been barbarously expelled by the government. The Congregation of St. Philip Neri took their place, but though

---

[9] Life, p. 121.

[1] Life, p. 104. He speaks (Evidences, p. 135) of two priests who died of *love*. "Love, long resisted, seized them, at length, like madness. Two I knew who died insane." Even granting it, I suppose it was love of *particular objects*. May not Protestants fall in love with persons who will not have them, or who are married? Dying for love is certainly an *idea* quite known in England, still more so, perhaps, in the South.

they did a great deal, they had not strength, single-handed, to stem the flood of corruption. Moreover you must consider the full number of clergy in a given place or neighbourhood, before you form a judgment upon their state as a whole. The whole number of clergy of Spain at this time amounted to 125,000 persons; of these the seculars were as many as 60,000. In the Cathedral of Seville alone 500 Masses were said daily; and the city was divided into twenty-six parishes, and contained besides between forty and fifty ecclesiastical establishments in addition to the monasteries.[2] The real question before us simply is, whether the proportion of bad priests at that time in the city and diocese of Seville was greater than the proportion of bad married clergy in England in the reign, we will say, of George the Second. It is to be remembered, too, that Catholic priests know each other far more intimately than is possible in the case of a married clergy; in a large city bad priests herd together: married clergymen, in respectable station, would sin each by himself, and no one of them can turn king's evidence against the rest.

This being the extent of Mr. Blanco White's evidence about the secular priests, about monks and friars he frankly tells us he knows next to nothing, though he thinks them "gross and vulgar." But here, as in the case of the secular clergy, he suspects and believes much evil which he does not know, and which those only will receive who have implicit reliance on his judgment. As to nuns, he speaks of those of them whom he knew, as being for the most part ladies of

---

[2] Laborde, vol. ii.

high character and unimpeachable purity;[3] though some were otherwise, at least to some extent. He seems to allow that reluctant nuns were comparatively few; though he says that many were tormented by scruples, and all would have been much happier had

---

[3] He has a most intense *notion* that they are "prisoners;" but that does not hinder his admitting that they are *willing* prisoners. He thinks the majority live in "*a dull monotony*" (Life, p. 67). It is not wonderful that he should take the formal Parliamentary view of nuns, considering that from his youth, as I have said, he, though a Catholic, had apparently as little sense of the Real Presence (*the true and sufficient Paraclete of a Nunnery*) as the House of Commons has. The following expressions sketch his idea of a nunnery; let it be observed, *vice* (except as an accident) is absent:—"The minute and anxious narrative of a **nervous recluse**" (p. 66). "A *sensible woman* confined for life" (Ibid.) "A soul troubled with all the fears of a *morbid conscience*" (p. 67). "The word Nunnery is a byword for **weakness of intellect**, *fretfulness, childishness*. In short, nun is the *superlative of old woman*" (p. 69). "Some of them were *women of superior good sense, and models of that fortitude* which," &c. (Ibid.) "One of *those excellent persons*" (Ibid.) "The *greater part* of the nuns whom I have known, were *beings of a much higher description, females whose purity* owed nothing to the strong gates and high walls of the cloister" (Evid. p. 135). "Some there are, I confess, among the nuns, who *never seem to long for freedom;* but the happiness boasted of in convents is generally the effect of an *honourable pride of* purpose, supported by a sense of utter *hopelessness*" (Ibid. p. 136). "Suppose but *one* nun in *ten thousand* wished vehemently for that liberty" (p. 137). "The *reluctant* nuns, you say, are *few;*—vain, unfeeling sophistry" (p. 139). "The *most sensitive, innocent, and ardent minds*" (Ibid. p. 141). "Crime *makes its way into*" (observe, not is congenial to) "those recesses" (Ibid. p. 135). "It is a *notorious fact,* that the nunneries in *Estremadura and Portugal*" (*not*, that are in Seville and Andalusia) "are *frequently* infected *with vice of the grossest kind*" (Ibid. p. 135). "*Souls* more polluted than those of *some* never fell within my observation, &c." (Life, vol. i. p. 70). Observe, "souls;" —to the soul he limits the sin, and he puts the word in italics, to show that this really is his meaning, and he adds "some." When it comes to the soul, the evidence is very vague; and this, out of 500, in Seville alone! Such on the whole is his evidence against convents: how little of fact, how much of suspicion, contempt, and hatred! how much, again, of involuntary admission in favour of their religious condition!

they married. But this is his opinion, as distinct from his testimony; and in like manner he has other strong opinions on the miseries inflicted on men and women by celibacy;[4] but I have no reliance on his judgment—nor had any one, I think, who knew him, he had so much prejudice, and so little patience—while I have the fullest confidence in his word, when he witnesses to facts, and facts which he knew.

Such is this remarkable evidence, remarkable in the witness, and in the things witnessed, remarkable as coming from a person who had special means of knowing a Catholic country, and whose honour you may depend upon; unlike such men as Ciocci and Achilli, and others, who also have left the Church and borne witness against her, whom no sensible man credits. Here is a man you can trust; and you see how little he has to say to the purpose of Protestantism after all. He makes the most indeed of his little, but he gives us the means of judging for ourselves. Here is no conspiracy of evil, no deep-laid treachery, no disguised agents prowling about, no horrible oaths, no secret passages, trapdoors, dungeons, axes, racks, and thumbscrews; no blood and fire, no screams of despair, no wailing of children, no spectres born of feverish guilt, and flitting before the mental eye. Here is little more than what happens

---

[4] The simple question is, whether *more* nuns are eaten up with scruples—*more* are restless and discontented—*more* are old women or old maids—*more* sin grossly, than unmarried women in a Protestant country. Here, as before, I am allowing for argument's sake, the worst side of things; and nothing of all this, be it observed, even if granted, disproves—(1.) the religiousness of the great majority; (2.) the angelical saintliness of many; (3.) the excellence and utility of the institution itself, after all drawbacks; which are the points a Catholic maintains.

every day in England; for I suppose that here in Protestant England there are secret unbelievers, and men who are fair and smooth, but inwardly corrupt, and many a single female wasted by weariness and sadness, and many a married woman cursing the day she ever took her vow; for these things must be, though they ought not to be, while the nature of man is the same. And moreover, as I have said, the popular voice seems to bear me out in the view I am taking; for this testimony, given under such favourable circumstances against the Church, has been let drop out of print; for it was after all tame; it did not do its work; it did not go far enough; it was not equal to the demand; it was not in keeping with the great Protestant Tradition.

5.

No, it must contain something huge, enormous, prodigious, because the people love story books, and do not like dry matter of fact. How dull is history, or biography, or controversy, compared with a good romance, the Lives of highwaymen, a collection of ghost stories, a melodrama, a wild-beast-show, or an execution! What would a Sunday newspaper be without trials, accidents, and offences? Therefore the poor Catholic is dressed up like a scarecrow to gratify, on a large scale, the passions of curiosity, fright, and hatred. Something or other men must fear, men must loathe, men must suspect, even if it be to turn away their minds from their own inward miseries. Hence it is, if a stranger comes to a small town, that he furnishes so inexhaustible a supply of gossip to his neighbours, about who he is, what he was, whom he knows, why he comes, and when he will go. If a house is empty for a while, it is sure to be haunted. When learning began to revive, your student was the object of curious horror; and Dr. Faustus, the printer and (as the nursery rhyme goes) schoolmaster, was made a magician, and is still drawn as such in poems and romances. When, then, a Catholic Church is opened in a place, or a monastic body takes up its abode there, its novelty and strangeness are a call for fiction on those who have a talent for invention; and the world would be seriously disappointed, if all sorts of superstition were not detected in the Church's rites, and all sorts of wickedness in her priests and nuns.

The popular appetite does not clamour long in vain. It asks, and it is answered. Look at that poor degraded creature, strolling about from village to village, from settlement to farmhouse, among a primitive and simple population. She has received an injury in her head when young; and this has taken away, in part, her responsibility, while it has filled her brain with wild ideas, and given it a morbid creative power. Ere she is grown up she leaves her home, and flits here and there, the prey of any one who meets with her. Catholics are all round about her; as a child she has been in a Catholic school, and perhaps she has from time to time wandered into Catholic churches. She enters, she peers about; still and demure, yet with wild curious eyes, and her own wanton thoughts. She sees, at first glance, the sanctity and gravity of the ceremonial: she is struck with the appearance of modesty, whether in the sacred ministers or in the nuns; but her evil heart instantly suggests that what shows so well is nothing but a show, and that close under the surface lies corruption. She contemplates the whole scene, she cannot forget it; but she asks herself, *What if* it be but a solemn mockery cloaking bad deeds? The words, the actions, so calm, so gentle, the words of peace, the sacramental actions, she carries them off with an accurate memory; those verses and responses, those sweet voices, those blessings, and crossings, and sprinklings, and genuflections. But what if they all be a cloak? And when the priest went out, or when he spoke to any one, what was it all about? And when he was in his confessional, and first one penitent, and then another came to him, what could they be saying? Ah, what indeed! what if it all be but a cloak for sin? There is the point. What if it be but a jest? Oh, the pleasant mischief! the stirring, merry fancy! to think that men can look so grave, yet love sin; that women, too, who pretend so much, need not be better than she is herself; that that meek face, or those holy hands, belong to a smooth hypocrite, who acts the angel and lives the devil! She looks closer and closer, measuring the limbs, scanning the gestures, and drinking in the words of those who unconsciously go about their duties in her presence; and imputing meanings to the most harmless and indifferent actions. It really is as she suspected, and the truth breaks upon her more and more. Her impure imagination acts upon her bodily vision, and she begins to see the image of her own suspicions in the objects she is gazing on. A sort of mirage spreads through the sacred building, or religious house, and horrors of all kind float across her brain.

She goes away, but they pursue her;—what may not have taken place amid those holy rites, or within those consecrated walls? The germ of a romance is already fermenting in her brain, and day after day it becomes more developed in its parts, and more consistent in its form.

Poor sinful being! She finds herself in a Penitentiary! no, sure, it is a religious house; so she will consider it, so will she henceforth speak of it; everything she sees there speaks to her of her feverish dream; the penitents become nuns; the very rooms, windows, passages, and stairs, she recognizes them as conventual, the very convent which her fancy has been framing. Things utterly separate from each other are confused together in her bewildered mind; and when she comes into the world again, she thinks herself a nun escaped from confinement, and she now begins to recollect scenes of indescribable horror, which gradually become clearer and clearer. Now, Protestant public, the hour is come; you have craved after lies, and you shall have your fill; you have demanded, and here is the supply. She opens her mouth; she lifts her voice; your oracle, your prophet, your idol, O Protestant public, is about to speak; she begins her "Awful Disclosures." Who is this hapless creature, very wicked, very mischievous, yet much to be pitied? It is Maria Monk.

My Brothers, in what I have been saying, I have but given substance in my own way to the facts recorded of her; but those facts are simply as I have stated them. The history of the wretched impostor was traced out and given to the world immediately on the publication of her romance. It was deposed by divers witnesses that she was born of parents who had lived at Montreal in Canada, about the year 1816. When about seven years old, she broke a slate pencil on her head, and had been strange ever since; at the age of eight she frequented a convent school; when about fourteen or fifteen she left her mother's roof; and is found successively in the service of several persons, an hotel-keeper, a farmer, a tradesman, and others, and then for a time was dependent on charity. From one of her mistresses she absconded with a quantity of wearing-linen; she was discharged by two others for her bad conduct, and was generally looked upon as a person of at least doubtful character. Then she made her appearance at Montreal itself, declaring she was daughter to Dr. Robertson, a magistrate of the city, who had kept her chained in a cellar for four years. This attempt failing, she next went off to the United States, appeared at New York, and then began a second and more successful tale against one of the convents of the city she had left, from which she said she had escaped. She was taken up by a party of New York Protestants, who thoroughly believed her, and reduced her story to writing. Who was the author is not quite certain; two names have been mentioned, one of them a person connected with this town. In this book, whoever wrote it, she gives a minute description of her imaginary convent in Montreal, and of some of the nuns and others she professed to have known there. On the slander making its way to Montreal, Protestants carefully went over the calumniated convent; and they reported, after minute inspection, that it in no respect answered to her account of it; indeed, it was certain she had never been within it. It was proved, on the other hand, that her description did distinctly answer to a Penitentiary of which she had lately been an inmate, and whence she was dismissed for bad conduct; and further, that the account she gave of her nuns in the convent answered to some of her fellow-penitents. Moreover, there is something about the book more remarkable still, not indeed as it concerns her, but as it concerns the argument I have in several of these Lectures been pursuing. I have insisted much on the traditional character of the fable, of which Catholics are the victims. It is the old lie, brought up again and again. Now this is most singularly exemplified in the infamous work I am speaking of. On its appearance the newspapers of the day asserted, without contradiction, that it was in great measure a mere republication of a work printed in the year 1731, under the title of "The Gates of Hell opened, or a Development of the Secrets of Nunneries." "Maria Monk's Pamphlet," says a Liverpool paper, "is a *verbatim* copy of that work, the only difference being a change of names." The editor of a Boston paper "pledged himself that this was the fact;" and the editor of another "was ready to make *affidavit* that the original work was in his possession a few months previously, when it had been lent to the publishers of Maria Monk's Disclosures." To show this he copied out passages from both works, which were the same word for word.[5]

Here, then, you have a witness who is prepared to

---

[5] For these facts, *vide* "A complete Refutation of Maria Monk's atrocious Plot," &c., by the Rev. R. W. Wilson (now Bishop of Hobart Town), Nottingham, 1837.

go any lengths in support of the Protestant Tradition, however truth or principle may lie in her way; and offensive as it will be to you to listen, and painful to me to read, you must, for the sake of the contrast between her and Mr. Blanco White, submit to one or two of those passages from her romance, which I am able without impropriety to quote.

Now, I will give you the key to the whole book considered as a composition, and its burden, and (what may be called) its moral, as addressed to the Protestant world. It is an idea, which, as I have already said, was naturally suggested to an impure mind, and forcibly addressed itself to a curious reader. Mankind necessarily proceeds upon the notion that what is within discloses itself by what is without; that the soul prompts the tongue, inspires the eye, and rules the demeanour; and such is the doctrine of Holy Writ, when it tells us that "out of the abundance of the heart the mouth speaketh." Hence, when strangers visit a nunnery, and see the order, cheerfulness, and quiet which reigns through it, they naturally take all this as the indication of that inward peace and joy which ought to be the portion of its inmates. And again, when strangers attend Mass, and observe the venerable and awful character of the rite, they naturally are led to think that the priest is "holding up pure hands," and is as undefiled in heart as he is grave in aspect. Now it is the object of this Narrative to reverse this natural association, to establish the contrary principle, and to impress upon the mind that what is within is always what the outward appearance is not, and that the more of saintliness is in the exterior, the more certainly is there depravity and guilt in the heart. Of course it must be confessed, there have been cases where what looked fair and beautiful was but a whited sepulchre, "full within of dead men's bones and of all filthiness;" such cases have been and may be, but they are unnatural surely, not natural; the exception, not the rule. To consider this as the rule of things, you must destroy all trust in the senses; when a man laughs, you must say he is sad; when he cries, you must say he is merry; when he is overbearing in words, you must call him gentle; and when he says foolish things, you must call him wise; all because sad hearts sometimes wear cheerful countenances, and divine wisdom sometimes has condescended to look like folly. It is reported to have been said by an able diplomatist, that the use of words is to disguise men's thoughts; but the very wit of the remark lies in the preposterous principle it ironically implies. Yet still to the run of readers there is something attractive in this perverted and morbid notion, both from a sort of malevolence and love of scandal, which possesses the minds of the vulgar, and from the wish to prove that others, who seems religious, are even worse than themselves; and besides, from the desire of mystery and marvel, which prompts them, as I have said before, to have recourse to some monstrous tale of priestcraft for excitement, as they would betake themselves to a romance or a ghost story.

Thus she says in one place, or rather the writers, whoever they may be:—"I have often reflected how grievously I had been deceived in my opinions of a nun's condition—all the holiness of their lives, I now found, was merely pretended. The appearance of sanctity and heavenly-mindedness which they had shown among us novices, I found was only a disguise, to conceal such practices as would not be tolerated in any decent society in the world; and, as for joy and peace like that of heaven, which I had expected to find among them, I learned too well that they did not exist there."[6]

Again, speaking of a picture of the infernal pit, at which the nuns were looking, she introduces a nun saying something so dreadful, that the reader hardly knows whether to laugh or to cry at it. "I remember she named the wretch who was biting at the bars of hell, with a serpent gnawing his head, with chains and padlocks on, Father Dufresne; and she would say, Does he not look like him, when he come in to catechism with his long solemn face, and begins his speeches with, 'My children, my hope is that you have lived very devout lives?'"[7]

In such passages, the object of the writer is to familiarise the reader's imagination to the notion that hypocrisy is the natural and ordinary state of things, and to create in him a permanent association between any serious act whatever and inward corruption. She makes the appearance of religion to be the presumption, not of reality, but of hollowness, and the very extravagance of her statements is their plausibility. The reader says, "It is so shocking, it must be true; no one could have invented it."

It is with a view to increase this unnatural plausibility that the writer or writers dwell minutely on various details which happen, or might easily happen, in Catholic churches and convents. For instance,

[6] P. 116. [7] P. 82.

they say, "The old priest ... when going to administer (the Blessed Sacrament) in any country place, used to ride with a man before him, who rang a bell as a signal. When the Canadians heard it, whose habitations he passed, they would come and prostrate themselves to the earth, worshipping it as God." Of course; it is so; Catholics do worship the Blessed Sacrament, because they believe It to be our Lord Himself. Therefore we will say so in our book, for we wish to lie naturally, we wish to root our imposture in a foundation of truth.

Again; "The bell rang at half-past six to awaken us. The old nun who was acting as night-watch immediately spoke aloud, 'Behold the Lord cometh!' The nuns all responded, 'Let us go and meet Him.' Presently, we then knelt and kissed the floor."[8]

Now observe the effect of all this. When a person, who never was in a Catholic church or convent, reads such particulars; when he reads, moreover, of the lattice-work of the confessional, of the stoup of holy water, and the custom of dipping the finger into it, of silence during dinner, and of recreation after it; of a priest saying Mass with his hands first joined together, and then spread, and his face to the altar; of his being addressed by the title of "my father," and speaking of his "children," and many other similar particulars; and then afterwards actually sees some Catholic establishment, he says to himself, "This is just what the book said;" "here is quite the very thing of which it gave me the picture;" and I repeat he has, in consequence of his reliance on it, so associated the acts of the ceremonial, the joined

[8] P. 39.

hands or the downcast eyes, with what his book went on slanderously to connect them, with horrible sin, that he cannot disconnect them in his imagination; and he thinks the Catholic priest already convicted of hypocrisy, because he observes those usages which all the world knows that he does observe, which he is obliged to observe, and which the Church has ever observed. Thus you see the very things, which are naturally so touching and so beautiful in the old Catholic forms of devotion, become by this artifice the means of infusing suspicion into the mind of the beholder.

Yes; all this outward promise of good is but a beautiful veil, hiding behind it untold horrors. Let us lift it, so far as we may do so without sharing in the writer's sin. Our heroine has passed through her noviciate, and proceeds to take the vows. Then she learns suddenly the horrors of her situation; she was, in fact, in a house of evil spirits; she represents herself, as was very natural, supposing she had been a religious person, overcome by distress, and unable to resign herself to her lot; and she was told by the Mother Superior, "that such feelings were very common at first, and that many other nuns had expressed themselves as I did, who had long since changed their minds. She even said, on her entrance into the nunnery she had felt like me. Doubts, she declared, were among our greatest enemies. They would lead us to question every path of duty, and induce us to waver at every step. They arose only from remaining imperfections, and were always evidences of sin; our only way was to dismiss them immediately, to repent, to confess them. They were deadly sins,

for the Protestant View. 171

and would condemn us to hell if we should die without confessing them. Priests, she insisted, could not sin. It was a thing impossible. Everything they did and wished was of course right." [9]

Now, my Brothers, you know there is a divine law written on the heart by nature, and that the Catholic Church is built on that law, and cannot undo it. No Priest, no Bishop, no Council can make that right which is base and shameful. In this passage the false witness would make the Protestant world believe that nuns are obliged to obey their confessors in commands strictly sinful, and horrible, and blasphemous. How different from the true witness, Mr. Blanco White! He said all he could against convents; he never hinted that religious women were taught by the priests that priests could not possibly sin, could not possibly issue a sinful command, could not possibly have a sinful wish; and therefore must be obeyed whatever they ask; he never hinted, from any experience of his, that in matter of fact they did make any sinful suggestions. His quarrel with the Catholic religion was that it was too strict, not that it was too lax; that it gave rise to nervousness, scruples, and melancholy. His utmost accusation (except as regards the unbelieving few) was that he knew some persons, and he believed there were others, who sinned, knew their sin, came and confessed it, and sinned again. There was no calling evil good, and good evil. Let her continue her revelations:—

"She also gave me another piece of information, which excited other feelings in me scarcely less dreadful. Infants were sometimes born in the con-

[9] P 35.

vent, but they were always baptised, and immediately strangled. This secured their everlasting happiness; for the baptism purified them from all sinfulness, and being sent out of the world before they had time to do anything wrong, they were at once admitted into heaven. How happy, she exclaimed, are those who secure immortal happiness for such little beings! Their little souls would thank those who killed their bodies, if they had it in their power.[1]

"So far as I know, there were no pains taken to preserve secrecy on this subject. . . . I believe I learned through the nuns that at least eighteen or twenty infants were smothered, and secretly buried in the cellar, while I was a nun."[2]

The nuns, according to her account, underwent the same fate, if they would not resign themselves to the mode of life in all its details, for which alone, as it would seem, the nunnery was set up. She gives an account of the murder of one of them; and after quoting this, I consider I may fairly be excused from quoting any more.

"I entered the door," she says, "my companions standing behind me, as the place was so small as hardly to hold five persons at a time. The young nun was standing alone, near the middle of the room; she was probably about twenty, with light hair, blue eyes, and a very fair complexion"[3] The poor victim is brought to the Bishop, who, the writer says, "it was easy to perceive, considered her fate to be sealed, and was determined she should not escape. In reply to some of the questions put to her she was silent; to others I heard her voice reply that she did not repent of

---
[1] P. 35.   [2] P. 120.   [3] P. 75.

words she had uttered, though they had been reported by some of the nuns who had heard them; that she had firmly resolved to resist any attempt to compel her to the commission of crimes which she detested. She added that she would rather die than cause the murder of harmless babes. 'That is enough, finish her!' said the Bishop. Two nuns instantly fell upon the woman; and in obedience to directions given by the Superior, prepared to execute her sentence. She still maintained all the calmness and submission of a lamb." Then they gag her and throw her on a bed. "In an instant," the narrative proceeds, "another bed was thrown upon her. One of the priests sprung like a fury upon it with all his force. He was speedily followed by the nuns, until there were as many upon the bed as could find room, and all did what they could, not only to smother, but to bruise her.... After the lapse of fifteen or twenty minutes, and when it was presumed that the sufferer had been smothered and crushed to death, (the priest) and the nuns ceased to trample upon her, and stepped from the bed. All was motionless and silent beneath it. They then began to laugh," &c.

But I surely need not continue trash such as this, which is as stupid as it is atrocious. In like manner she tells us the number of nuns killed, the number who killed themselves, the various penances and tortures which were common, gags, hot irons, glass chewing, and the "cap;" the cells, and everything which is proper furniture of such an abode. She concludes the book with a solemn reflection, how hard it is to think aright after thinking wrong. "The Scriptures," she is made to say, "always affect me powerfully when I read them; but I feel that I have but just begun to learn the great truths, in which I ought to have been early instructed. . . . The first passage of Scripture that made any serious impression on my mind, was the text on which the chaplain preached on the Sabbath after my introduction into the house, 'Search the Scriptures:'"—and so the book ends.

I have now described, first, the character of the writer, next, the character of her book; one point alone remains, its reception by the public. The calumny first appeared in 1836, it still thrives and flourishes in 1851. I have made inquiries, and I am told I may safely say that in the course of the fifteen years that it has lasted, from 200,000 to 250,000 copies have been put into circulation in America and England. The edition I have used is printed at Nottingham in the *present* year. A vast number of copies has been sold at a cheap rate, and given away by persons who ought to have known it was a mere blasphemous fiction. At this very time the book is found, I believe, in some of the parochial lending libraries of this place, and I hear rumours concerning some of the distributors, which, from the respect I wish to entertain towards their names, I do not know how to credit. Nor have these various efforts been without visible fruit, at least in America. A nunnery was burned down at Charlestown; and at New York fifty houses, inhabited by Catholics, were also destroyed by fire, which extended to the Cathedral.

6.

And thus I have completed, my Brothers, the contrast I proposed to set before you. A writer of name, of character, of honour, of gentleman-like feeling, who has the *entrée* of the first and most intellectual circles of the metropolis, and is the friend of the first Protestant ecclesiastics of his day, records his testimony against Catholicism; it is in the main true, and it fails:—a worthless stroller gets her own testimony put into writing; it is a heap of fables, and it triumphantly succeeds. Let, then, the Protestant public be itself the judge:—its preference of Maria Monk to Blanco White reveals a great fact;—truth is not equal to the exigencies of the Protestant cause; falsehood is its best friend.

Nor let it be imagined, my Brothers, that I have unfairly selected my examples, in order to serve a purpose. Inhabitants of Birmingham ought, more than others, to acquit me of this. Only two years have I been here, and each of these two has been signalised by accusations against Catholics, similar, in the disreputableness of their authors, and in the enormity of their falsehood, and in the brilliancy of their success, to the calumnies of Maria Monk. Two years ago it was Jeffreys; last year it was Teodore. You recollect how Jeffreys acted his part, how he wept, and prayed, and harangued, and raised a whole population against an innocent company of monks; and how he was convicted of fraud, and confessed his guilt, and was sent to prison. You also recollect how an impostor, called Teodore, declaimed such shocking things, and wrote such indecent pamphlets against us, that they cannot have been intended for any other purpose than to afford merriment to the haunts of profligacy and vice; yet he was followed for a time, was admitted into Protestant places of worship, and honoured as a truth-telling oracle, till at length he was plainly detected to be what every one from the first would have seen he really was, were it usual to do the same common justice to Catholics which every Protestant considers his due ;—for falsehood is the basis of the Protestant Tradition.

On the other hand, I might give you other instances similar to that of Mr. Blanco White. I might point to Mr. Steimnitz, who, within the last ten years, began his noviciate among the Jesuits, left them, turned Protestant, and published an account of the community he had quitted. He wrote to expose them, and abounded in bitterness and invective; but as to his facts, so little had he to produce from his own personal knowledge to the disadvantage of the Institution he was attacking, and so severely did he disappoint the Protestants for whom he wrote, that they considered his work what they called a Jesuitical trick, and said that he was pretending to attack the good fathers in order really to set them off to advantage; for truth does but prejudice the Protestant Tradition.

Falsehood succeeds for a generation, or for a period; but there it has its full course and comes to an end. Truth is eternal; it is great, and will prevail. The end is the proof of things. Brothers of the Oratory, surely we shall succeed, because " they say all manner of evil against us falsely for His Name's sake."

LECTURE V.

LOGICAL INCONSISTENCY OF THE PROTESTANT VIEW.

A CONSIDERATION was incidentally introduced into the argument which engaged our attention last week, Brothers of the Oratory, which deserves insisting on, in the general view which I am taking of the present position of the Catholic Religion in England. I then said that, even putting aside the special merits and recommendations of the Catholic rule of celibacy, as enjoined upon the Priesthood and as involved in Monachism, (with which I was not concerned,) and looking at the question in the simple view of it, to which Protestants confine themselves, and keeping ourselves strictly on the defensive, still, when instances of bad priests and bad religious are brought against us, we might fairly fall back upon what may be called the previous question. I mean, it is incumbent on our opponents to show, that there are fewer cases of scandal among the married clergy than among unmarried; fewer cases of mental conflict, of restlessness, of despondency, of desolation, of immorality, and again of cruel slavery and hopeless suffering, among Protestant women, whether unmarried or wives than among Catholic nuns. It must be shown that in such instances of guilt or sorrow which can be adduced, the priests accused have fallen into sin, the nuns compassionated have passed from happiness to misery, distinctly *by virtue* of the vow which binds them to a single life :—for till this is proved nothing is proved. Protestants, however, for the most part find it very pleasant to attack others, very irksome and annoying to defend themselves ; they judge us by one rule, themselves by another ; and they convict us of every sin under heaven for doing sometimes what they do every day.

This one-sidedness, as it may be called, is one of the very marks or notes of a Protestant ; and bear in mind, when I use the word Protestant, I do not mean thereby all who are not Catholics, but distinctly the disciples of the Elizabethan Tradition. Such an one cannot afford to be fair ; he cannot be fair if he tries. He is ignorant, and he goes on to be unjust. He has always viewed things in one light, and he cannot adapt himself to any other ; he cannot throw himself into the ideas of other men, fix upon the principles on which those ideas depend, and then set himself to ascertain how those principles differ, or whether they differ at all, from those which he acts upon himself ; and, like a man who has been for a long while in one position, he is cramped and disabled, and has a difficulty and pain, more than we can well conceive, in stretching his limbs, straightening them, and moving them freely.

I.

This narrow and one-sided condition of the Protestant intellect might be illustrated in various ways.

(1.) For instance, as regards the subject of Education. It has lately been forcibly shown that the point which the Catholic Church is maintaining against the British Government in Ireland, as respects the Queen's Colleges for the education of the middle and upper classes, is precisely that which Protestantism maintains, and successfully maintains, against that same Government in England—viz., that secular instruction should not be separated from religious.[1] The Catholics of Ireland are asserting the very same principle as the Protestants of England; however, the Minister does not feel the logical force of the fact; and the same persons who think it so tolerable to indulge Protestantism in the one country, are irritated and incensed at a Catholic people for asking to be similarly indulged in the other. But how is it that intelligent men, who can ascend in their minds from the fall of an apple to the revolution of a comet, who can apply their economical and political inductions from English affairs to the amelioration of Italy and Spain—how is it that, when they come to a question of religion, they are suddenly incapable of understanding that what is reasonable and defensible in one country, is not utterly preposterous and paradoxical in another? What is true under one degree of longitude, is true under another. You have a right indeed to say that Catholicism itself is not true; but you have no right, for it is bad logic, to be surprised that those who think it true act consistently with that supposition; you do not well to be angry with those who resist a policy in Ireland which your own friends

---

[1] *Vide Tablet* Newspaper, May 31, 1851.

and supporters cordially detest and triumphantly withstand in England.

(2.) Take again a very different subject. A Protestant blames Catholics for showing honour to images; yet he does it himself. And first, he sees no difficulty in a mode of treating them, quite as repugnant to his own ideas of what is rational, as the practice he abominates; and that is, the offering insult and mockery to them. Where is the good sense of showing dishonour, if it be stupid and brutish to show honour? Approbation and criticism, praise and blame go together. I do not mean, of course, that you dishonour what you honour; but that the two ideas of honour and dishonour so go together, that where you *can* apply—(rightly or wrongly, but still) —where it is *possible* to apply the one, it is possible to apply the other. Tell me, then, what is meant by burning Bishops, or Cardinals, or Popes in *effigy*? has it no meaning? is it not plainly intended for an insult? Would any one who was burned in effigy feel it no insult? Well, then, how is it *not* absurd to feel pain at being dishonoured in effigy, *yet* absurd to feel pleasure at being honoured in effigy? How is it childish to honour an image, if it is not childish to dishonour it? This only can a Protestant say in defence of the act which he allows and practises, that he is used to it, whereas to the other he is not used. Honour is a new idea, it comes strange to him; and, wonderful to say, he does not see that he has admitted it in principle already, in admitting dishonour, and after preaching against the Catholic who crowns an image of the Madonna, he complacently goes his way, and sets light to a straw effigy of Guy Fawkes.

But this is not all; Protestants actually set up images to represent their heroes, and they show them honour without any misgiving. The very flower and cream of Protestantism used to glory in the statue of King William on College Green, Dublin; and, though I cannot make any reference in print, I recollect well what a shriek they raised some years ago, when the figure was unhorsed. Some profane person one night applied gunpowder, and blew the king right out of his saddle; and he was found by those who took interest in him, like Dagon, on the ground. You might have thought the poor senseless block had life, to see the way people took on about it, and how they spoke of his face, and his arms, and his legs; yet those same Protestants, I say, would at the same time be horrified, had I used "he" and "him" of a crucifix, and would call me one of the monsters described in the Apocalypse, did I but honour my living Lord as they their dead king.

(3.) Another instance:—When James the Second went out, and the aforesaid William came in, there were persons who refused to swear fidelity to William, because they had already sworn fidelity to James; and who was to dispense them from their oath? yet these scrupulous men were the few. The many virtually decided that the oath had been conditional, depending on their old king's good behaviour, though there was nothing to show it in the words in which it ran: and that accordingly they had no need to keep it any longer than they liked. And so, in a similar way, supposing a Catholic priest, who has embraced the Protestant persuasion, to come over to this country and marry a wife, who among his new co-religionists would dream of being shocked at it? Every one would think it both natural and becoming, and reasonable too, as a protest against Romish superstition; yet the man has taken the vow, and the man has broken it. "Oh! but he had no business to make such a vow; he did it in ignorance, it was antichristian, it was unlawful." There are then, it seems, after all, such things as unlawful oaths, and unlawful oaths are not to be kept, and there are cases which require a dispensation; yet let a Catholic say this, and he says nothing more—(rather he says much less than the Protestant; for he strictly defines the limits of what is lawful and what is unlawful! he takes a scientific view of the matter, and he forbids a man to be judge in his own case),—let a Catholic, I say, *assert* what the Protestant *practises*, and he has furnished matter for half-a-dozen platform speeches, and a whole set of Reformation Tracts.

These are some of the instances, which might be enlarged upon, of the blindness of our opponents to those very same acts or principles in themselves, which they impute as enormities to us; but I leave them for your consideration, my Brothers, and proceed to an instance of a different character.

2.

What is a more fruitful theme of declamation against us than the charge of persecution? The Catholic Church is a persecuting power; and every one of us is a persecutor; and, if we are not by nature persecutors, yet we are forced to be persecutors by the necessity we lie under of obeying a persecuting Church. Now let us direct a careful attention to this Protestant land, which has so virtuous a horror of persecution, and so noble a loathing of persecutors, and so tender a compassion for the persecuted, and let us consider whether the multitude of men are not, to say the least, in the same boat with us; whether there is anything which we are said to do which they do not do also, anything which we are said to have done which they have not done, and therefore, whether, with this theoretical indignation of persecution on the one hand, and this practical sanction of it on the other, they are not in the very position of that great king, in his evil hour, who sentenced a transgressor, when he himself was "the man."

Now I suppose, when men speak of persecution, and say that Catholics persecute, they mean that Catholics, on the score of religious opinions, inflict punishment on persons, property, privileges, or reputation; that we hate, calumniate, mock, mob and distress those who differ from us; that we pursue them with tests, disabilities, civil penalties, imprisonment, banishment, slavery, torture and death; that we are inflexible in our tempers, relentless in our measures, perfidious in our dealings, and remorseless in our inflictions. Something of this kind will be said, with a good deal of exaggeration even at very first sight; but still, as even a candid man may perhaps fancy, with some truth at the bottom. Well, see what I propose to do. I shall not discuss any point of doctrine or principle; such a task would not fall within the scope of these Lectures; I am not going to assume that savage cruelty, ruthless animosity, frantic passion, that the love of tormenting and delight in death are right, nor am I going to assume that they are wrong; I am not entering upon any question of the moral law;—moreover I will not discuss how far Catholics fairly fall in fact under the charge of barbarity, mercilessness, and fanaticism, and for this reason, because it is not my concern; for I mean to maintain, that the acts imputed to Catholics, whatever be their character, so very closely resemble in principle what is done by Protestants themselves, and in a Protestant's judgment is natural, explicable, and becoming, that Protestants are just the very last persons in the world who can with safety or consistency call Catholics persecutors, for the simple reason, that they should not throw stones who live in glass houses.

I am maintaining no paradox in saying this; it is a truth which is maintained by intelligent Protestants themselves. There is Dr. Whately, the present Protestant Archbishop of Dublin, one of the first writers of the day, and a most violent opponent of Catholicism; listen how he speaks, at the very time he is inveighing against our Holy Religion. "The Romish Church," he says, "which has so long and so loudly been stigmatized as a persecuting Church, is, indeed, deeply stained with this guilt, but cannot with any reason be reckoned the originating cause of it. . . . This, as well as the other Romish errors, has its root in the evil heart of the unrenewed man. Like the rest, it neither began with Romanism, nor can reasonably be expected to end with it."[2]

Now, what I shall do is, to take the Protestant in his house, his family, and his circle of friends, in his occupation, and his civil and political position, as a

[2] Whately on Romanism, p. 225.

good kind father, as a liberal master, as a useful member of society; and to consider, as regards this matter of persecution, whether, could he see himself in a looking-glass, he would not mistake himself for a Catholic.

For instance, what is the first and natural act on the part of a Protestant father of a family, when he receives the intelligence that his son or daughter, grown up to man's or woman's estate, nay, long since come of age, has become, or is on the point of becoming a Catholic? Of course there are exceptions; but in most cases his conduct is so uniform, so suggestive of a general law, to which particular cases belong, that I almost fear to describe it, lest, what is farthest from my wish, I seem to be personal, and to be indulging in satire, when I am but pursuing an argument. "My dear John or James," the father says, calling him by his Christian name, "you know how tenderly I love you, and how indulgent I have ever been to you. I have given you the best of educations, and I have been proud of you. There is just one thing I cannot stand, and that is Popery; and this is the very thing you have gone and taken up. You have exercised your right of private judgment; I do not quarrel with you for this; you are old enough to judge for yourself; but I too have sacred duties, which are the unavoidable result of your conduct. I have duties to your brothers and sisters;—never see my face again; my door is closed to you. It wounds me to come to this decision, but what can I do? My affection for you is as strong as ever it was, but you have placed yourself under influences hostile to your father's roof and your own home, and you must take the consequences."

No one can look round him, who has much to do with conversions and converts, without seeing this fulfilled often to the letter, and *mutatis mutandis*, in a variety of parallel cases. Protestants have felt it right, just, and necessary, to break the holiest of earthly ties, and to inflict the acutest temporal suffering on those who have exercised their private judgment in the choice of a religion. They have so acted, and they so act daily. A sense of duty to religious opinions, and of the supposed religious interests of those intrusted to them, has triumphed over the feelings of nature. Years have passed, perhaps death has come, without any signs of recognition passing from the father to the son. Sometimes the severance and its consequences may be sterner still: the wife may be sent away, her children taken from her, because she felt a call in conscience to join the Catholic Church. The son has been cut off (as they say) to a shilling. The daughter has been locked up, her books burned, the rites of her religion forbidden her. The malediction has been continued to the third generation; the grandchildren, the child unborn, has not been tolerated by the head of the family, because the parents were converts to the faith of their forefathers.

Nature pleads; and therefore, to fortify the mind the various reasons for such severity must be distinctly passed before it, and impressed upon it, and passion must be roused to overcome affection. " Such a base, grovelling, demoralising religion, unworthy of a man of sense, unworthy of a man! I could have borne his turning Drummondite, Plymouth-Brother, or Mormonite. He might almost have joined the

Agapemone. I would rather see him an unbeliever; yes, I say it deliberately, Popery is worse than Paganism. I had rather see him dead. I could have borne to see him in his coffin. I cannot see him the slave of a priest. And then the way in which he took the step: he never let me know, and had been received before I had had a hint about it;" or "he told me what he meant to do, and then did it in spite of me;" or, "he was so weak and silly," or "so headstrong," or "so long and obstinately set upon it." "He had nothing to say for himself," or "he was always arguing." "He was inveigled into it by others," or "he ought to have consulted others, he had no right to have an opinion. Anyhow he is preferring strangers to his true friends; he has shown an utter disregard of the feelings of his parents and relations; he has been ungrateful to his father."

These are a few out of the many thoughts which pass through the Protestant's mind under the circumstances I have supposed, and which impel him to inflict a severe penalty on a child for a change of religion. And if there be Protestant fathers who demur to the correctness of this representation (and I am using the word Protestant in its proper sense, as I have noticed several times before), I beg to ask such parents whether, in fact, they have themselves suffered the affliction I have supposed,—I mean, that of their children becoming Catholics; and, if they have not, I entreat them to fancy such an affliction for a moment, and how they would feel and act if it really took place. Rather they will not be able to get themselves to fancy it; I am sure that most of them will revolt from the thought in indignation; the very supposition irritates them. "I should like to see any son or daughter of mine turning Papist!" is the thought which spontaneously rises to their mind.

I have been speaking of the upper and middle classes: in the lower the feeling is the same, only more uncourteously expressed, and acted on more summarily. The daughter, on her return home, tells the mother that she has been attending, and means to attend, the Catholic chapel; whereupon the mother instantly knocks the daughter down, and takes away from her her bonnet and shawl, and the rest of her clothes to keep her in-doors: or if it is the case of a wife, the husband falls to cursing, protests he will kill her if she goes near the Catholics, and that if the priest comes here, he will pitch him out of window. Such are specimens of what Dr. Whately truly calls, 'the evil heart of the unrenewed man."

Perhaps, however, the one party or the other gives way; milder counsels prevail with the persecutor, or the persecuted is menaced into submission. A poor child is teased and worried, till, to escape black looks, sharp speeches, petty mortifications, and the unsympathizing chill of the domestic atmosphere, she consents to go to Protestant worship; and is forced to sit, stand, and kneel, in outward deference to a ceremonial, which she utterly disbelieves, and perhaps hates. At length, doing violence to her conscience, she loses her sense of the reality of Catholicism, grows indifferent to all religion, sceptical of the truth of everything, and utterly desponding and sick at heart and miserable. Her friends suspect her state, but it is better than Popery; their detestation of the

Catholic religion is so intense, that, provided their child is saved from its influence, for them she may believe anything or nothing ; and as to her distress of mind, time will overcome it—they will get her married. Such is a Protestant's practical notion of freedom of opinion, religious liberty, private judgment, and those other fine principles which he preaches up with such unction in public meetings, and toasts so enthusiastically at public dinners.

Perhaps, however, there is a compromise. Terms are made, conditions extracted ; the parties who have made the mistake of thinking they might judge for themselves, are taken into favour again,—are received under the paternal roof on the rigid stipulation that no sign of Catholicism is to escape them ; their mouths are to be sealed ; their devotional manuals to be hid ; their beads must never escape from their pocket ; their crucifix must lie in a drawer ; Opinion is to be simply put down in the family.

As to domestic servants whose crime it is to be Catholics, far more summary measures are taken with them, not less cruel in effect, though more plausible in representation. They are the first to suffer from a popular cry against the Catholic religion. Perhaps some reverend person, high in station, draws public attention to this defenceless portion of the community, —not to protect them from those moral dangers which benevolent statesmen are striving to mitigate, —but to make them the objects of suspicion, and to set their masters and mistresses against them. Suddenly a vast number of young persons are thrown out of their situations, simply because they are Catholics—because, forsooth, they are supposed to be emissaries of the Jesuits, spies upon the family, and secret preachers of Popery. Whither are they to go? home they have none; trial and perils they have without number, which ought to excite remorse in the breasts of those who, at the gain of a smart argument in controversy, or a telling paragraph in a speech or a charge, are the cause of their misfortunes. They look about in vain for a fresh place; and their only chance of success is by accepting any wages, however poor, which are offered them, and going into any service, however hard, however low, however disadvantageous. Well, but let us suppose the best that can befall them: they shall be tolerated in a household and not discharged; but what is the price they pay for this indulgence! They are to give up their religious duties; never to go to confession; only once or twice a year to mass; or an arrangement is made, as a great favour, to allow them to go monthly. Moreover, they are had up into the parlour or drawing-room for family prayers, or to hear tracts and treatises, abusive of their religion, or to endure the presence of some solemn Protestant curate, who is expressly summoned to scare and browbeat, if he cannot persuade, a safe victim, whom her hard circumstances have made dependent on the tyranny of others.

Now, I would have every Protestant, to whom my words may come, put his hand on his heart and say, first, whether scenes such as I have been describing, whether in high life or in low, are not very much what he would call persecution in Catholics, and next, whether they can, by any the utmost ingenuity, be referred, in the cases supposed, to any Catholic influence as their cause. On the contrary, they come out of the very depths and innermost shrine of the Protestant heart: it is undeniable, the very staunchest Protestants are the actors in them : nay, the stauncher they are, the more faithfully do they sustain their part: and yet, I repeat, if a similar occurrence were reported of some Catholic family in Italy or Spain, these very persons whose conduct I have been describing would listen with great satisfaction to the invectives of any itinerant declaimer, who should work up the sternness of the father, the fury of the mother, the beggary of children and grandchildren, the blows struck, the imprecations uttered, the imprisonment, the over-persuasion, or the compulsory compromise, into a demonstration that Popery was nothing else than a persecuting power, which was impatient of light, and afraid of inquiry, and which imposed upon fathers, mothers, and husbands, under pain of reprobation, the duty of tormenting their children, and discharging their servants at an hour's warning.

Let us walk abroad with those children or servants, who, by the spirit of Protestantism, have been sent about their business for being Catholics, and we shall see fresh manifestations of its intolerance. Go into the workshops and manufactories, you will find it in full operation. The convert to Catholicism is dismissed by his employer; the tradesman loses his custom; the practitioner his patients; the lawyer has no longer the confidence of his clients; pecuniary aid is reclaimed, or its promise recalled; business is crippled, the shop cannot be opened; the old is left without provision, the young without his outfit—he must look about for himself; his friends fight shy of him; gradually they drop him, if they do not disown him at once. There used to be pleasant houses open to him, and a circle of acquaintance. People were glad to see him, and he felt himself, though solitary, not lonely; he was by himself, indeed, but he had always a refuge from himself, without having recourse to public amusements which he disliked. It is now all at an end; he gets no more invitations; he is not a welcome guest. He at length finds himself in *Coventry;* and where his presence once was found, now it is replaced by malicious and monstrous tales about him, distorted shadows of himself, freely circulated, and readily believed. What is his crime?—he is a Catholic among Protestants.

3.

If such is the conduct of Protestant society towards individuals, what is it not against the Priest? what against the Catholic Name itself? Do you think it is with the good will of Establishment, Wesleyan Connection, and various other denominations of religion, that Catholics are in Birmingham at all? do we worship—have we a place of worship,—with or against the will of the bodies in question? Would they not close all our churches and chapels to-morrow, would they not cut the ground from under us, if they could? what hinders them from turning us all out of the place, except that they can't? Attend to this, my Brothers, and observe its bearing. You know what an outcry is raised, because the Roman Government does not sell or give ground to Protestants to build a Protestant Church in the centre of Rome; that government hinders them there, because it is able; Protestants do not hinder us here, because they are not able. Can they, in the face of day, deny this?—they cannot. Why, then, do they find fault with others who do, because they can, what they themselves would do if they could? Do not tell me, then, that they are in earnest when they speak of the "intolerance of Catholics" abroad; they ought to come into court with clean hands. They do just the same themselves, as far as they can; only, since they cannot do it to their mind's content, they are determined it shall form an article of impeachment against us; and they eagerly throw a stone that comes to hand, though it is only by an accident that it does not fall back on themselves.

It has lately been reported in the papers that the Catholics of Italy are going to build a church in London for their poor countrymen, who in great numbers are found there. Let them go to the Board of Woods and Forests (and less equitable bodies might be found), and try to negotiate a purchase of ground for a site; would Government for a moment entertain the proposal? would it not laugh at their impudence in asking? would the people suffer the Government, even if it were disposed? would there not be petitions sent up to the two Houses, enough to break the tables on which they were ranged,—petitions to the Queen, enough to block up the Home Office? would not the whole press, both daily and weekly, in town and in country, groan and tremble under the portentous agitation such a project would occasion? Happily for Catholics, other ground is to be had. But would not Court and Ministry, Establishment, Wesleyans, almost every political party, almost all the denominations of

London, the Court of Aldermen, the Common Council, the City Companies, the great landlords, the Inns of Court, and the Vestries, hinder any Catholic Church if they could? Yet these are the parties to cry out against a line of conduct in Rome, which they do their best to imitate in London.

But this is not all: in spite of their manifesting, every day of their lives, an intense desire to do us all the harm in their power, wonderful to say, they go on to reproach us with ingratitude. We evince no gratitude, say the Protestant Bishops, for the favours which have been shown us. Gratitude for what? What favours have we received? the Frenchman's good fortune, and nothing else. When he boasted the king had spoken to him, he was naturally asked what the king had said: and he answered that his Majesty had most graciously cried out to him, "Fellow, stand out of the way." Statesmen would ignore us if they could; they recognise us in order to coerce; they cannot coerce without recognising, therefore at last they condescend to recognise. When there was a proposal, several years ago, for an interchange of ministers between England and the Pope, then they would not have his name mentioned; he was not to be called by any title of his own, but by a new-fangled name, framed for the occasion. He was to be known as "Sovereign of the Roman States;" a title which pretty well provided, should occasion occur, for treating with some other sovereign power in his States who should not be he. Now that they wish to do him an injury, forthwith they wake up to the fact of his existence. Our statesmen affect to know nothing of the greatest power on earth, the most ancient dynasty in history, till it comes right across their path, and then they can recognise as foes, what before they could not recognise as gentlemen.

Indeed, if the truth must be told, so one-sided is this Protestantism, that its supporters have not yet admitted the notion into their minds, that the Catholic Church has as much right to make converts in England, as any other denomination. It is a new idea to them; they had thought she ought to be content with vegetating, as a sickly plant, in some back-yard or garret window; but to attempt to spread her faith abroad—this is the real insidiousness, and the veritable insult. I say this advisedly. Some public men, indeed, have even confessed it; they have been candid enough to admit distinctly, that the Penal Bill is intended to throw a damper on our energies; and others imply it who dare not say it. There are words, for instance, imputed to the Prime Minister, with reference to a publication of my own, which put the matter in a very clear point of view. I have to acknowledge his civility to myself personally; and I am sure, though I have an aversion to his party and his politics, of twenty, nay thirty years' standing, yet I bear nothing but goodwill to himself, except as the representative of the one and of the other. But now consider what he said. It appears he had laid it down, that his only object in his Parliamentary measure was to resist any temporal pretensions of the Pope; and in proof, observe, that such pretensions were made, what does he do, but quote some words which I used in a sermon preached at Chad's last October, on occasion of the Establishment of the Hierarchy. Now what was that sermon about? was there a word in it about Catholics exercising or gaining temporal power in England, which was the point on which he was insisting?—not a syllable. I may confidently say, for I know my own feelings on the subject, that the notion of any civil or political aggrandisement of Catholicism never came into my head. From the beginning to the end of the sermon, I spoke simply and purely of conversions—of conversions of individuals, of the spread of the Church by means of individual conversions, by the exercise of private judgment, by the communication of mind with mind, by the conflict of opinion, by the zeal of converts, and in the midst of persecution; not by any general plan of operation, or by political movement, or by external influence bearing upon the country. Such a growth of Catholicism, intellectual, gradual, moral, peaceable, and stable, I certainly predicted and predict, and such only: yet this, though the fruit of free opinion and disputation, is adduced by the Premier as an intelligible, as a sufficient, reason for introducing a measure of coercion.

An intellectual movement must be met by Act of Parliament. Can a clearer proof be required, that not our political intrigues—for we are guilty of none—but our moral and argumentative power, is the real object of apprehension and attack? they wish to coerce us because we are zealous, and they venture to coerce us because we are few. They coerce us for the crime of being few and wishing to be many. They coerce us while they can, lest they should not dare to coerce when another twenty years has passed over our heads. "Hit him, he's down!" this is the cry of the Ministry, the country gentlemen, the Establishment, and Exeter Hall. *Therefore* are we ultramontanes; *therefore* are we aggressive; *this* is our conspiracy, that we have hearts to desire what we believe to be for the religious wellbeing of others, and heads to compass it. Two centuries ago, all England, you know, was in terror about some vast and mysterious Popish plot, which was to swallow up the whole population, without any one knowing how. What does the historian Hume—no Catholic, certainly,—say on the subject? "Such zeal of proselytism," he observes, "actuates that sect (meaning us) that its missionaries have penetrated into every nation of the globe; and in one sense there is a Popish plot perpetually carrying on against all states, Protestant, Pagan, and Mahometan."[3] The simple truth! this is the unvarnished account of the matter: we do surpass in zeal every other Religion, and have done so from the first. But this, surely, ought to be no offence, but a praise: that Religion which inspires the most enthusiasm has a right to succeed. If to cherish zeal, if to deal the blows of reason and argument, if this be political, if this be disloyal, certainly we deserve worse punishment than the deportation suggested by one member of Parliament, and the £500 penalty proposed by another.

Had indeed the ruling powers of the country, when coercion was in their power, refrained from coercion, and turned a host of controversialists in upon us instead; had a gracious answer come from the Throne

---

[3] Charles the Second, ch 67.

in return for the loyal address of the Protestant Bishops, commanding them to refute us, and never to enter the royal closet again without a tail of twenty converts apiece; had a Parliamentary Committee been appointed to inquire into the best means of denying our facts, and unravelling our arguments; had a reward of some £1000 been offered for our scientific demolition, in Bridgewater Treatise or Warburton Lecture, we should have felt gratitude towards those who had rather fail in their end than be ungenerous in their measures. But for years and years the case has been just the reverse; they have ever done us all the harm that they could, they have not done only what they could not. They have only made concessions under the influence of fear. Small thanks for scanty favours; such thanks as Lazarus's for the rich man's crumbs which could not help falling from the table: it is no virtue to grant what you cannot deny. Now, what is the state of the case; Protestant sects quarrel among themselves, they scramble for power, they inflict injuries on each other; then at length they come to think it would be well to bear and forbear. They establish the great principle of toleration, not at all for our sakes, simply for the sake of each other, one and all devoutly wishing that they could tolerate each other without tolerating us. We, born Britons and members of the body politic as much as they, accidentally come under the shadow of a toleration which was meant for others. When they find that common sense and fairness are too strong for them, and that they cannot keep us out, and, moreover, that it is dangerous to do so, they make a merit of letting us in, and they wish us to be grateful for a privilege which is our birthright as much as it is theirs.

I know well there is a rising feeling, there are emergent parties in this country, far more generous and equitable, far more sensible, than to deserve these imputations; but I am speaking all along of the dominant faction, and of the children of the Tradition. As for the latter, it will be long before they realise the fact that we are on a social equality with themselves, and that what is allowable in them is allowable in us. At present, it is a matter of surprise to them that we dare to speak a word in our defence, and that we are not content with the liberty of breathing, eating, moving about, and dying in a Protestant soil. That we should have an opinion, that we should take a line of our own, that we should dare to convince people, that we should move on the offensive, is intolerable presumption, and takes away their breath. They think themselves martyrs of patience if they can keep quiet in our presence, and condescending in the heroic degree, if they offer us any lofty civility. So was it the other day, when the late agitation began; the hangers-on of Government said to us, "Cling tight to our coat-tails; we are your best friends; we shall let you off easy; we shall only spit upon you; but beware of those rabid Conservatives;" and they marvelled that we did not feel it to be the highest preferment for the Catholic Church to wait in the ante-chambers of a political party. So it is with your Protestant controversialist, even when he shows to best advantage; his great principle of disputation is that he is up, and the Catholic is down; and his great duty is to show it.

He is intensely conscious that he is in a very eligible situation, and his opponent in the gutter; and he lectures down upon him, as if out of a drawing-room window. It is against his nature to be courteous to those for whom he feels so cordial a disdain, and he cannot forgive himself for stooping to annihilate them. He mistakes sharpness for keenness, and haughtiness for strength; and never shows so high and mighty in manner as when he means to be unutterably conclusive. It is a standing rule with him to accuse his opponent of evasion and misstatement; and, when in fault of an argument, he always can impugn his motives, or question the honesty of his professions.

Such is the style of that writer to whom Cardinal Wiseman alludes in his late Appeal to the English people. The person I speak of is a gentleman and a scholar, nay, one of the most distinguished Protestant theologians of the day; but that did not hinder him, on the occasion alluded to by the Cardinal, from strutting about with indignation that a Catholic should intrude himself into the quarrels of the Establishment, and from fancying that rudeness would be an indication of superiority. In his title-page he describes his pamphlet as "A letter to N. Wiseman, D.D., *calling himself* Bishop of Melipotamus;" then he addresses him, not "Rev. Sir," but "Sir," and talks of it being reported that he has "received the form of episcopal consecration at Rome," and tells him this is no excuse for his "acting in opposition to his legitimate diocesan, the [Protestant] Bishop of Worcester." He proceeds to speak of Dr. Wiseman's "characteristic sagacity," and of the "leaders of his party;" reminds him that "in the eyes of his superiors the end sanctifies the means," and says that a mistake of fact, of which he accuses him, "appears to be not quite unintentional." He is ever upon stilts, and, as the pamphlet proceeds, there is an ever-thickening recurrence of such rhetoric as "Excuse me, Sir," and "Now, Sir," and "Such, Sir," and "But, Sir," and "Yes, Sir," and "No, Sir." I should not notice this pamphlet, which is of some years' standing, did I think the writer at all repented of its tone, and might not any day publish just such another. After all, it is but an instance in detail of the Protestant Tradition; for such has been the received style of the Church of England ever since the days of such considerable men as Laud, Taylor, Stillingfleet, and Ussher. Moreover, it is emphatically the gentleman-like manner of conducting the controversy with us, in contrast to that of the pulpit or the platform, where the speaker considers himself a sort of theological Van Amberg, scares us with his eye, and hits up to and fro with his cudgel.

4.

Now for another department of this petty persecution. That able writer, Dr. Whately, whom I have already quoted in this Lecture, and whom, for the love I bear him, from all memories, in spite of our religious differences, I take pleasure in quoting, whenever I can do so with any momentary or partial agreement with him—the Protestant Archbishop of Dublin, I say, writing on the subject of persecution, is led to speak of insult and abuse, calumny, ridicule, and blasphemy, as directed by the professors of one religion against those of another; and he uses the following remarkable words:—" Undoubtedly," he says, " they ought to enjoy this protection, not only of their persons and property, but of their comfort and feelings also. The State is both authorised and bound to prohibit and to guard against, by her own appropriate penalties, not only everything that may tend to a breach of the peace, but also everything that unnecessarily interferes with the comfort, and molests the feelings of any one. I say, unnecessarily, because it may be painful indeed to a man's feelings to have his opinions controverted, and to be obliged to encounter opponents; but then free discussion is necessary for the attainment and maintenance of truth. *Not so with ridicule and insult;* to forbid these can be no violation of religious liberty, since no man can be bound in conscience to employ such weapons: they have manifestly no tendency to advance the cause of truth; they are, therefore, analogous to the slaughter of women and children, and other non-belligerents, which is regarded by all civilized nations as a violation of the laws of war; these being unnecessary cruelties, since they have no direct tendency to bring the war to a conclusion." And then he goes on to say, " It is evident that all this reasoning applies with equal force to the case of persons of *every religious persuasion*, whether Christians of various sects, or Jews, or Mahometans. All of these, though they must be prepared indeed to encounter fair argument, should be protected, not only from persecution, but from *insult, libel, and mockery*, as occasioning a useless interruption of public or of domestic peace and comfort; and this being an offence against society, may justly be prohibited and punished by human laws."[4]

Here, you will observe, a writer, setting down his thoughts on persecution twenty-five years ago, when the present state of the controversy was as yet in the womb of the future, distinctly tells us that insult, abuse, and mockery, are inconsistent with religious liberty, and that they should be prohibited by law, even as directed against Mahometans. Now I accept the sentiment, though I will not adopt it without an explanation. I consider then, that in applying it to the existing state of things, we must distinguish between religious objects and rites, and the persons who acknowledge them. I cannot reprobate, in a free country like this, the ridicule of individuals, whoever they are; and I think it would be a very evil day when it was forbidden. From the Lord Chancellor and Prime Minister, to the ephemeral charlatan or quack, who astonishes the world with his impudence and absurdity, it is desirable that all should be exposed to the ridicule of any who choose to make them the objects of it. In no other way are various abuses, or encroachments, or nuisances, or follies, so easily and gently got rid of; it is a most healthy expression of public opinion; it is a safety-valve for feelings, which if not allowed so harmless an escape, might end in a serious explosion. Moreover, it is our boast among the nations, that, while elsewhere it is dangerous, with us it is positively healthy. In France or in Italy, I suppose, no Government could stand against public ridicule; the Anglo-Saxon is good-natured in his

---

[4] Letters on the Church, p. 53. I am told (1872) the Archbishop never owned the authorship of this able volume.

satire ; and he likes his rulers not at all the worse, or rather the better, that he can distort them into attitudes, and dress them up in masquerade. And this permission must be suffered to extend to the case of persons who bear a religious profession, as well as that of others ; though in this case the line will sometimes be difficult to draw. It will be painful, indeed, to those who look up to them, to see one whom they revere, or who is associated with what is sacred in their minds, made the subject of insult and buffoonery, as it may be annoying to the private circle and painful to the relatives of a statesman or public man, who undergoes a similar ordeal ; but, as matters go in this country, there is no sufficient ground for prohibiting, nor much wisdom in complaining. But the case is very different when the religious rite is insulted, and the individual for the sake of the rite. For example, were England a Catholic country, I can fancy a caricature of a fat monk or a fanatical pilgrim being quite unobjectionable ; it would argue no disrespect to the Religion itself, but would be merely a blow at an abuse of religion, in the instance of certain individuals who were no ornament to it ; on the other hand, in a Protestant land, it would or would not be an insult to Catholicism, according to the temper of the moment, and the colouring and details of the satire. However, my business is not to draw the line between what is allowable and what is unfair as regards ridicule in matters of religion, but merely to direct your attention to this point, that I have no wish, when it can be helped, to shelter the persons of religious men under the sacredness of the Religion itself.

With this explanation, then, in favour of ridicule, I

accept Dr. Whately's doctrine as reasonable and true; but consider, my Brothers, its application to ourselves. What a remarkable light does it cast on the relative position of Protestants and Catholics in England during the current year! Our author tells us that insult and mockery, in religious controversy, is as cowardly and cruel as the slaughter of women and children in war, and he presses on us the duty of the State to prohibit by penalties such interference with the comforts and feelings of individuals; now, I repeat, what a remarkable illustration have Protestants supplied to this doctrine of a Protestant divine since Michaelmas last! The special champions of toleration, the jealous foes of persecution, how studiously and conscientiously, during nine long months, have they practised what they preached! What a bright example have they set to that religious communion which they hold in such abhorrence on the ground of its persecuting spirit! Oh, the one-sided intellect of Protestantism! I appeal in evidence of it to a great banquet, where, amid great applause, the first judge of the land spoke of trampling Cardinal Wiseman's hat under his feet. I appeal to the last fifth of November, when jeers against the Blessed Sacrament and its rites were chalked up in the Metropolis with impunity, under the very shadow of the Court, and before the eyes of the Home Office and the Police. I appeal to the mock processions to ridicule, and bonfires to burn, what we hold most venerable and sacred, not only Pope, and Cardinal and Priest, but the very Mother of our Lord, and the Crucifix itself. I appeal to those ever-growing files of newspapers, whose daily task, in the tedious succession of months, has been to cater for the gross palate of their readers all varieties of disgusting gossip, and of bitter reproach, and of extravagant slander, and of affronting, taunting, sneering, irritating invective against us. I appeal to the buckram nuns of Warwickshire, Nottingham, and Clapham, to the dungeons of Edgbaston, and the sin-table of St. Gudule's. I appeal to the outrageous language perpetrated in a place I must not name, where one speaker went the length of saying, what the reporters suppressed for fear of consequences, that a dear friend and brother of mine, for whose purity and honour I would die, mentioning him by name, went about the country, as the words came to the ears of those present, seducing young women. I appeal to the weekly caricatures, not of persons only and their doings, but of all that is held sacred in our doctrines and observances, of our rites and ceremonies, our saints and our relics, our sacred vestments and our rosaries. I appeal to the popular publication, which witty and amusing in its place, thought it well to leave its "sweetness" and its "fatness," to change make-believe for earnest, to become solemn and sour in its jests, and awkwardly to try its hand at divinity, because Catholics were the game. I appeal to the cowardly issue of a cowardly agitation, to the blows dealt in the streets of this very town upon the persons of the innocent, the tender, and the helpless;—not to any insult or affliction which has come upon ourselves, for it is our portion, and we have no thought of complaining,—but to the ladies and the school-girls, who, at various times, up to the day I am recording it, because they are Catholics, have been the victims of these newspaper sarcasms, and these platform blasphemies. I appeal to the stones striking sharply upon the one, and the teeth knocked out of the mouths of the other. Dr. Whately's words have been almost prophetic; mockery and insult have literally terminated in the bodily injury of those non-belligerents, who are sacred by the laws of all civilised warfare. Such are some of the phenomena of a Religion which makes it its special boast to be the Prophet of Toleration.

5.

And in the midst of outrages such as these, my Brothers of the Oratory, wiping its mouth, and clasping its hands, and turning up its eyes, it trudges to the Town Hall to hear Dr. Achilli expose the Inquisition. Ah! Dr. Achilli, I might have spoken of him last week, had time admitted of it. The Protestant world flocks to hear him, because he has something to tell of the Catholic Church. He *has* a something to tell, it is true; he *has* a scandal to reveal, he *has* an argument to exhibit. It is a simple one, and a powerful one, as far as it goes—and it is *one*. That one argument is himself; it is his presence which is the triumph of Protestants; it is the sight of him which is a Catholic's confusion. It is indeed our great confusion, that our Holy Mother could have had a priest like him.[5] He feels the force of the argument, and he shows himself to the multitude that is gazing on him. "Mothers of families," he seems to say, "gentle maidens, innocent children, look at me, for I am worth looking at. You do not

---

[5] *Vide Dublin Review* for July, 1850, and "Authentic Brief Sketch of the Life of Dr. Giacinto Achilli." Richardsons.

see such a sight every day. Can any Church live over the imputation of such a birth as I am?"[6]

* * * * * *

Yes, you are an incontrovertible proof that priests may fall and friars break their vows. You are your own witness; but while you *need* not go out of yourself for your argument, neither are you *able*. With you the argument begins; with you too it ends: the beginning and the ending you are both, When you have shown yourself, you have done your worst and your all; you are your best argument and your sole. Your witness against others is utterly invalidated by your witness against yourself You leave your sting in the wound; you cannot lay the golden eggs, for you are already dead.

For how, Brothers of the Oratory, can we possibly believe a man like this in what he says about persons, and facts, and conversations, and events, when he is of the stamp of Maria Monk, of Jeffreys, and of Teodore, and of others who have had their hour, and then been dropped by the indignation or the shame of mankind? What call is there on Catholics to answer what has not yet been proved? what need to answer the evidence of one who has not replied to the Police reports of Viterbo, Naples, and Corfu? He tells me that a Father Inquisitor said to him, "Another time," that you are "shut up in the Inquisition," "you" will not "get away so easily."[7] I do not believe it was said to him. He reports that a Cardinal said of him, "We must either make him a Bishop, or shut him up

---

[6] The paragraphs omitted are those which were decided by jury to constitute a libel, June 24, 1852.

[7] Dealings with the Inquisition, p. 2.

in the Inquisition."[8] I do not believe it. He bears witness, that "the General of the Dominicans, the oldest of the Inquisitors, exclaimed against him before the council, 'This heretic, we had better burn him alive.'"[9] I don't believe a word of it. "Give up the present Archbishop of Canterbury," says he, "amiable and pious as he is, to one of these rabid Inquisitors; he must either deny his faith, or be burned alive. Is my statement false? Am I doting?"[1] Not doting, but untrustworthy. "Suppose I were to be handed over to the tender mercy of this Cardinal [Wiseman], and he had full power to dispose of me as he chose, without losing his character in the eyes of the nation, ... should I not have to undergo some death more terrible than ordinary?" Dr. Achilli does not dote; they dote who trust him.

Why do I so confidently assert that he is not to be believed?—first, because his life for twenty years past creates no prepossession in favour of his veracity; secondly, because during a part of that period, according to his own confession, he spoke and argued against doctrines, which at the very time he confessed to be maintained by the communion to which he belonged; thirdly, because he has ventured to deny in the general, what official documents prove against him in the particular; fourthly, because he is not simple and clear enough in his narrative of facts to inspire any confidence in him; fifthly, because he abounds in misstatements and romance, as any one will see who knows anything of the matters he is writing about; sixthly, because he runs counter to facts known and confessed by all.

[8] Ibid. p. 27.   [9] Ibid. p. 46.   [1] Ibid. p. 75.

6.

Indeed, I should not finish my Lecture to-night, my Brothers, if I went through the series of historical facts which might be detailed in contradiction of the statements which this author advances, and in proof of the utterly false view which Protestants take of the Inquisition, and of the Holy See in connection with it. I will set down a few. A recent Catholic controversialist, a Spanish writer of great name, Dr. Balmez, goes so far as to say "that the Roman Inquisition has never been known to pronounce the execution of capital punishment, although the Apostolic See has been occupied, during that time, by Popes of extreme rigour and severity in all that relates to the civil administration."[2]—"We find," he continues, "in all parts of Europe scaffolds prepared to punish crimes against religion; scenes which sadden the soul were everywhere witnessed. Rome is an exception to the rule;—Rome, which it has been attempted to represent as a monster of intolerance and cruelty. . . . The Popes, armed with a tribunal of intolerance, have not spilt a drop of blood; Protestants and philosophers have shed torrents." Moreover, the Spanish Inquisition, against which, and not the Roman, it is more common to inveigh, though Dr. Achilli writes about the Roman, the Spanish Inquisition, which really was bloody, is confessed by great Protestant authorities, such as Ranke, and Guizot, to have been a political, not an ecclesiastical institution; its officials, though ecclesiastics, were

---

[2] Balmez' Protestantism, transl., p. 166.—I am rather surprised that this is stated so unrestrictedly, *vide* Life of St. Philip Neri, vol. i.; however, the fact is substantially as stated, even though there were some exceptions to the rule.

"appointed by the crown, responsible to the crown, and removable at its pleasure."[3] It had, indeed, been originally authorised by the Pope, who, at the instance of the civil power, granted it a bull of establishment; but as soon as it began to act, its measures so deeply shocked him, that he immediately commenced a series of grave remonstrances against its proceedings, and bitterly complained that he had been deceived by the Spanish Government. The Protestant Ranke distinctly maintains that it was even set up *against* the Pope and the Church. "As the jurisdiction of the Court," he says, "rested on the Royal Supremacy, so its exercise was made available for the maintenance of the Royal authority. It is one of those *spoliations* of the ecclesiastical power, by which this government rose into strength; . . . in its nature and its object, it was a purely political institute." Moreover, the Pope, anxious and displeased at what was going on, appointed a new functionary to reside on the spot, with the office of Judge of Appeals from the Inquisition, in favour of the condemned: and when this expedient was evaded, he appointed special judges for particular cases; and lastly, when the cruelty of the Spanish Government and its officials, lay and ecclesiastical, defeated this second attempt to ameliorate the evil, then he encouraged the sufferers to flee to Rome, where he took them under his protection.[4] In this way it is recorded, that in one

---

[3] *Vide* an able article in the Dublin Review, June, 1850,—which is my authority for this and other facts.

[4] Gieseler says that "the Popes at first tried *to draw some advantage* from the new Institution by selling [ecclesiastical] absolution for the crime of apostasy."—Vol. iii. p. 335. It is easy to throw out such insinuations as to objects and motives.

year he rescued 230 persons, and 200 in another. Sometimes he directly interfered in Spain itself; in the beginning of one year he liberated fifty heretics; and fifty more a month or two later; three further interpositions of mercy are recorded within the year. Sometimes he set aside and annulled the judgments passed: sometimes he managed to rescue the condemned from the infamy and civil consequences of the sentence; sometimes he actually summoned, censured, and excommunicated the Inquisitor; and often he took the part of the children of those whose property was forfeited to the crown. Moreover he refused to allow the Spanish Government to introduce their Inquisition into Naples, or the Milanese, which then belonged to Spain, from his disapprobation of its rigour.

Such conduct as this is but in accordance with the historical character of the Holy See, in all times and in all countries. Doubtless in the long course of eighteen hundred years, there are events which need explanation, and which Catholics themselves might wish otherwise: but the general tenor and tendency of the traditions of the Papacy have been mercy and humanity. It has ever been less fierce than the nations, and in advance of the age: it has ever moderated, not only the ferocity of barbarians, but the fanaticism of Catholic populations. Let the accusations which can be made against it be put in form; let the formal charges be proved: let the proved offences be counted up; and then Protestants themselves will be able to determine what judgment is to be passed on the language in which they indulge themselves against it. "An actual hell," says their present oracle, Dr. Achilli, "seems to be at the command of this Church, and it may be known by the name of the Inquisition. . . . The Inquisition is truly a hell, invented by priests. . . . Christianity suffers more now than in former times under this harsh slavery."[5] The Inquisition, it seems, is a hell; then there are many other hells in the world present and past, and worse hells, though this is the only one of which Dr. Achilli has had experience. He, indeed, may be excused for not knowing that, in his reprobation of the Inquisition, he is in fact virtually reflecting upon the nation, at whose good opinion he is aiming; but Protestants, had they the caution of ordinary disputants, would have known better than to accept a field of controversy, far less dangerous to their enemy than to themselves. Judgment and justice, like charity, begin at home: and before they commiserate culprits two thousand miles away, they would do well to feel some shame at victims of their own making. They are shocked, forsooth, at religious ascendancy and religious coercion at Rome; as if the ideas and the things were foreign to a British soil and a British policy. The *name* alone of the Inquisition, says Dr. Achilli, "is sufficient to incite in the minds of all rational beings a sentiment of horror and repugnance, little inferior to what Christians experience with respect to hell itself."[6] A true word! what is the Inquisition *but* a name? What is the Court of Queen's Bench but a name? why should not, in this matter, the names be interchanged? what has the Inquisition done at Rome, which the Royal name and authority has not done in England? The question is, not what a tribunal is called, but what has been its

---

[5] Inquisition, pp. 5, 11. [6] Ibid. p. 5.

work. Dr. Achilli, it seems, has been imprisoned by the Inquisition, for preaching in Rome against the religion of Rome: and has no one ever been put in prison, or fined, or transported, or doomed to death in England, for preaching against the religion of England? Those adversaries, indeed, of Catholicism pleaded that Catholicism was rebellion: and has Dr. Achilli had nothing to do with a party not only dangerous, but actually and contemporaneously subversive of the Pontifical Government? It seems never to occur to a Protestant, that he must not do in his own case what he blames in another; and should he at any time leave off a practice, he is surprised that every one else has not left it off at the same moment, and he has no mercy on any that has not;—like converted prodigals, who are sternly unforgiving towards the vices they have only just abandoned themselves.

7.

It is in my own memory, that a popular writer was convicted in the King's Bench, and sentenced to fine and imprisonment, for parodying passages of the Anglican Prayer Book. It is within my own memory, that an unbeliever in Christianity incurred a similar sentence, for exposing and selling his publications in a shop in Fleet Street. Why is Christianity to be protected by law, if Catholicism is not? What has the Inquisition done to Dr. Achilli, which the King's Bench did not do, and more, to Hone and Carlyle? Why is that so shocking to-day, which came so natural to you thirty years ago? Not many years have passed since Unitarian worship was a legal offence: the Unitarian creed was felony, and Unitarian congregations incurred the penalty of transportation. "If the civil magistrate," says Dr. Whately, "have no rightful jurisdiction whatever in religious concerns, it is quite as much an act of injustice, though of far less cruelty, to fine a Socinian, as to burn him."[7] Nor, indeed, was burning absent; five men were burnt in Elizabeth's reign for denying the Holy Trinity, of whom the Protestant Bishop of Norwich burnt three. In the next reign, the Protestant Bishop of London burnt one, and the Protestant Bishop of Lichfield another. A third was sentenced, but the compassion of the people saved him. Catholics have fared even worse; they have not, indeed, been burned, but they have been tortured, hung, cut down alive, cut open alive, quartered, and boiled. Nay, it is only quite lately, that heavy penal inflictions have been taken off the daily acts of our religion. Many of us, my Brothers, as you know well, wear about us crosses, pictures, medals, beads, and the like, blessed by the Pope; they are still illegal; an *Agnus Dei* is still illegal. Nay, five years have not fully passed, since the bringing them into the kingdom, and the giving them away, and the receiving and wearing them was punishable, by outlawry, forfeiture of all goods and chattels to the Queen, and imprisonment for life. Yet British Law is the wonder of the world, and Rome is Antichrist!

Nor has this prohibition been at all times an empty menace, as it is to-day: time was, when it was followed out into its extreme consequences. The possession of an *Agnus Dei* was the foremost charge in the indictment brought against the first of our

[7] Letters on the Church, p. 42.

Martyrs among the Missionary Priests in the reign of bloody Elizabeth. "As soon as the Sheriff came into the chamber," say the Acts of the martyrdom of Cuthbert Maine, "he took Mr. Maine by the bosom, and said to him, What art thou? he answered, I am a man. Whereat the Sheriff, being very hot, asked if he had a coat of mail under his doublet; and so unbuttoned it, and found an *Agnus Dei* case about his neck, which he took from him, and called him traitor and rebel, with many other opprobrious names."[8] Maine was hanged, cut down alive, falling from a great height, and then quartered. He was the first-fruit of a sanguinary persecution, which lasted a hundred years. John Wilson, while they tore out his heart said, "I forgive the Queen, and all that are the cause of my death." Edward Campion was cruelly torn and rent upon the rack divers times. "Before he went to the rack, he used to fall down at the rack-house door, upon both knees, to commend himself to God's mercy; and upon the rack he called continually upon God, repeating often the holy name of Jesus. His keeper asked him the next day, how he felt his hands and feet, he answered, 'Not ill, because not at all.' He was hanged and embowelled at Tyburn." Ralph Sherwin came next; the hangman, taking hold of him with his bloody hands, which had been busy with the bowels of the martyred priest who preceded him, said to him, thinking to terrify him, "Come, Sherwin, take thou also thy wages." But the holy man, nothing dismayed, embraced him with a cheerful countenance, and reverently kissed the blood that stuck to his hands; at

---

[8] Challoner's Missionary Priests.

which the people were much moved. He had been twice racked, and now he was dealt with as his brother before him. Thomas Sherwood, after six months' imprisonment in a dark and filthy hole, was hanged, cut down alive, dismembered, bowelled, and quartered. Alexander Brian had needles thrust under his nails, was torn upon the rack, hanged, and beheaded. George Haydock was suffered to hang but a very little while, when the Sheriff ordered the rope to be cut, and the whole butchery to be performed upon him while he was alive, and perfectly sensible. John Finch was dragged through the streets, his head beating all the way upon the stones; was then thrust into a dark and fetid dungeon, with no bed but the damp floor; was fed sparingly, and on nothing but oxen's liver. Here he was left first for weeks, then for months; till at length he was hanged, and his quarters sent to the four chief towns of Lancashire. Richard White, being cut down alive, pronounced the sacred name of Jesus twice, while the hangman had his hands in his bowels. James Claxton was first put into *little ease*, that is, a place where he could neither stand, lie, nor sit; there he was for three days, fed on bread and water. Then he was put into the mill to grind; then he was hanged up by the hands, till the blood sprang forth at his fingers' ends: at length he was hanged, dying at the age of twenty-one years. These are the acts, these are the scenes, which Protestants, stopping their ears, and raising their voices, and casting dust into the air, will not let us inflict upon them. No, it is pleasanter to declaim against persecution, and to call the Inquisition a hell, than to consider their own devices, and the work of their own hands. The catalogue reaches to some hundred names. One was killed in this manner in 1577, two in 1578, four in 1581, eleven in 1582, thirteen in 1583 and 1584, nineteen in 1585 and 1586, thirty-nine in 1587 and 1588, and so on at intervals to the end of the seventeenth century; besides the imprisonments and transportations, which can hardly be numbered. What will the Protestants bring against the Holy See comparable to atrocities such as these? not, surely, with any fairness, the burnings in Queen Mary's reign, the acts, as they were, of an English party, inflamed with revenge against their enemies, and opposed by Cardinal Pole, the Pope's Legate, as well as by the ecclesiastics of Spain.

8.

My time is run out, Brothers of the Oratory, before my subject is exhausted. One remark I will make in conclusion. The horrors I have been describing are no anomaly in the history of Protestantism. Whatever theoretical differences it has had on the subject with the Catholic Religion, it has, in matter of fact, ever shown itself a persecuting power. It has persecuted in England, in Scotland, in Ireland, in Holland, in France, in Germany, in Geneva. Calvin burnt a Socinian, Cranmer an Anabaptist, Luther advised the wholesale murder of the fanatical peasants, and Knox was party to bloody enactments and bloody deeds. You would think that with scandals such as these at their door, Protestants would find it safest to let history alone, and not meddle with the question of persecution at all, from a lively consciousness of deeds identical with those which they impute to the Catholic Church. Not a bit of it. What then is their view of the matter? Strange to say, they make it their plea of exculpation, and the actual difference between Catholics and them, that they condemn persecution on principle; in other words, they bring their own inconsistency as the excuse for their crime. Now I grant them, I am far from disputing it, that a man who holds a right principle, and occasionally, nay often, offends against it, is better than he who holds the opposite wrong principle, and acts consistently upon it; but that is not the present case. The case before us is that of persons who never once have acted on the principle they profess—never once; for they cannot produce their instance, when Protestants, of whatever denomination, were in possession of national power for any sufficient time, without persecuting some or other of their polemical antagonists. So it has been, so it is now. Three centuries ago Protestantism in England set off on its course with murdering Catholic priests; only a few months have passed since a clergyman of the Establishment gave out to his congregation that transportation was too good for us, and he thought we all ought to be put to death. So far from the Protestant party feeling any real shock at this avowal, a little while after, a second clergyman, as influential in Manchester as the first mentioned is in Liverpool, repeated the sentiment; and still no shock or sensation in the Protestant public was the result. Doubtless they gave their *reasons* for wishing it, sufficient in their own judgment, and so too did the Protestant Elizabeth, so too did Gardiner and the other advisers of the

Catholic Mary; but still such was the upshot of their reasons, death to every Catholic priest. The present case then is not of an individual, or a ruler, or a body politic laying down a good principle, and not being able at times and under circumstances, through passion or policy, to act up to it; no, it is the case of a religion saying one thing, and on every actual and possible occasion doing another. Can such a religion extenuate its acts on the ground of its professions? Yet this is the excuse, nay, this is the boast, the glory, of the Protestant party:—"We always do one thing, and we always say another; we always preach peace, but we always make war; we have the face of a lamb, and the claws of a dragon. And we have another boast; to be sure, we persecute, but then, as a set off, you see, we always denounce in others what we are in the practice of doing ourselves; this is our second great virtue. Observe, we, persecutors, protest against persecution,—virtue one; next, we, persecutors, blacken and curse the Papists for persecuting,—virtue two; and now for a third virtue —why, we are so superlatively one-sided, that we do not even see our own utter inconsistency in this matter, and we deny, that what is a stigma in their case is even a scandal in ours. We think that profession and denunciation make up a good Christian, and that we may persecute freely, if we do but largely quote Scripture against it."

And now I might leave Protestants to explain this matter if they can, and to unravel the mystery how it is that, after all their solemn words against persecution, they have persecuted, as I have shown, whenever, wherever, and however they could, from Elizabeth down to Victoria, from the domestic circle up to the Legislature, from black looks to the extremity of the gibbet and the stake; I might leave them, but I am tempted to make them one parting suggestion. I observe, then, it is no accident that they unite in their history this abjuration with this practice of religious coercion; the two go together I say it boldly and decidedly, and do not flinch from the avowal—Protestants attempt too much, and they end in doing nothing. They go too far; they attempt what is against nature, and therefore impossible. I am not proving this; it is a separate subject; it would require a treatise. I am only telling the Protestant world why it is they ever persecute, in spite of their professions. It is because their doctrine of private judgment, as they hold it, is extreme and unreal, and necessarily leads to excesses in the opposite direction. They are attempting to reverse nature, with no warrant for doing so; and nature has its ample revenge upon them. They altogether ignore a principle which the Creator has put into our breasts, the duty of maintaining the truth; and, in consequence, they deprive themselves of the opportunity of controlling, restraining and directing it. So was it with the actors in the first French Revolution: never were there such extravagant praises of the rights of reason; never so signal, so horrible a profanation of them. They cried, "Liberty, Equality, Fraternity," and then proceeded to massacre the priests, and to hurry the laity by thousands to the scaffold or the river-side.

Far other is the conduct of the Church. Not to put the matter on higher and doctrinal grounds, it is plain, if only to prevent the occurrence of injustice and cruelty, she must—to use a phrase of the day—

direct impulses, which it is impossible from the nature of man to destroy. And in the course of eighteen hundred years, though her children have been guilty of various excesses, though she herself is responsible for isolated acts of most solemn import, yet for one deed of severity with which she can be charged, there have been a hundred of her acts, repressive of the persecutor and protective of his victims. She has been a never-failing fount of humanity, equity, forbearance, and compassion, in consequence of her very recognition of natural ideas and instincts, which Protestants would vainly ignore and contradict: and this is the solution of the paradox stated by the distinguished author I just now quoted, to the effect that the Religion which forbids private judgment in matters of Revelation, is historically more tolerant than the Religions which uphold it. His words will bear repetition: "We find, in all parts of Europe, scaffolds prepared to punish crimes against religion; scenes which sadden the soul were everywhere witnessed. Rome is one exception to the rule; Rome, which it has been attempted to represent a monster of intolerance and cruelty. It is true, that the Popes have not preached, like the Protestants, universal toleration; but the facts show the difference between the Protestants and the Popes. The Popes armed with a tribunal of intolerance, have scarce spilt a drop of blood; Protestants and philosophers have shed it in torrents." [9]

---

[9] Since this Lecture has been in type, I have been shown De Maistre's Letters on the Inquisition, and am pleased to see that in some places I have followed so great a writer.

LECTURE VI.

PREJUDICE THE LIFE OF THE PROTESTANT VIEW.

IN attributing the extreme aversion and contempt in which we Catholics are held by this great Protestant country, to the influence of falsehood and misrepresentation, energetic in its operation and unbounded in its extent, I believe in my heart I have referred it to a cause, which will be acknowledged to be both real and necessary by the majority of thoughtful and honest minds, Catholics or not, who set themselves to examine the state of the case. Take an educated man, who has seen the world, and interested himself in the religious bodies, disputes, and events of the day, let him be ever so ill-disposed towards the Catholic Church, yet I think, if he will but throw his mind upon the subject, and then candidly speak out, he will confess that the arguments which lead him to his present state of feeling about her, whatever they are, would not be sufficient for the multitude of men. The multitude, if it is to be arrested and moved, requires altogether a different polemic from that which is at the command of the man of letters, of thought, of feeling, and of honour. His proofs against Catholicism, though he considers them sufficient himself, and considers that they ought to be sufficient for the multitude, have a sobriety, a delicacy, an exactness, a nice adjustment of parts, a width and breadth, a philosophical cumulativeness, an indirectness and circuitousness, which will be lost on the generality of men. The problem is, how to make an impression on those who have never learned to exercise their minds, to compare thought with thought, to analyse an argument, or to balance probabilities. Catholicism appeals to the imagination, as a great fact, wherever she comes; she strikes it; Protestants must find some idea equally vivid as the Church, something fascinating, something capable of possessing, engrossing, and overwhelming, if they are to battle with her hopefully; their cause is lost, unless they can do this. It was then a thought of genius, and, as I think, preternatural genius, to pitch upon the expedient which has been used against the Church from Christ's age to our own; to call her, as in the first century, Beelzebub, so in the sixteenth, Anti-Christ; it was a bold, politic, and successful move. It startled men who heard; and whereas Anti-Christ, by the very notion of his character, will counterfeit Christ, he will therefore be, so far, necessarily like Him; and if Anti-Christ is like Christ, then Christ, I suppose, must be like Anti-Christ; thus there was, even at first starting, a felicitous plausibility about the very charge, which went far towards securing belief, while it commanded attention.

This, however, though much, was not enough; the charge that Christ is Anti-Christ must not only be made, but must be sustained; and sustained it could not possibly be, in the vastness and enormity of its idea, as I have described it, by means of truth. Falsehood then has ever been the indispensable condition of the impeachment which Protestants have made; and the impeachment they make is the indispensable weapon wherewith to encounter the antagonist whom they combat. Thus you see that calumny and obloquy of every kind is, from the nature of the case, the portion of the Church, while she has enemies, that is, in other words, while she is militant,—her portion, that is, if she is to be argued with at all; and argued with she must be, because man, from his very moral constitution, cannot content himself, in his warfare of whatever kind, with the mere use of brute force. The lion rends his prey, and gives no reason for doing so; but man cannot persecute without assigning to himself a reason for his act: he must settle it with his conscience; he must have sufficient reasons, and if good reasons are not forthcoming, there is no help for it; he must put up with bad. How to conflict with the moral influence of the Church, being taken as the problem to be solved, nothing is left for him but to misstate and defame; there is no alternative. Tame facts, elaborate inductions, subtle presumptions, will not avail with the many; something which will cut a dash, something gaudy and staring, something inflammatory, is the rhetoric in request; he must make up his mind then to resign the populace to the action of the Catholic Church, or he must slander her to her greater confusion. This, I maintain,'*is* the case; this I consider, *must* be the case;—bad logic, false facts; and I really do think that candid men, of whatever persuasion, though they will not express themselves exactly in the words I have used, will agree with me in substance; will allow, that, putting aside the question whether Protestantism can be supported by any other method than controversy, for instance, by simple establishment, or by depriving Catholics of education, or by any other violent expedient, still, if popular controversy *is* to be used, then fable, not truth, calumny, not justice, will be its staple. Strip it of its fallacies and its fiction, and where are you? It is no accident then that we are the victims of slander.

So much in corroboration of what I have said in former Lectures; but I have not yet stated the full influence in the controversy, or (as it may be called) the full virtue, of this system of misrepresentation. The question may have occurred to you, my Brothers, as a philosophical difficulty, how it is that able, cultivated, enlarged minds should not only be the organs of the grossest slanders about us, but should refuse to retract them, when they have been absolutely silenced and exposed. The very courtesy of civilized life demands from them a retraction; it is the rule among gentlemen that, even when an accuser adheres in his heart to what he has advanced against another, yet on that other's denying it, he accepts the denial and withdraws his words. It is otherwise in the contest with Catholics; when we deny what is charged against our character or conduct, and deny it with irresistible arguments, we not only have reason to desiderate that outward consideration which the laws of society enforce, but probably are bluntly told that we lie, and there we are left, and the matter too. Doubtless this phenomenon is traceable in part to that characteristic of the human kind, noticed by philosophers, to crouch to what is in the ascendant, and to insult what is down in the world; but it partly arises from a cause to which I have not yet referred, and which I mean to make the subject of this Lecture. This cause is so obvious, that you may wonder I am so circuitous in introducing it, and why I have not treated of it before; but it properly comes in this place. I allude to the power of *Prejudice*, which is to be reckoned a principal reason why our most triumphant refutations of the facts and arguments urged against us by our enemies avail us so little; for in reality, those facts and arguments have already done their work, before their demolition arrives and in spite of their subsequent demolition, by impressing the minds of the persons who have heard and have used them with a *prejudice* against us.

I.

Now, first I must explain what Prejudice is, and how it is produced, before I go on to consider its operation. Prejudice, you know, means properly a pre-judgment, or judgment by anticipation; a judgment which is formed prior to the particular question submitted to us, yet is made to bear upon it. Thus, if a man is accused of theft, and I already believe him to be an habitual thief, I am naturally led to think that this particular charge is well-founded before going into the evidence which is actually adducible for it. In this way, previous good or bad name has so much to do with the decisions in courts of justice; slight evidence will be enough to convict a reputed thief; on the other hand, a person under accusation, in order to repel it, brings witnesses to his character. When we have this previous knowledge of persons, we say, —when their actions or they themselves come under consideration,—on the one hand, that we cannot help being "prejudiced" *against* one, and on the other, "prejudiced" or "prepossessed" *in favour* of another. Now there is nothing unfair in all this; what is past naturally bears on the future; from what has been, we conjecture what will be; it is reasonable and rational to do so; and hence, persons who have all their lives long heard nothing but what is bad of Catholics, naturally and fairly entertain a bad opinion of them; and when a new charge is made against them, are disposed to credit it without stopping to consider the evidence. And it matters not, whether the previous judgment, which influences their belief, be a judgment of their own forming, or be inherited; let it be the tradition of their country; still there is nothing strange, there is nothing wrong, in their being influenced by it.

But then observe this;—after all, a previous judgment, conclusion, or belief such as this, in which consists their *prejudice*, is but vague and general; it is not more than an opinion or inference, of greater or less strength, as the case may be, and varying with the trustworthiness of the reasons or testimony which has created it. It cannot reasonably, and must not, be taken as infallible;—did the persons in question so simply rest upon it, that they would not hear what could be said on the other side, as if they were quite sure nothing could be said to the purpose, they would cease to act rationally, they would be simply obstinate. And this is Prejudice in its bad and culpable sense, the sense in which the word is commonly used, and in which I am using it here, and am imputing it to Protestants. I accuse them of making too much of the Tradition which has come down to them; they not only take it at first sight as true, and act upon it as true (a proceeding against which nothing can fairly be said), but they put such implicit confidence in it, that they cannot bring themselves to hear what can be said on the other side. They make the Tradition practically infallible, as if it had settled the view they are to take of the subject of it once for all and for ever.

How can any one, you will say, act so absurdly, who has any pretensions to good sense and good feeling? yet it may happen in a measure to any one of us, and in the following way. Now I hope I shall not be taxing your attention, my Brothers, more than I have a right to do on an occasion such as this, in what I am going to say in explanation. Prejudice then is something more than an act of judgment; it is not a mere act, it is a habit or state of mind. I must refer to a peculiarity, not of the English character, but of our mental constitution generally. When, then, we hear a thing said again and again, it makes what may be called an impression upon us. We not only hold it in our mind as an opinion or belief, as separate from us, as depending on the information or grounds on which we have received it, and as admitting of being thrown off the next minute at our will, should we have reasons for discarding it, but it has acted upon our mind itself, it has sunk into it, it has impressed it. No longer at our disposal as before, to keep or throw away, it becomes one of our habitual and invariable modes of judging and believing, something like the ideas we have of good and evil, and of religious duty. The idea, for instance, that justice is a virtue, or that there is a Divine Providence, is imprinted in our minds; it is congenial to our nature, and it is true, and that, because it is found in all times and places, with exceptions too rare or inconsiderable to be worth noticing. Such an idea, I say, is true; still there may also be impressions, similar in permanence, which yet are false and are uncongenial to our nature, and they are characterized, first, in *not* being common to all; next, in *not* being found in the mind from the first (if I may so speak), in *not* coming thither no one knows how, that is, from heaven itself, but formed in us by the accidental occurrence of things which we have seen or heard, and another has not. These impressions are commonly created in the mind by the repetition of something striking it from without. A fact or argument is not stronger in its own nature by being repeated; but the effect on any mind, which is passive under the infliction, *is* stronger and stronger every time it is repeated. In this way almost any idea whatever may be impressed on the mind; a man will begin at length to think himself a fool or a knave, if every one tells him so.

This then is what comes of the perpetual talk against Catholics. It does not become truer because it is incessant; but it continually deepens the impression in the minds of those who hear it, that Catholicism is an imposture. I say, there is no increase of logical cogency; a lie is a lie just as much the tenth time it is told as the first; or rather more, it is ten lies instead of one; but it gains in rhetorical influence. Let it be repeated again and again; it matters not; the utterer has only to go on steadily proclaiming it, and first one, then another, will begin to believe it, and at length it will assume the shape of a very respectable fact or opinion, which is held by a considerable number of well-informed persons. This is what is meant by the proverb, "Fling dirt enough and some will stick." And if even one pertinacious slanderer has the prospect of such success in his slander, from this peculiarity of our nature, what must be the effect when vast multitudes of men are incessantly crying out to each other, with unwearied and sleepless energy, fables and fallacies against the Catholic Religion? Why, each is convincing the other, and deepening the hostile impression in his mind with a keenness and precision which it is appalling to contemplate; and thus the meetings and preachings which are ever going on against us on all sides, though they may have no argumentative force whatever, are still immense factories for the creation of prejudice,—an article, by means of these exertions, more carefully elaborated, and more lasting in its texture, than any specimens of hardware, or other material productions, which are the boast of a town such as this is.

Now the peculiarity of these mental impressions is, that they do not depend afterwards upon the facts or reasonings by which they were produced, any more than a blow, when once given, has any continued connexion with the stone or the stick which gave it. To burn the stick will not salve the sore: and to demolish the argument, as I have already said, does not obliterate the prejudice. Suppose I have been told that my neighbour is a thief; suppose the idea has rested on my mind, and I have accustomed myself to it; and suppose I hear what it was that made my informant assert it, and examine into this, and find it to be utterly untrue; why I *may* indeed cast off my feeling against my neighbour at once and altogether, but I *may* have a great difficulty in doing so. The idea may still cling to me, and I may find it impossible, except by degrees, to overcome the associations with which he is connected in my mind, and the repugnance I feel to him; there is something I have to struggle against. And thus, even though a slander be perfectly cleared up, even though it be brought into a court of justice, and formally disconnected from the person who has been the victim of it, he is not what he was. It was a saying of the greatest of the Romans, "that Cæsar's wife should not be suspected." The slander has, as it were, stained the minds of the hearers, and only time, if even time, can wipe it out. This, then, is properly a prejudice,—not an opinion which is at our own disposal, and dependent for its presence or its dismissal on our will, but an impression, which reason indeed can act upon, and the will can subdue, but only by degrees and with trouble. It sank into the mind by the repetition of untrue representations, it must be effaced by an opposite process, by a succession of thoughts and deeds antagonistic to it. We must make it up to the injured party by acts of kindness, by friendly services, by good words, by praising him, by the desire and attempt to please and honour him, and thus gradually we shall lose all recollection of our former hard thoughts of him. On the other hand, it is quite possible to shut ourselves up in ourselves; to keep at a distance from him, and to cherish coldness or ill-will; and then, in spite of the calumnies having been triumphantly refuted, and of our nominal acquiescence, we shall be as suspicious or jealous as ever. We shall say that we are not, after all, satisfied; that we cannot, indeed, give our grounds, but that things have a suspicious appearance; and we shall look about diligently for some fresh ground of accusation against him, to justify us in such thoughts and such conduct.

Now you may recollect, Brothers of the Oratory, that, in speaking of prejudice in its first and most simple sense, as a mere anticipation or previous opinion in disparagement of another, I said there was no harm in it. It is a mere judgment, formed on previous grounds, like any judgment, which the owner puts away at once, as soon as its unsoundness is detected. But prejudice, in its second and ordinary sense, in which I have now for some time been using it—viz., as an impression or stain on the mind is not at all innocent or excusable, just the reverse. This may surprise you; you may say, How can a man help his impressions? he is passive under them; they come of themselves; he is as little answerable for what is actually stamped upon his mind, as for a wound which is inflicted on his body; but this is very far from the case, as a little consideration will show. The will goes with a prejudice; there is no compulsion or necessity; those who have prejudices are unwilling to give them up; there is no prejudice without the will; we are prejudiced, I say, because we will;

and therefore, if we did not will, we should not be prejudiced. I do not say we could get rid of the prejudice in a day by wishing to do so; but we should, in that case, be tending to get rid of it. Scripture speaks of those who "loved darkness rather than the light;" and it is impossible for us to deny, from what we see on all sides, that as regards the Protestant view of Catholics, men love to be left to their own dark thoughts of us; they desire to be able with a good reason and a good conscience to hate us; they do not wish to be disabused, they are loth that so pleasant an error should be torn from them. First, then, I say, that prejudice depends on the will; now, secondly, if it does depend on the will, it is not, cannot be, innocent, because it is directed, not against things, but against persons, against God's rational creatures, against our fellows, towards all of whom we owe the duties of humanity and charity. There is a natural law, binding us to think as well as we can of every one; we ought to be glad when imputations are removed and scandals cleared up. And this law is observed by every generous mind: such a mind is pained to believe that bad things can be said of others with any plausibility, and will rejoice to be able to deny them, will hope they are not true, and will give the subject of them the benefit of its doubts. Every hour, then, as it passes, bears with it protests against prejudice, when there is generosity, from the natural striving of the heart the other way. Jealousy, suspicion, dislike, thinking ill, are feelings so painful to the rightly disposed, that there is a constant reclamation going on within them, an uneasiness that they should be obliged to entertain them, and an effort to get rid of them. Nay, there are persons of such kind and tender hearts, that they would believe there is no evil at all in the world, if they could : and it is a relief to them whenever they can knock off, so to say, any part of the score of accusations which the multitude of men bring against each other. On the other hand, to close the ears to an explanation, and to show a desire that the worst may be true,—unless indeed the innocence of the individual who at present lies under a cloud involves the guilt of a vast many others instead, so that one has to strike a balance of crimes,—I say, to resolve that rumours or suspicions, for which no distinct grounds are alleged, shall be true, is simple malevolence, deplorable, shocking, inexcusable.

I do not know how any one can deny the justice of these remarks; but observe what a melancholy comment they form on the treatment which Catholics receive in this Protestant country. Where are the tender hearts, the kind feelings, the upright understandings of our countrymen and countrywomen? where is the generosity of the Briton, of which from one's youth up one has been so proud? where is his love of fair play, and his compassion for the weak, and his indignation at the oppressor, when we are concerned? The most sensible people on the earth, the most sensitive of moral inconsistency, the most ambitious of propriety and good taste, would rather commit themselves in the eyes of the whole world, would rather involve themselves in the most patent incongruities and absurdities, would rather make sport, as they do by their conduct, for their enemies in the four quarters of the earth, than be betrayed into any portion—I will not say of justice, I will not say of humanity and mercy, but of simple reasonableness and common sense, in their behaviour to the professors of the Catholic Religion; so much so, that to state even drily and accurately what they do daily is to risk being blamed for ridicule and satire, which, if anywhere, would be simply gratuitous and officious in this matter, where truth most assuredly, "when unadorned," is "adorned the most." This risk, as far as I am incurring it myself in these Lectures, I cannot help; I cannot help if, in exposing the prejudice of my countrymen, I incur the imputation of using satire against them; I do not wish to do so; and, observe, that nothing I have said, or shall say, is levelled at the matter or the rites of Protestant worship. I am concerned with Protestants themselves; moreover not with Protestants quiescent and peaceable, but with Protestants malevolent, belligerent, busy, and zealous in an aggression upon our character and conduct. *We* do not treat *them* with suspicion, contempt, and aversion: this is their treatment of *us*; our only vengeance, surely it is not a great one, is to make a careful analysis of that treatment.

2.

The Prejudiced man, then—for thus I shall personify that narrow, ungenerous spirit which energizes and operates so widely and so unweariedly in the Protestant community—the Prejudiced man takes it for granted, or feels an undoubting persuasion,—not only that he himself is in possession of divine truth, for this is a matter of opinion, and he has a right to his own,—but that we, who differ from him, are universally impostors, tyrants, hypocrites, cowards, and slaves. This is a first principle with him; it is like divine faith in the Catholic, nothing can shake it. If he meets with any story against Catholics, on any or no authority, which does but fall in with this notion of them, he eagerly catches at it. Authority goes for nothing; likelihood, as he considers it, does instead of testimony; what he is now told is just what he expected. Perhaps it is a random report, put into circulation merely because it has a chance of succeeding, or thrown like a straw to the wind: perhaps it is a mere publisher's speculation, who thinks that a narrative of horrors will pay well for the printing: it matters not, he is perfectly convinced of its truth; he knew all about it beforehand; it is just what he always has said; it is the old tale over again a hundred times. Accordingly he buys it by the thousand, and sends it about with all speed in every direction, to his circle of friends and acquaintance, to the newspapers, to the great speakers at public meetings; he fills the Sunday and week-day schools with it; loads the pedlars' baskets, perhaps introduces it into the family spiritual reading on Sunday evenings, consoled and comforted with the reflection that he has got something fresh and strong and undeniable, in evidence of the utter odiousness of the Catholic Religion.

Next comes an absolute, explicit, total denial or refutation of the precious calumny, whatever it may be, on unimpeachable authority. The Prejudiced Man simply discredits this denial, and puts it aside, not receiving any impression from it at all, or paying it the slightest attention. This, if he can: if he cannot, if it is urged upon him by some friend, or brought up against him by some opponent, he draws himself up, looks sternly at the objector, and then says the very same thing as before, only with a louder voice and more confident manner. He becomes more intensely and enthusiastically positive, by way of making up for the interruption, of braving the confutation, and of showing the world that nothing whatever in the universe will ever make him think one hair-breadth more favourably of Popery than he does think, than he ever has thought, and than his family ever thought before him, since the time of the fine old English gentleman.

If a person ventures to ask the Prejudiced Man what he knows of Catholics personally—what he knows of individuals, of their ways, of their books, or of their worship, he blesses himself that he knows nothing of them at all, and he never will; nay, if they fall in his way, he will take himself out of it; and if unawares he shall ever be pleased with a Catholic without knowing who it is, he wishes by anticipation to retract such feeling of pleasure. About our state of mind, our views of things, our ends and objects, our doctrines, our defence of them, our judgment on his objections to them, our thoughts about him, he absolutely refuses to be enlightened: and he is as sore if expostulated with on so evident an infirmity of mind, as if it were some painful wound upon him, or local inflammation, which must not be handled ever so tenderly. He shrinks from the infliction.

However, one cannot always make the whole world take one's own way of thinking; so let us suppose the famous story, to which the Prejudiced Man has pledged his veracity, utterly discredited and scattered to the winds by the common consent of mankind :— this only makes him the more violent. For it *ought*, he thinks, to be true, and it is mere special pleading to lay much stress on its not having all the evidence which it might have? for if it be not true, yet half a hundred like stories are. It is only impertinent to ask for evidence, when the fact has so often been established. What is the good of laboriously vindicating St. Eligius, or exposing a leading article in a newspaper, or a speaker at a meeting, or a popular publication, when the thing is notorious; and to deny it is nothing else than a vexatious demand upon his time, and an insult to his common sense. He feels the same sort of indignation which the Philistine champion, Goliath, might have felt when David went out to fight with him. " Am I a dog, that thou comest to me with a staff? and the Philistine cursed him by his gods." And, as the huge giant, had he first been hit, not in the brain, but in the foot or the shoulder, would have yelled, not with pain, but with fury at the insult, and would not have been frightened at all or put upon the defensive, so our Prejudiced Man is but enraged so much the more, and almost put beside himself, by the presumption of those who, with their doubts or their objections, interfere with the great Protestant Tradition about the Catholic Church. To bring proof against us is, he thinks, but a matter of time; and we know in affairs of everyday, how annoyed and impatient we are likely to become, when obstacles are put in our way in any such case. We are angered at delays when they are but accidental, and the issue is certain; we are not angered, but we are sobered, we become careful and attentive to impediments, when there is a doubt about the issue. The very same difficulties put us on our mettle in the one case, and do but irritate us in the other. If, for instance, a person cannot open a door, or get a key into a lock, which he has done a hundred times before, you know how apt he is to shake, and to rattle, and to force it, as if some great insult was offered him by its resistance: you know how surprised a wasp, or other large insect is, that he cannot get through a window-pane; such is the feeling of the Prejudiced Man, when we urge our objections—not softened by them at all, but exasperated the more; for what is the use of even incontrovertible arguments against a conclusion which he already considers to be infallible?

This, you see, is the reason why the most overwhelming refutations of the calumnies brought against us do us no good at all with the Protestant community. We were tempted, perhaps, to say to ourselves, "What *will* they have to say in answer to this? now at last the falsehood is put down for ever, it will never show its face again?" Vain hope! just the reverse: like Milton's day-star, after sinking into the ocean, it soon "repairs its drooping head,"

"And tricks its beams, and with new-spangled ore
Flames in the forehead of the morning sky."

Certainly; for it is rooted in the mind itself; it has no uncertain holding upon things external; it does not depend on the accident of time, or place, or testimony, or sense, or possibility, or fact; it depends on the will alone. Therefore, "unhurt amid the war of elements," it "smiles" at injury, and "defies" defeat? for it is safe and secure, while it has the man's own will on its side. Such is the virtue of prejudice—it is ever reproductive; in vain is Jeffreys exposed; he rises again in Teodore; Teodore is put down; in vain, for future story-tellers and wonder-mongers, as yet unknown to fame, are below the horizon, and will come to view, and will unfold their tale of horror, each in his day, in long succession; for these whispers, and voices, and echoes, and reverberations, are but the response, and, as it were, the expression of that profound inward persuasion, and that intense illusion, which wraps the soul and steeps the imagination of the Prejudiced Man.

However, we will suppose him in a specially good humour, when you set about undeceiving him on some point on which he misstates the Catholic faith. He is determined to be candour and fairness itself, and to do full justice to your argument. So you begin your explanation;—you assure him he misconceives your doctrines; he has got a wrong view of facts. You appeal to original authorities, and show him how shamefully they have been misquoted; you appeal to history and prove it has been garbled. Nothing is wanted to your representation; it is triumphant. He is silent for a moment, then he begins with a sentiment. "What clever fellows these Catholics are!" he says, "I defy you to catch them tripping; they have a way out of everything. I thought we had you, but I fairly own I am beaten. This is how the Jesuits got on; always educated, subtle, well up in their books; a Protestant has no chance with them." You see, my Brothers, you have not advanced a step in convincing him.

R

Such is the Prejudiced Man at best advantage; but commonly under the same circumstances he will be grave and suspicious. "I confess," he will say, "I do *not* like these very complete explanations; they are too like a made-up case. I can easily believe there was exaggeration in the charge; perhaps money was only sometimes taken for the permission to sin, or only before the Reformation, but our friend professes to prove it never was taken; this is proving too much. I always suspect something behind, when everything is so very easy and clear." Or again, "We see before our eyes a tremendous growth of Popery; *how* does it grow? You tell me you are poor, your priests few, your friends without influence; then how does it *grow?* It could not grow without means! it is bad enough if you can assign a cause; it is worse if you cannot. Cause there must be somewhere, for effects imply causes. How did it get into Oxford? tell me that. How has it got among the Protestant clergy? I like all things above board; I hate concealment, I detest plots. There is evidently something to be accounted for; and the more cogently you prove that it is not referable to anything which we see, the graver suspicions do you awaken, that it is traceable to something which is hidden." Thus our Prejudiced Man simply ignores the possible existence of that special cause to which Catholics of course refer the growth of Catholicism, and which surely, if admitted, is sufficient to account for it—viz., that it is true. He will not admit the power of truth among the assignable conjectural causes. He would rather, I am sure, assign it to the agency of evil spirits, than suspect the possibility of a religion being true which he wills should be a falsehood.

3.

One word here as to the growth of Catholicism, of conversions and converts;—the Prejudiced Man has his own view of it all. First, he denies that there are any conversions or converts at all. This is a bold game, and will not succeed in England, though I have been told that in Ireland it has been strenuously maintained. However, let him grant the fact, that converts there are, and he has a second ground to fall back upon: the converts are weak and foolish persons,—notoriously so; all their friends think so; there is not a man of any strength of character or force of intellect among them. They have either been dreaming over their folios, or have been caught with the tinsel embellishments of Popish worship. They are lack-a-daisical women, or conceited young parsons, or silly squires, or the very dregs of our large towns, who have nothing to lose, and no means of knowing one thing from another. Thirdly, in corroboration:—they went over, he says, on such exceedingly wrong motives; not any one of them but you may trace his conversion to something distinctly wrong; it was love of notoriety, it was restlessness, it was resentment, it was lightness of mind, it was self-will. There was trickery in his mode of taking the step or inconsiderateness towards the feelings of others. They went too soon, or they ought to have gone sooner. They ought to have told every one their doubts as soon as ever they felt them, and before they knew whether or not they should overcome them or no: if they had clerical charges in the

Protestant Church, they ought to have flung them up at once, even at the risk of afterwards finding they had made a commotion for nothing. Or, on the other hand, what, forsooth, must these men do when a doubt came on their mind, but at once abandon all their clerical duty and go to Rome, as if it were possible anywhere to be absolutely certain? In short, they did not become Catholics at the right moment; so that, however numerous they may be, no weight whatever attaches to their conversion. As for him, it does not affect him at all; he means to die just where he is; indeed these conversions are a positive argument in favour of Protestantism; he thinks still worse of Popery, in consequence of these men going over, than he did before. His fourth remark is of this sort: they are sure to come back. He prophesies that by this time next year, not one of them will be a Catholic. His fifth is as bold as the first;—they *have* come back. This argument, however, of the Prejudiced Man admits at times of being shown to great advantage, should it so happen that the subjects of his remarks have, for some reason or other, gone abroad, for then there is nothing to restrain his imagination. Hence, directly a new Catholic is safely lodged two or three thousand miles away, out comes the confident news that he has returned to Protestantism; when no friend has the means to refute it. When this argument fails, as fail it must, by the time a letter can be answered, our Prejudiced Man falls back on his sixth common-place, which is to the effect that the converts are very unhappy. He knows this on the first authority; he has seen letters declaring or showing it. They are quite altered men, very much disappointed with Catholicism, restless, and desirous to come back except from false shame. Seventhly, they are altogether deteriorated in character; they have become harsh, or overbearing, or conceited, or vulgar. They speak with extreme bitterness against Protestantism, have cast off their late friends, or seem to forget that they ever were Protestants themselves. Eighthly, they have become infidels;—alas! heedless of false witness, the Prejudiced Man spreads the news about, right and left, in a tone of great concern and distress; he considers it very awful.

Lastly, when every resource has failed, and in spite of all that can be said, and surmised, and expressed, and hoped, about the persons in question, Catholics they have become, and Catholics they remain, the Prejudiced Man has a last resource, he simply forgets that Protestants they ever were. They cease to have antecedents; they cease to have any character, any history to which they may appeal: they merge in the great fog, in which to his eyes everything Catholic is enveloped: they are dwellers in the land of romance and fable; and, if he dimly contemplates them plunging and floundering amid the gloom, it is as griffins, wiverns, salamanders, the spawn of Popery, such as are said to sport in the depths of the sea, or to range amid the central sands of Africa. He forgets he ever heard of them; he has no duties to their names, he is released from all anxiety about them; they die to him.

Now, my Brothers, unless I should be obliged to allude to myself, I could, without bringing in other instances, show you, from my own experience, that there is no exaggeration in what I have been saying.

I will go so far as to mention four facts about me, as they have been commonly reported. First, when I became a Catholic, grave persons, Protestant clergymen, attested (what they said was well known to others besides themselves) that either I was mad, or was in the most imminent danger of madness. They put it into the newspapers, and people were sometimes quite afraid to come and see me. Next, they put about, what they had prophesied beforehand as certain to be, that I had already the gravest differences with one from whom I had received nothing but kindness, and whom I regarded, and still regard, with no other feelings than those of gratitude and affection, Cardinal Wiseman. They had predicted it, and therefore so it must be, whether there was evidence of it or not. I will quote to you the words of an eminent pulpit and platform clergyman, one of those two eloquent defenders of Protestantism, who lately gave out that every Catholic Priest ought to be hanged. "He believed," said the *Manchester Courier*, reporting his speech, "that already some of those reverend gentlemen, who had betaken themselves to Rome, under the idea that they were going to a scene of beauty and piety, had found that dark was the place behind the scenes that they had painted as so beautiful. So he believed it was with Mr. Newman. (Hear, hear.) He (the speaker) was told that Mr. Newman had a most sovereign contempt for Dr. Wiseman; and he was told that Dr. Wiseman had the utmost hatred for Mr. Newman. And he believed that result was brought about from Mr. Newman having seen Dr. Wiseman more closely, and Dr. Wiseman having found out that Mr. Newman saw through the mask, and discerned him as he was." You see "the wish was father to the thought." Thirdly, when I went to Rome, then at once a long succession of reports went about, to the effect that I had quarrelled with the ecclesiastical authorities there, and had refused to be ordained on their conditions; moreover, that I was on the point of turning Protestant, and that my friends about me had done so already. The list of good stories had not run out by the time I came back; they were too precious to be lost, any one of them; so it was circulated, when I came here to Birmingham, that I was suspended by the present Bishop of the diocese, and not allowed to preach. Fourthly and lastly, it has lately been put into the papers, under the sanction of respectable names, that I am not a believer in the Catholic doctrines; and broader still in private letters, that I have given up Revealed Religion altogether. I mention these instances, not for their own sake, but to illustrate the power of prejudice. Men are determined they will *not* believe that an educated Protestant can find peace and satisfaction in the Catholic Church; and they invent catastrophes for the occasion, which they think too certain to need testimony or proof. In the reports I have been setting down, there was not even a rag or a shred of evidence to give plausibility to them.

I have been setting forth as yet the resources of the Prejudiced Man, when he has no facts whatever on his side, but all against him; but now let us suppose he has something or other to show; in that case it is plain that he finds it very much easier to maintain his position. If he could do so much with no materials at all, to what will he be unequal when he has really something or other, external and objective, to bring forward in his justification? "Trifles light as air," says the poet,

> "Are to the jealous confirmation strong
> As proofs of Holy Writ."

You may be sure he makes the most of them. A vast number of matters, we easily may understand, are of daily occurrence, which admit of an interpretation this way or that, and which are, in fact, interpreted by every one according to his own existing opinions. Rival philosophers seize on new discoveries, each as being in favour of his own hypothesis; it is not indeed, many instances which are critical and decisive. Are we told of some strange appearance at night in some solitary place? Those who are fond of the marvellous, think it an apparition; those who live in the rational and tangible, decide that it has been some gleam of the moonbeam, or some wayfarer or beggar, or some trick intended to frighten the passer-by. Thus history also reads in one way to one, in another to another. There are those who think the French at the bottom of all the mischief which happens in England and Ireland; others lay it to the Russians. Our Prejudiced Man of course sees Catholics and Jesuits in everything, in every failure of the potato crop, every strike of the operatives, and every mercantile stoppage. His one idea of the Catholic Church haunts him incessantly, and he sees whole Popery, living and embodied, in every one of its professors, nay, in every word, gesture and motion of each. A Catholic Priest cannot be grave or gay, silent or talkative, without giving matter of offence or suspicion. There is peril in his frown, there is greater peril in his smile. His half sentences are filled up; his isolated acts are misdirected; nay, whether he eats or sleeps, in every mouthful and every nod he ever has in view one and one only object, the aggrandizement of the unwearied, relentless foe of freedom and of progress, the Catholic Church. The Prejudiced Man applauds himself for his sagacity, in seeing evidences of a plot at every turn; he groans to think that so many sensible men should doubt its extension all through Europe, though he begins to entertain the hope that the fact is breaking on the apprehension of the Government.

4

The Prejudiced Man travels, and then everything he sees in Catholic countries only serves to make him more thankful that his notions are so true; and the more he sees of Popery, the more abominable he feels it to be. If there is any sin, any evil in a foreign population, though it be found among Protestants also, still Popery is clearly the cause of it. If great cities are the schools of vice, it is owing to Popery. If Sunday is profaned, if there is a Carnival, it is the fault of the Catholic Church. Then, there are no private homes, as in England, families live on staircases; see what it is to belong to a Popish country. Why do the Roman labourers wheel their barrows so slow on the Forum? why do the Lazzaroni of Naples' lie so listlessly on the beach? why, but because they are under the *malaria* of a false religion. Rage, as is well-known, is in the Roman like a falling sickness, almost as if his will had no part in it, and he had no responsibility; see what it is to be a Papist. Bloodletting is as frequent and as much a matter of course in the South, as hair-cutting in England ; it is a trick borrowed from the convents, when they wish to tame down refractory spirits.

The Prejudiced man gets up at an English hour, has his breakfast at his leisure, and then saunters into some of the churches of the place ; he is scandalized to have proof of what he has so often heard, the infrequency of communions among Catholics. Again and again, in the course of his tour, has he entered them, and never by any chance did he see a solitary communicant :— hundreds, perhaps, having communicated in those very churches, according to their custom, before he was out of his bedroom. But what scandalizes him most, is that even bishops and priests, nay, the Pope himself, does not communicate at the great festivals of the Church. He was at a great ceremonial, a High Mass, on Lady Day, at the Minerva ; not one Cardinal communicated ; Pope and Cardinals, and every Priest present but the celebrant, having communicated, of course, each in his own Mass, and in his own chapel or church early in the morning. Then the churches are so dirty ; faded splendour, tawdriness, squalidness are the fashion of the day ;—thanks to the Protestants and Infidels, who, in almost every country where Catholicism is found, have stolen the revenues by which they were kept decent. He walks about and looks at the monuments, what is this? the figure of a woman: who can it be? His Protestant cicerone at his elbow, who perhaps has been chosen by his good father or guardian to protect him on his travels from a Catholic taint, whispers that it is Pope Joan, and he notes it down in his pocket-book accordingly. I am alluding to an accident, which in its substance befell a most excellent person, for whom I had and have a great esteem, whom I am sure I would not willingly offend, and who will not be hurt at this cursory mention of an unintentional mistake. He was positive he had seen Pope Joan in Rome,—I think, in St. Peter's; nay, he saw the inscription on the monument, beginning with the words, "Joannæ Papissæ." It was so remarkable a fact, and formed so plausible an argument against the inviolateness of the chair of St. Peter, that it was thought worth inquiring into. I do not remember who it was that the female, thus elevated by his imagination, turned into in the process of investigation, whether into the Countess Matilda, or Queen Christina, or the figure of Religion in the vestibule of St. Peter's; but certainly into no lady who had any claim on the occupation of the Ecumenical See.

This puts me in mind of another occurrence, of which the publications of the day have recently been full. A lady of high literary reputation deposed that Denon and other French savans had given her the information that, in the days of the Republic or Consulate, they had examined St. Peter's chair in the Vatican Basilica, and had found that it unquestionably had come from the East, long after the age of the Apostle, for it had inscribed upon it the celebrated confession of Islamism, " There is one God, and Mahomet is his prophet." Her prejudices sharpened her memory, and she was positive in her testimony. Inquiry was made, and it turned out that the chair of which she had spoken was at Venice, not at Rome; that it had been brought thither by the Crusaders from the East, and therefore might well bear upon it the

Mahometan inscription; and that tradition gave it the reputation of being, by no means the Roman, but the Antiochene Chair of the Apostle. In this, as in other mistakes, there was no deliberate intention to deceive; it was an ordinary result of an ordinary degree of prejudice. The voucher of the story was so firmly convinced, I suppose, of the "childish absurdity and falsehood of all the traditions of the Romish Church," that she thought it unnecessary to take pains to be very accurate, whether in her hearing or her memory.

Our Prejudiced Man might travel half his life up and down Catholic Europe, and only be confirmed in his contempt and hatred of its religion. In every place there are many worlds, quite distinct from each other: there are good men and bad, and the good form one body, the bad another. Two young men, as is well known, may pass through their course at a Protestant University, and come away with opposite reports of the state of the place: the one will have seen all the bad, the other all the good; one will say it is a sober, well-conducted place, the other will maintain that it is the home of every vice. The Prejudiced Man takes care to mix only in such society as will confirm his views; he courts the society of Protestants and unbelievers, and of bad Catholics, who shelter their own vice under the imputations they cast on others, and whose lives are a disgrace to the Church prior to their testimony. His servants, couriers, *laquais de place*, and acquaintance, are all of his own way of thinking, and find it for their interest to flatter and confirm it. He carries England with him abroad; and, though he has ascended mountains and traversed cities, knows scarcely more of Europe than when he set out.

But perhaps he does not leave England at all ; he never has been abroad ; it is all the same ; he can scrape together quite as good evidence against Catholicism at home. One day he pays a visit to some Catholic chapel, or he casually finds the door open, and walks in. He enters and gazes about him, with a mixed feeling of wonder, expectation and disgust ; and according to circumstances, this or that feeling predominates, and shows itself in his bearing and his countenance. In one man it is curiosity ; in another, scorn ; in another, conscious superiority ; in another, abhorrence ; over all of their faces, however, there is a sort of uncomfortable feeling, as if they were in the cave of Trophonius or in a Mesmerist's lecture-room. One and all seem to believe that something strange and dreadful may happen any moment ; and they crowd up together, if some great ceremony is going on, tiptoeing and staring, and making strange faces, like the gargoyles or screen ornaments of the church itself. Every sound of the bell, every movement of the candles, every change in the grouping of the sacred ministers and the assistants, puts their hands and limbs in motion, to see what is coming next ; our own poor alleviation, in thinking of them, lying in this,—that they are really ignorant of what is going on, and miss, even with their bodily eyes, the distinctive parts of the rite. What is our ground of comfort, however, will be their ground of accusation against us ; for they are sure to go away and report that our worship consists of crossings, bowing, genuflections, incensings, locomotions, and revolvings, all about nothing.

5.

In this matter, my Brothers, as I have already said, the plain truth is the keenest of satires; and therefore, instead of using any words of my own, I shall put before you a Protestant's account of a Benediction of the Blessed Sacrament, which he went to see in the Chapel of the Fathers of the Oratory in London. I quote his words from a publication of an important body, the British Reformation Society, established in the year 1827, and supported, I believe, by a number of eminent persons, noblemen, gentlemen, and ministers of various denominations. The periodical I speak of is called "*The British Protestant, or Journal of the Religious Principles of the Reformation.*" It would seem to be one of the Society's accredited publications, as it has its device upon the title-page. In the 62nd Number of this work, being the Number for February, 1850, we are presented with "Extracts from the Journal of a Protestant Scripture Reader." This gentleman, among his missionary visits to various parts of London, dropt in, it seems, on Tuesday, January 8th, to the Roman Catholic Chapel in King William Street; which, he commences his narrative by telling us, for "the large roses of every colour, and laurel," "was more like the flower-shops in the grand row of Covent Garden than a place of worship." Well, he had a right to his opinion here as much as another; and I do not mean to molest him in it. Nor shall I say anything of his account of the Sermon, which was upon one of the January Saints, and which he blames for not having in it the name of Jesus, or one word of Scripture from beginning to end; not dreaming that a Rite was to follow, in which we not only bow before the Name, but worship the real and substantial Presence of our exalted Lord.

I need hardly observe to you, my Brothers, that the Benediction of the Blessed Sacrament is one of the simplest rites of the Church. The priests enter and kneel down; one of them unlocks the Tabernacle, takes out the Blessed Sacrament, inserts it upright in a Monstrance of precious metal, and sets it in a conspicuous place above the altar, in the midst of lights, for all to see. The people then begin to sing; meanwhile the Priest twice offers incense to the King of heaven, before whom he is kneeling. Then he takes the Monstrance in his hands, and turning to the people, blesses them with the Most Holy, in the form of a cross, while the bell is sounded by one of the attendants to call attention to the ceremony. It is our Lord's solemn benediction of His people, as when He lifted up His hands over the children, or when He blessed His chosen ones when He ascended up from Mount Olivet. As sons might come before a parent before going to bed at night, so, once or twice a week the great Catholic family comes before the Eternal Father, after the bustle or toil of the day, and He smiles upon them, and sheds upon them the light of His countenance. It is a full accomplishment of what the Priest invoked upon the Israelites, "The Lord bless thee and keep thee; the Lord show His face to thee and have mercy on thee; the Lord turn His countenance to thee and give thee peace." Can there be a more touching rite, even in the judgment of those who do not believe in it? How many a man, not a Catholic, is moved, on seeing it, to say "Oh, that I did but believe it!" when he sees the Priest take up the Fount of Mercy, and the people bent low in adoration! It is one of the most beautiful, natural, and soothing actions of the Church—not so, however, in the judgment of our young Protestant Scripture Reader, to whom I now return.

This Protestant Scripture Reader then, as he calls himself, enters the chapel, thinking, of course, he knows all about everything. He is the measure of everything, or at least of everything Popish. Popery he knows perfectly well, in substance, in spirit, in drift, in results; and he can interpret all the details when they come before him at once, by this previous, or what a theologian might term "infused," knowledge. He knows, and has known from a child, that Popery is a system of imposture, nay, such brazen imposture, that it is a marvel, or rather miracle, that any one can be caught by it—a miracle, that is, of Satan: for without an evil influence it is quite impossible any single soul could believe what the Protestant Scripture Reader would call so "transparent a fraud." As a Scripture Reader he knows well the text, Second of Thessalonians, chapter two, verse eleven, "He shall send them strong delusion that they should believe a lie," and he applies it to the scene before him. He knows that it is the one business of the Priest to take in the people, and he knows that the people are so inconceivably brutish that nothing is too gross or absurd a trick to take them in withal. If the Priest were to put up a scarecrow, they, like the silly birds, would run away as if it were a man; and he has only to handle his balls or cards, and flourish them about, and they take him for a god. Indeed, we all know, he gives out he *is* a god, and can do what he pleases, for it is sin to doubt it. It is most wonderful, certainly, as to this Popery, that in spite of the Parliament all in a bustle, passing laws, as if against typhus or cholera, ye there it is, and spread it will; however, Satan is the father of lies; that is sufficient. With this great principle, I say, clearly impressed upon his mind, he walks into the chapel, knowing well he shall find some juggling there; accordingly, he is not at all surprised at the scene which passes before him. He looks on at his ease, and draws up his own account of it, all the time that the Catholic people are bowing and singing, and the Priest incensing; and his account runs thus:—

After the sermon, he tells us (I am quoting the very words of his Journal), "another young priest came in with a long wand in his hand, and an extinguisher on the top of it, and a small candle, and he began to light others." "*Another* young priest:" he thinks we are born priests; "priest" is a sort of race, or animal, or production, as oxen or sheep may be, and there are young priests and old priests, and black priests and white priests, and perhaps men priests and women priests; and so in came this "other young priest" with a wand. "With a wand:" he evidently thinks there is something religious about this lighter and extinguisher; it is a conjuror's wand; you will, I think, see presently I am borne out in saying this. He proceeds: "The next part of the play was four priests coming to the altar" (it is as I said; everything is a priest), "four priests and

Gordon in the middle:" this is a mistake, and an unwarrantable and rude use of the name of one of the Fathers of the London Oratory, my dear brother and friend, the Reverend Philip Gordon—for it was not he, and he was not a priest; accordingly, I should leave the name out, except that it adds a good deal to the effect of the whole. "One of them," he proceeds, "took from a small cupboard on the altar," that is, from the tabernacle, "a gold star;" this is the *head* of the Monstrance, in which is placed the Blessed Sacrament, "and screwed it on to a candlestick," that is, the *foot* of the Monstrance, "and placed it on the top of the altar, under the form of a beehive, supported by four pillars," that is, under the canopy. He calls the head of the Monstrance a star, because it consists of a circle surrounded by rays; and he seems to think it in some way connected with the season of the year, the Epiphany, when the Star appeared to the Wise Men.

"The Star," he proceeds, "glittered like diamonds, for it had a round lamp in the middle of it;" I suppose he means the glass covering the Blessed Sacrament, which reflected the light, and you will see clearly, as he goes on, that he actually thinks the whole congregation was worshipping this star and lamp. "This Star glittered like diamonds, for it had a round lamp in the middle of it; when placed under the beehive, the four priests began to burn incense, waving a large thing like a lanthorn" (the thurible) "towards the Star, and bowing themselves to kiss the foot of the altar before the Star." Now observe, my Brothers, I repeat, I am not blaming this person for not knowing a Catholic rite, which he had no means of knowing, but for thinking he knows it, when he does not know it, for coming into the chapel, with this most coxcombical idea in his head, that Popery is a piece of mummery, which any intelligent Protestant can see through, and therefore being not at all surprised, but thinking it very natural, when he finds four priests, a young priest with a wand, and a whole congregation, worshipping a gold star glittering like diamonds with a lamp in it. This is what I mean by *prejudice*.

Now you may really have a difficulty in believing that I have interpreted him rightly; so let me proceed. "The next piece acted was, one of them went to bring down the Star, and put it on the altar, while another put something like a white shawl round Gordon's shoulders." True; he means the veil which is put upon the Priest, before he turns round with the Blessed Sacrament in his hand. "Gordon next takes the Star, and, turning his face to the people, to raise up the Star, with part of the shawl round the candlestick, the other two priests, one on each side of him, drawing the shawl, it showed a real piece of magic art." Now what makes this so amusing to the Catholic is, that, as far as the priest's actions go, it is really so accurately described. It is the description of one who has his eyes about him, and makes the best of them, but who, as he goes on, is ever putting his own absurd comment on everything which occurs in succession. Now, observe, he spoke of "magic;" let us see what the magic is, and what becomes of the Star, the lamp, and the candlestick with the shawl round it.

"As Gordon raised the Star, with his back to all

the lighted candles on the altar, he clearly showed the Popish deceit, for *in the candlestick there is a bell."* Here is his first great failure of fact; he could not be looking at two places at once; he heard the bell, which the attendant was ringing at one side; he did not see it; where could it be? his ready genius, that is, the genius of his wonderful prejudice about us, told him at once where it was. It was a piece of priestcraft, and the bell was concealed inside the foot of the candlestick;—listen. "As Gordon raised the Star, with his back turned to all the lighted candles on the altar, he clearly showed the Popish deceit; for in the candlestick there is a bell, that rung three times of its own accord, to deceive the blind fools more; and the light through the shawl showed so many colours, as Father Gordon moved his body; the bell ringing they could not see, for the candlestick was covered with part of this magic shawl, and Gordon's finger at work underneath."

Such is his account of the rite of Benediction; he is so densely ignorant of us, and so supremely confident of his knowledge, that he ventures to put in print something like the following rubrical direction for its celebration :—

☞ *First, a young priest setteth up a golden, diamond-like star, with a lamp in it, sticking it on to the top of a candlestick, then he lighteth fifty candles by means of a wand with an extinguisher and wax candle upon it; then four priests bow, burn incense, and wave a lanthorn before the star; then one of the priests, hiding what he is at, by means of a great shawl about his hands and the foot of the candlestick, taketh up said candlestick, with the lamp and gold star glittering like diamonds, and beginneth secretly to tinkle with his finger a bell hid in its foot; whereupon the whole congregation marvelleth much, and worshippeth star, lamp and candlestick incontinently.*

He ends with the following peroration:—" This is the power of priests; they are the best play actors in this town. I should be glad to see this published, that I might take it to Father Gordon, to see if he could contradict a word of it." Rather, such is the power of prejudice, by good luck expressed in writing, and given to the world, as a specimen of what goes on, without being recorded, in so many hundred thousands of minds. The very confidence with which he appeals to the accuracy of his testimony, only shows how prejudice can create or colour, where facts are harmless or natural. It is superior to facts, and lives in a world of its own.

Nor would it be at all to the purpose to object, that, had he known what the rite really meant, he would quite as much, or even more, have called it idolatry. The point is not what *he* would think of our rites, if he understood them exactly, for I am not supposing his judgment to be worth anything at all, or that we are not as likely to be right as an individual Scripture Reader; the question is not, what he would judge, but what he did think, and how he came to think it. His prejudice interpreted our actions.

6.

Alas, my Brothers, though we have laughed at the extravagance which shows itself in such instances of prejudice, it is in truth no matter for a jest. If I laugh, it is to hide the deep feelings of various kinds which it necessarily excites in the mind. I laugh at what is laughable in the displays of this wretched root of evil, in order to turn away my thoughts from its nature and effects, which are not laughable, but hateful and dangerous—dangerous to the Catholic, hateful to the Supreme Judge. When you see a beast of prey in his cage, you are led to laugh at its impotent fury, at its fretful motions and its sullen air and its grotesque expressions of impatience, disappointment, and malice, if it is baulked of its revenge. And, as to this Prejudice, Brothers of the Oratory, really in itself it is one of the direst, most piteous, most awful phenomena in the whole country; to see a noble, generous people the victims of a moral infirmity, which is now a fever, now an ague, now a falling sickness, now a frenzy, and now a St. Vitus's dance! Oh, if we could see as the angels see, thus should we speak of it, and in language far more solemn. I told you why in an earlier part of this Lecture;—not simply because the evil comes from beneath, as I believe it does; not only because it so falls upon the soul, and occupies it, that it is like a bad dream or nightmare, which is so hard to shake off;—but chiefly because it is one of the worst sins of which our poor nature is capable. Perhaps it is wrong to compare sin with sin, but I declare to you, the more I think of it, the more intimately does this prejudice seem to me to corrupt the soul, even beyond those sins which are commonly called most deadly, as the various forms of impurity or pride. And why? because, I repeat it, it argues so astonishing a want of mere natural charity or love of our kind. It is piercing enough to think what little faith there is in the country; but it is quite heartrending to witness so utter a deficiency in a mere natural virtue. Oh, is it possible, that so many, many men, and women too, good and kind otherwise, should take such delight in being quite sure that millions of men have the sign and seal of the Evil One upon them! Oh, is it conceivable that they can be considerate in all matters of this life, friendly in social intercourse, indulgent to the wayward, charitable to the poor and outcast, merciful towards criminals, nay, kind towards the inferior creation, towards their cows, and horses, and swine; yet, as regards us, who bear the same form, speak the same tongue, breathe the same air, and walk the same streets, ruthless, relentless, believing ill of us, and wishing to believe it! I repeat it, they wish us to be what they believe us to be; what a portentous fact! They delight to look at us, and to believe that we are the veriest reptiles and vermin which belied the human form divine. It is a dear thought, which they cannot bear to lose. True, it may have been taught them from their youth, they never may have had means to unlearn it,—that is not the point; they have never *wished* better things of us, they have never *hoped* better things. They are tenacious of what they believe, they are impatient of being argued with, they are angry at being contradicted, they are disappointed when a point is cleared up; they had rather that *we* should be guilty than *they* mistaken; they have no wish at all we should not be blaspheming hypocrites, stupid idolaters, loathsome profligates, unprincipled rogues and bloodthirsty demons. They are kinder even to their dogs and their cats than to us. Is it not true? can it be denied? is it not portentous? does it not argue an incompleteness or hiatus in the very structure of their moral nature? has not something, in their case, dropped out of the list of natural qualities proper to man?

And hence it is, that, calm as may be the sky, and gentle the breeze, we cannot trust the morning: at any moment a furious tempest may be raised against us, and scatter calamity through our quiet homes, as long as the Prince of the power of the air retains this sovereignty. There is ever a predisposition in the political and social atmosphere to lour and thicken. We never are secure against the access of madness in that people, whose name and blood we share. Some accident,—a papal bull, worded as papal documents have been since the beginning of time, a sudden scandal among our priests or in our convents, or some bold and reckless falsehood, may raise all England against us. Such also was our condition in the first age of the Church: the chance of the hour brought the Pagan Romans upon us. A rash Christian tore down an Imperial manifesto from its place; the horrible Dioclesian persecution was the consequence. A crop failed, a foe appeared, it was all through the poor Christians. So speaks the Early Christian Apologist, the celebrated Tertullian, in his defence of us, about a hundred years after St. John's time. "They think the Christians," he says, "to be the cause of every public calamity, of every national ill. If the Tiber cometh up to the walls, if the Nile cometh not up to the fields, if the rain hath not fallen, if the earth hath been moved, if there be any famine, if any pestilence, *Christianos ad leonem*—to the lion with the Christians—is forthwith the cry." No limit could be put to the brutishness of the notions then entertained of us by the heathen. They believed we fed on children; they charged us with the most revolting forms of incest; they gave out that we worshipped beasts or monsters. "Now a new report of our God hath been lately set forth in this city," says the same Tertullian, "since a certain wretch put forth a picture with some such title as this,—The god of the Christians conceived of an ass. This was a creature with ass's ears, with a hoof on one foot, carrying a book and wearing a gown. We smiled both at the name and the figure." Not indeed the same, but parallel, are the tales told of us now. Scottish absurdities are gravely appropriated as precious truths. Our very persons, not merely our professions, are held in abhorrence; we are spit at by the malevolent, we are passed with a shudder of contemptuous pity by the better-natured; we are supposed to be defiled by some secret rites of blood by the ignorant. There is a mysterious pollution and repulsion about us, which makes those who feel its influence curious or anxious to investigate what it can be. We are regarded as something unclean, which a man would not touch, if he could help it; and our advances are met as would be those of some hideous baboon, or sloth, or rattlesnake, or toad, which strove to make itself agreeable.

7.

Is it wonderful, with this spirit of delusion on the faculties of the many, that charges against us are believed as soon as made? So was it two centuries ago; one or two abandoned men, Titus Oates, whom the Protestant Hume calls "the most infamous of mankind," William Bedloe, who, the same writer says, was, "if possible, more infamous than Oates," and some others, aided by the lucky accident of the assassination of a London magistrate, whose murderers were never discovered, were sufficient, by a bold catalogue of calumnies, to put the whole kingdom into a paroxysm of terror and suspicion. The fit had been some time coming on, when "the cry of a plot," says Hume, "all on a sudden, struck their ears. They were awakened from their slumber, and, like men affrighted in the dark, took every figure for a spectre. The terror of each man became a source of terror to another; and a universal panic being diffused, reason and argument, and common sense, and common humanity, lost all influence over them."

Oates and Bedloe came forward to swear against us the most atrocious and impossible falsehoods. The Pope and Propaganda had claimed possession of England; and he had nominated the Jesuits to be his representatives here, and to hold the supreme power for him. All the offices of government had been filled up under the seal of this Society, and all the dignities of the Protestant Church given away, in great measure, to Spaniards and other foreigners. The king had been condemned to death as a heretic. There had been a meeting of fifty Jesuits in London during the foregoing May, when the king's death was determined on. He was to be shot or to be poisoned. The confessor of the French king had sent to London

£10,000 as a reward for any one who would assassinate him; a Spanish ecclesiastic had offered £10,000 more; and the Prior of the Benedictines £6,000. The Queen's physician had been offered £10,000, and had asked £15,000 for the job, and had received an instalment of £5,000. Four Irish ruffians had been hired by the Jesuits at twenty guineas a-piece, to shoot the king at Windsor. Two others were also engaged, one at £1,500; the other, being a pious man, preferred to take out the money in masses, of which he was to receive 30,000. Another had been promised canonization and £500, if he was successful in the enterprise. There was a subscription going on among the Catholics all through England, to collect sums for the same purpose. The Jesuits had determined to set fire to London, Southwark, and all the chief cities of the country. They were planning to set fire to all the shipping in the Thames. Twenty thousand Catholics were to rise in London in twenty-four hours' time, who, it was estimated, might cut the throats of 100,000 Protestants. The most eminent divines of the Establishment were especially marked for assassination. Ten thousand men were to be landed from abroad in the North, and were to seize Hull; and 20,000 or 30,000 religious men and pilgrims from Spain were to land in Wales.

Is all this grave history?—it is. Do not think I have added aught of my own; it is unnecessary. Invention cannot run with prejudice. Prejudice wins. Do not my true stories of Protestantism beat the fables against Catholicism of Achilli and Maria Monk? they are a romance, true and terrible.

What came of these wild allegations, preferred by men of infamous character, and favoured by the accident of Sir Edmonsbury Godfrey's murder, by unknown assassins? "Without further reasoning," says Hume, "the cry rose that he had been assassinated by the Papists, on account of his taking Oates's evidence. The clamour was quickly propagated, and met with universal belief. Each hour teemed with new rumours and surmises. To deny the reality of the plot was to be an accomplice; to hesitate was criminal. Royalist, republican, churchman, sectary, courtier, patriot, all parties concurred in the illusion. The city prepared for its defence, as if the enemy were at its gates; the chains and posts were put up. . . . The dead body of Godfrey was carried into the city, attended by vast multitudes. . . . Seventy-two clergymen marched before; above a thousand persons of distinction followed after; and, at the funeral sermon, two able-bodied divines mounted the pulpit, and stood on each side of the preacher, lest, in paying the last duties to this unhappy magistrate, he should, before the whole people, be murdered by the Papists."

A recent historian adds to the picture:[1] "Everywhere," he says, "justices were busied in searching houses and seizing papers. All the gaols were filled with Papists. London had the aspect of a city in a state of siege. The trainbands were under arms all night. Preparations were made for barricading the great thoroughfares. Patrols marched up and down the streets. Cannon were placed round Whitehall.

---

[1] Macaulay, History, vol. i. p. 235.

No citizen thought himself safe, unless he carried under his coat a small flail loaded with lead to brain the Popish assassins."

The Parliament kept pace with the people, a solemn fast was voted, and a form of prayer drawn up; five Catholic peers were committed to the Tower on charge of high treason; a member of the Commons, who in private society spoke strongly against the defenders of the plot, was expelled the House; and both Houses, Lords and Commons, voted, almost in the form of a dogmatic decree, "that there is, and hath been, a damnable and hellish plot, contrived and carried on by the Popish recusants, for assassinating the King, for subverting the Government, and for rooting-out and destroying the Protestant succession." Titus Oates was called the Saviour of his country; was lodged in Whitehall, protected by guards, and rewarded with a pension of £1,200 a year.

I will not pursue the history of this remarkable frenzy into its deeds of blood, into the hangings, and embowellings, and the other horrors of which innocent Catholics were in due course the victims. Well had it been had the pretended plot ended with the worldly promotion of its wretched fabricators, whom at this day all the world gives up to reprobation and infamy. Oates and Bedloe were the Maria Monk, the Jeffreys, the Teodore, the Achilli of their hour, on a larger field; they spoke then as Protestant champions speak now, to the prejudices of the people: they equalled our own slanderers in falsehood and assurance,—in success they surpassed them.

We live in a happier age than our forefathers; at least, let us trust that the habits of society and the self-interest of classes and of sects will render it impossible that blind prejudice and brute passion should ever make innocence and helplessness their sport and their prey, as they did in the seventeenth century.

LECTURE VII.

ASSUMED PRINCIPLES THE INTELLECTUAL GROUND OF THE PROTESTANT VIEW.

I.

THERE is a great and a growing class in the community, who wish to be fair to us, who see how cruelly we are dealt with, who are indignant at the clamour, and see through the calumnies, and despise the prejudice, which are directed against us, who feel themselves to be superior to the multitude in their feelings and their judgments, who aim at thinking well of all men, all persuasions, all schools of thought, and of Catholics in the number, and to like each for what is good in it, though they may not follow it themselves. Being thus candid, and, in a certain sense, unbiassed, they readily acknowledge the grandeur of the Catholic Religion, both in history and in philosophy; they wish to be good friends with it; they delight to contemplate its great heroes; they recognise, perhaps, with almost enthusiastic admiration, the genius and other gifts of the intellect, which in every age have been so profusely found among its adherents. They know and they like individual Catholics; they have every desire to like us in all respects; they set their minds towards liking us, our principles, our doctrines, our worship and our ways. As far as can be said of men, they really have no prejudice. In this interesting and excellent state of mind, they take up one of our books, sincerely wishing to get on with it; alas, they are flung back at once; they see so much which they cannot abide at all, do what they will. They are annoyed at themselves, and at us; but there is no help for it; they discover, they feel that between them and us there is a gulf. So they turn from the subject in disgust, and for a time perhaps are in bad humour with religion altogether, and have a strong temptation to believe nothing at all. Time passes; they get over the annoyance, and perhaps make a second attempt to adjust their own feelings with our doctrines, but with no better success. They had hoped to have found some middle term, some mode of reconciliation; they did not expect agreement, but at least peace; not coincidence, but at least a sort of good understanding and concurrence :—whereas they find antagonism. No: it is impossible; it is melancholy to say it, but it is no use disguising the truth from themselves; they cannot get over this or that doctrine or practice; nay, to be honest, there is no part they can acquiesce in; each separate portion is part of a whole. They are disappointed, but they never can believe, they never can even approve; if the Catholic system be true, faith in it must be a gift, for reason does not bear it out.

What are the things which so offend the candid and kindly-disposed persons in question? So many, that they do not know where to begin, nor where to end.

It is the whole system of Catholicism; our miracles, and our relics, and our legends of saints; and then our doctrine of indulgences, and our purgatory; and our views of sin, and of the virtue of penances; and our strange formalities in worship; in a word, all is extravagant, strained, unnatural, where it is not directly offensive, or substantially impossible. They never could receive any part of it, they are sure; they would find it as hard to receive one part as the whole. They must lose their moral identity, and wake up with a new stock of thoughts, principles, and argumentative methods, ere they could ever endure it.

If such is the feeling of even candid and kind men, what will be the impression produced by Catholicism on the prejudiced? You see it is a cause of shrinking from us quite independent of prejudice, for it exists among those who are not prejudiced; but it may be joined with prejudice, and then the aversion and abhorrence entertained towards us will be intense indeed. In that case, reason (that is, what the person in question takes to be such)—reason and passion will go together.

Further, consider that it is not individuals merely, here and there, but vast multitudes who are affected precisely in the same way at hearing our doctrines; millions, whole nations. Each member of them bears witness to the rest; there is the consent, intimate, minute, exact, absolute, of all classes, all ranks, all ages, all dispositions. All this is a fact; we see it before us: do we require anything more to account for the position we hold in a Protestant country? So strong does the persuasion become, that Catholicism is indefensible, that our opponents become aggressive;

T

they not only spurn our creed and our worship themselves, but they are (as they think) in a condition to maintain that we too in our hearts despise both the one and the other as really as they. They will not believe that educated men can sincerely accept either; *they* do not hold them, therefore no one else can hold them. They conclude, therefore, that we *disbelieve* what we teach and practise; and in consequence, that we are *hypocrites*, as professing one thing, and thinking another. Next they come to a third conclusion, that since no one acts without motives, we must have a motive in professing without believing, and it must be a *bad motive;* for instance, gain or power: accordingly we are, first, unbelievers; secondly, liars; thirdly, cheats and robbers. And thus you have fullblown Priestcraft; here you have Popery simply detected and uncloaked: and observe the course of the argument;—Catholic Priests are infidels, are hypocrites, are rogues, why? simply, because Protestants think Catholic doctrine and Catholic worship irrational.

2.

Here then, Brothers of the Oratory, you see I have pointed out to your notice a cause of the feeling which is cherished towards us and our religion, altogether distinct from any other I have hitherto mentioned; and perhaps the most important of all. I say the most important, because it influences not only the multitude of men, but the men of thought, of education, of candour, those who are conscious they do wish to do us justice. The instinctive rising of the mind, of the intellect, of the reason (so they would say themselves, though, of course, and, as you will see, I am not going to allow it), opposes itself to the Catholic system. Is not our cause hopeless? how can we ever overcome so overwhelmingly formidable a fact?

I acknowledge its force is very great; this is the argument to which men mean to point, when they talk of education, light, progress, and so on, being the certain destruction of Catholicism. They think our creed is so irrational that it will fall to pieces of itself, when the sun of reason is directed in upon the places which at present it is enveloping. And I repeat (without of course allowing for an instant that this spontaneous feeling, if so it may be called, is synonymous with reason), I acknowledge that it is a most tremendous obstacle in the way of our being fairly dealt with. And our enemies, I say again, are in great triumph about it; they say, "Let in education upon them; leave them to reason; set the schoolmaster upon them." Well, I allow this "reason" (to use for the moment their own designation of it), *is* a serious inconvenience to us: it is a hindrance in our path; but I do not think it so invincible a weapon as they consider it; and on this simple ground,—because, if it were so ready, so safe, and so complete a method as they would have it, I consider they would have been slower to take *other* methods; for instance, slower to hang, to disembowel, to quarter, to imprison, to banish. If this "reason" would do their work for them so well, I do not think they would have established their "reason," instead of leaving it to fight its own battles; I do not think we should have had so many laws passed in favour of "Reason," and against us the Irrational. If this "Reason," as they choose to call it, made such short work with Catholicism, they would not have been so frightened at what they call "Popish Aggression," or have directed a stringent Act of Parliament against a poor twentieth part of the population of England. If this innate common sense, as they desire to consider it, were so crushing, so annihilating to our claims, to our existence, why the thousands of fables, fictions, falsehoods, fallacies, put out against us? why Maria Monk, and Jeffreys, and Teodore, and Achilli? Allowing, then, as I do, the importance of the phenomenon which I have been mentioning, feeling most fully that it requires careful consideration, granting that we may be fairly asked what we have to say to it, and that we ought to account for its existence,—nevertheless, I do not think it is so decisive an argument as its own upholders would make it, else it ought to have altogether superseded all others.

In truth, the spontaneous feeling against our doctrines and worship, of which I have been speaking, has far greater influence with educated men than with the many; it is to the educated class what absurd fiction and false-witness are to the multitude: the multitude is credulous, the educated classes are speculative; the multitude is sensitive of facts, true or false, the educated classes of theories, sound or unsound; though I do not deny that the educated classes are credulous too, and the multitude theorists. This, then, is pretty much the state of the case; and as in former Lectures I have directed your attention, my Brothers, to the fables and falsehoods circulated against us, as one special cause of the odium which attaches to the Catholic Name, so this evening I propose to give you some description of those views theories, principles, or whatever they are to be called, which imbue the educated and active intellect, and lead it, as it were, instinctively and spontaneously, first to pronounce the creed and worship of Catholicism absurd, and next by inference to pronounce its professors hypocritical.

I fear I have got upon a dry subject; I must make some demand on your attention, yet I cannot help it. All subjects are not equally amusing, equally easy; still it is too important a subject to omit. Did I do so, I should be said to be evading the most difficult part of the whole controversy. It is, indeed, the most important of all I have to treat; so important, that I cannot do justice to it in one Lecture, which is all I mean to give to it. So I have a double difficulty about it; one lies in my writing, the other in your attending; but I must do my best.

3

You may recollect, that, in my Lecture last week, in speaking of prejudice, I alluded to opinions and conclusions, which often went by the name of prejudices, yet should more properly be called Prejudgments or Presumptions; for this reason, because they rest on argumentative grounds, and are abandoned by their upholders when those grounds fail them, whereas a Prejudice is held tenaciously against reason. Thus a man may hold as a general fact, that Blacks are inferior to Whites in the gifts of intellect, and might thereby be led to expect that a certain Black, whom he met, would be unequal to play his part in English society; but he might yield at once when evidence was brought in proof of the ability of the particular individual in question ; or again, he might yield to argument directed against his view altogether. Here would be a presumption without a prejudice. On the other hand, if he still persisted that the particular Black was weak-minded and incapable, against fact, or if he refused to reconsider his grounds, when there was reason for his doing so, then certainly he would be justly called prejudiced.

There is no difficulty so far; but, observe, there are opinions and beliefs which do not depend on previous grounds, which are not drawn from facts for which no reasons can be given, or no sufficient reasons, which proceed immediately from the mind, and which the holder considers to be, as it were, part of himself. If another person doubts them, the holder has nothing to show for their truth except that he is sure that they *are* true: he cannot say, "I will reconsider my reasons," for he has no reasons to consider. What, then, is to make him abandon them? what is to touch them? He holds them, and continues to hold them, whatever is urged against him to the contrary; and thus these opinions and beliefs look like prejudices, though they are not. They are not prejudices, because prejudices are opinions formed upon grounds, which grounds the prejudiced person refuses to examine; whereas these opinions which I am speaking of have from the first no grounds at all, but are simple persuasions or sentiments, which came to the holder he cannot tell how, and which apparently he cannot help holding, and they are in consequence commonly called First Principles. For instance, that all Blacks are unintellectual would be a prejudice, if obstinately held against facts; whereas the obstinate belief that God cannot punish in hell is rather a first principle than a prejudice, because (putting aside the authority of Revelation) it can hardly be said to come within the reach of facts at all. From what I have said, it is plain that First Principles may be false or true; indeed, this is my very point, as you will presently see. Certainly they are not necessarily true; and again, certainly there *are* ways of unlearning them when they are false: moreover, as regards moral and religious First Principles which are false, of course a Catholic considers that no one holds them except by some fault of his own; but these are further points, and some of them beyond my present subject, which is not theological; however, I mention them to prevent misconception.

Now that there must be such things as First Principles—that is, opinions which are held without proof as if self-evident,—and, moreover, that every one must have some or other, who thinks at all, is evident from the nature of the case. If you trace back your reasons for holding an opinion, you must stop somewhere; the process cannot go on for ever; you must come at last to something you cannot prove; else, life would be spent in inquiring and reasoning, our minds would be ever tossing to and fro, and there would be nothing to guide us. No man alive, but has some First Principles or other. Even if he declares that nothing can be known for certain, then that is his First Principle. He has got his place in philosophy ready marked out for him; he is of the sect called Academics or Pyrrhonists, as the case may be, and his dogma is either "Nothing can be known in itself," or "Nothing can be known even for practical purposes." Any one may convince himself of the truth of what I am saying, who examines his own sentiments; for instance, supposing, on meeting a particular person, you said you would have nothing to do with him politically, and gave as your reason, *because* he belonged to a certain political party. And, supposing, on being asked why you disliked that party, you answered, *because* their very principle was to stand upon their own rights; and then supposing you were asked why it was wrong to stand on one's own rights, and you answered again, *because* it was selfish and proud; and being asked once more, why selfishness and pride were wrong, supposing you answered that selfishness and pride were bad feelings, *because* they were the feelings of the bad angels, who stood upon their supposed rights against their Maker; or, to sum up the whole in Dr. Johnson's famous saying, because "the devil was the first Whig,"—why, in that case, you see, you would have come to a First Principle, beyond which you could not get. I am not saying whether your reasoning, or your First Principle, was true or false; that is quite another matter; I am but illustrating what is meant by a First Principle, and how it is that all reasoning ultimately rests upon such. It would be your First Principle, in the case supposed, a principle for which no reason could be given, that the bad angels are to be avoided; *thence* it would follow that what is like them is to be avoided; and *from that* again, it followed that pride and selfishness are to be avoided; and *from that* again, that the particular political party in question is to be avoided. This, I repeat, is what is called a First Principle, and you see what a bearing it has both upon thought and upon action.

It is a First Principle that man is a social being;

a First Principle that he may defend himself; a First Principle that he is responsible; a First Principle that he is frail and imperfect; a First Principle that reason must rule passion.

I will set down one or two other instances of First Principles by way of further illustration.

The celebrated Roman patriot Cato stabbed himself when besieged at Utica, rather than fall into the hands of Cæsar. He thought this a very great action, and so have many others besides. In like manner Saul, in Scripture, fell on his sword when defeated in battle; and there have been those who have reproached Napoleon for not having blown out his brains on the field of Waterloo. Now, if these advocates of suicide had been asked why they thought such conduct, under such circumstances, noble, perhaps they would have returned the querist no answer, as if it were too plain to talk about, or from contempt of him, as if he were a person without any sense of honour, any feeling of what becomes a gentleman, of what a soldier, a hero, owes to himself. That is, they would not bring out their First Principle from the very circumstance that they felt its power so intensely; that First Principle being, that there is no evil so great in the whole universe, visible and invisible, in time and eternity, as humiliation.

Again, supposing a medical man were to say to his patient that he could not possibly get well unless he gave up his present occupation, which was too much for his health; supposing him to say, "As to the *way* of your doing this—how you are to make your livelihood if you give it up; or again, how you are to become a proficient in your present trade, or art, or intellectual pursuit; or again, how, if you take that step, you can keep up your religious connections; all these questions I have nothing to do with; I am only speaking to you *as* a medical man;"—nothing could be kinder or more sensible than such language; he does not make his own medical enunciations First Principles; he delivers his opinion, and leaves it to the patient to strike the balance of advantages. But it is just possible, to take an extreme case, that he might take another line. He might be so carried away by his love for his own science (as happens commonly to men in any department of knowledge), as to think that everything ought to give way to it. He might actually ridicule religious scruples as absurd, and prescribe something which would be simply unlawful to a religious man; and he might give as a reason for such advice, that nature required it, and there was an end of the matter. In such case he would be going so far as to make the principles of his own science First Principles of conduct; and he would pronounce it impossible that moral duty ought in any case to interfere with or supersede the claims of animal nature.

I will take a third instance:—I believe that some time ago various benevolent persons exerted themselves in favour of the brute creation, who endure so much wanton suffering at the hands of barbarous owners. Various speculations were set afloat in consequence, and various measures advocated. I think I have heard that one doctrine was to the effect that it was wrong to eat veal, lamb, and other young meat, inasmuch as you killed creatures which would have enjoyed a longer life, and answered the purpose of food better, had you let them live to be beef and mutton. Again, shrimp sauce, it was said, ought to give way to lobster; for in the latter case you took one life away, in the former a hundred. Now the world laughed at all this, and would not condescend to reason; perhaps could not, though it had the best of the question; that is, perhaps it had not put its ideas sufficiently in order to be able to reason. However, it *had* reasons, and these reasons will be found traceable up to this First Principle, which expresses the common theory of all mankind in their conduct towards the inferior animals—viz., that the Creator has placed them absolutely in our hands, that we have no duties to them, and that there is as little sin except accidentally, and in the particular case, in taking away a brute's life, as in plucking a flower or eating an orange. This being taken for granted, all questions are in their substance solved, and only accidental difficulties remain.

I have said enough to show you what important, what formidable matters First Principles are. They are the means of proof, and are not themselves proved; they rule and are not ruled; they are sovereign on the one hand, irresponsible on the other: they are absolute monarchs, and if they are true, they act like the best and wisest of fathers to us: but, if they are false, they are the most cruel and baneful of tyrants. Yet, from the nature of our being, there they are, as I have said; there they must ever be. They are our guides and standards in speculating, reasoning, judging, deliberating, deciding, and acting; they are to the mind what the circulation of the blood and the various functions of our animal organs are to the body. They are the conditions of our mental life; by them we form our view of events, of deeds, of persons, of lines of conduct, of aims, of moral qualities, of religions. They constitute the difference between man and man; they characterize him. As determined by his First Principles, such is his religion, his creed, his worship, his political party, his character, except as far as adventitious circumstances interfere with their due and accurate development; they are, in short, the man.

One additional remark must be made, quite as important as the foregoing. I just now said that these First Principles, being a man's elementary points of thinking, and the ideas which he has prior to other ideas, might be considered as almost part of his mind or moral being itself. But for this very reason, because they are so close to him, if I may so speak, he is very likely not to be aware of them. What is far off, your bodily eyes see; what is close up to you is no object for your vision at all. You cannot see yourself; and, in somewhat the same way, the chance is that you are not aware of those principles or ideas which have the chief rule over your mind. They are hidden for the very reason they are so sovereign and so engrossing. They have sunk into you; they spread through you; you do not so much appeal to them as act from them. And this in great measure is meant by saying that self-knowledge is so difficult; that is, in other words, men commonly do not know their First Principles.

Now to show you that they have this subtle and recondite character. For instance, two persons begin to converse; they come upon some point on which they do not agree: they fall to dispute. They go on arguing and arguing perhaps for hours; neither makes way with the other, but each becomes more certain his own opinion is right. Why is this? How is it to be explained? They cannot tell. It surprises them, for the point is so very clear; as far as this they are agreed, but no further; for then comes the difference, that where one says yes, the other says no, and each wonders that the other is not on his side. How comes each to be so positive when each contradicts the other? The real reason is, that each starts from some principle or opinion which he takes for granted, which he does not observe he is assuming, and which, even if he did, he would think too plain to speak about or attempt to prove. Each starts with a First Principle, and they differ from each other in first principles.

For instance, supposing two persons to dispute whether Milton was or was not a poet; it might so happen, that they both took for granted that every one knew what a poet was. If so, they might go on arguing to the end of time and never agree, because they had not adjusted with each other the principles with which they started.

Now, here the mistake is very obvious; it might, however, very easily be a First Principle which did not come so prominently forward in the discussion. It might come in by the by, neither party might see it come in at all, or even recognise it to himself as a proposition which he held in the affirmative or negative, and yet it might simply turn the decision this way or that.

Thus again it happens, to take an instance of

another kind, that we cannot tell why we like some persons and dislike others, though there are reasons, if we could reach them; according to the lines,—

> "I do not like thee, Dr. Fell;
> The reason why I cannot tell."

Or a person says, "I do not know how it is that this or that writer so comes home to me, and so inspires me; I so perfectly agree with him," or "I can so easily follow his thoughts." Both feelings may be accounted for, at least in many cases, by a difference or agreement in First Principles between the speaker and the person spoken of, which shows itself in the words, or writings, or deeds, or life of the latter, when submitted to the criticism of the former.

Sometimes two friends live together for years, and appear to entertain the same religious views; at the end of the time they take different courses; one becomes an unbeliever, the other a Catholic. How is this? Some latent and hitherto dormant First Principle, different in each, comes into play, and carries off one to the East, the other to the West. For instance, suppose the one holds that there is such a thing as sin; the other denies it,—denies it, that is, really and in his heart, though at first he would shrink from saying so, even to himself, and is not aware he denies it. At a certain crisis, either from the pressure of controversy or other reason, each finds he must give up the form of religion in which he has been educated; and then this question, the nature of sin, what it is, whether it exists, comes forward as a turning-point between them; he who does not believe in it becomes an unbeliever; he who does, becomes a Catholic.

Such, then, are First Principles; sovereign, irresponsible, and secret;—what an awful form of government the human mind is under from its very constitution!

4.

There are many of these First Principles, as I have called them, which are common to the great mass of mankind, and are therefore true, as having been imprinted on the human mind by its Maker. Such are the great truths of the moral law, the duties, for instance, of justice, truth, and temperance. Others are peculiar to individuals, and are in consequence of no authority; as, for instance, to take a case which cannot often occur, the opinion that there is no difference between virtue and vice. Other principles are common to extended localities; men catch them from each other, by education, by daily intercourse, by reading the same books, or by being members of the same political community. Hence nations have very frequently one and the same set of First Principles, of the truth of which each individual is still more sure, because it is not only his own opinion, but the opinion of nearly every one else about him. Thus, for instance, it was the opinion of the ancient pagan Romans, that every one should follow the religion of his own country, and this was the reason why they persecuted the first Christians. They thought it exceedingly hard that the Christians would take up a religion of their own, and that, an upstart religion, lately imported from Palestine. They said, " Why cannot you be contented to be as your ancestors? we are most liberal on the point of religion; we let a Jew follow Jewish rites, and an Egyptian the rites of Egypt, and a Carthaginian the Punic; but you are ungrateful and rebellious, because, not content with this ample toleration, you *will* be introducing into your respective countries a foreign religion." They thought all this exceedingly sensible, and, in fact, unanswerable; statesmen of all parties and all the enlightened men and great thinkers of the Empire gave in their adhesion to it; and on this First Principle they proceeded to throw our poor forefathers to the beasts, to the flame, and to the deep, after first putting them to the most varied and horrible tortures. Such was the power of an imperial idea, and a popular dogma; such is the consequence of a First Principle being held in common by many at once; it ceases to be an opinion; it is at once taken for truth; it is looked upon as plain common sense; the opposite opinions are thought impossible; they are absurdities and nonentities, and have no rights whatever.

In the instance I have mentioned, the folly and the offence, in the eyes of the Romans, was *proselytising;* but let us fancy this got over, would the Christian system itself have pleased the countrymen of Cato at all better? On the contrary, they would have started with his First Principle, that humiliation was immoral, as an axiom; they would not have attempted to prove it; they would have considered it as much a fact as the sun in heaven; they would not have even enunciated it, they would have merely implied it. Fancy a really candid philosopher, who had been struck with the heroic deaths of the Martyrs, turning with a feeling of good will to consider the Christian ethics; what repugnance would he not feel towards them on rising up from the study! to crouch, to turn the cheek, not to resist, to love to be lowest! Who ever heard of such a teaching? It was the religion of slaves, it was unworthy of a man; much more of a Roman; yet that odious religion in the event became the creed of countless millions. What philosophers so spontaneously and instinctively condemned has been professed by the profoundest and the noblest of men, through eighteen centuries;—so possible is it for our First Principles to be but the opinions of a multitude, not truths.

Now be quite sure, my Brothers, that I make clear to you the point on which I am animadverting in these instances. I am not blaming Cato and his countrymen for using their First Principles, whatever they were, while they believed them: every one must use such opinions as he has; there is nothing else to be done. What I should blame in them would be their utterly despising another system with which they did not sympathize, and being so sure that they were right; their forgetting that the Christians might have First Principles as well as they, and opposite ones; their forgetting that it was a *question* of First Principles; that the contest was not ended—that it had not begun. They viewed Christianity with disgust, at first sight. They were repelled, thrown back, they revolted from the Religion, and they took that mere feeling of theirs as an evidence that the Religion really was wrong and immoral. No, it only showed that *either* the Religion *or* they were wrong, which of the two had still to be determined. Christians had their First Principles also; "blessed are the meek," "blessed are the persecuted," "blessed are the pure-hearted." These First Principles the Pagans had no right to ignore. They chose to apply their own First Principles, as decisive tests, to the examination of the precepts and practice of the Church, and by means of them they condemned her; but if they had applied Christian principles as the measure of her precepts and her practice, they would, on the contrary, have been forced to praise her. All depends on which set of principles you begin by assuming.

The same thing takes place now. A dispassionate thinker is struck with the beauty and the eloquence of the rites and ceremonies of the Catholic Church; he likes to be present at them, but he says they are addressed of course only to the imagination, not to the reason. They are indefensible in the eye of reason. What does he mean? Why this, when he explains himself:—he says he cannot understand how the Divine Being needs propitiating—is He not good? what can be the use of these ceremonies? why, too, such continual prayer? why try to get others to pray for you too, and for your object, whatever it is? what the use of *novenas?* why betake yourselves to saints? what can they do for you? So he might go on, speaking against the whole system of deprecatory and intercessory prayer, and we might be grieved and perplexed at such a line of thought in so candid a man, and we should ask ourselves how it came to be. Now if it turned out at length that the said critic disbelieved the virtue of prayer altogether, or that the Divine Being was really moved by it, or that it was of any good whatever beyond the peace and sereneness which the exercise poured over the soul, I think you would consider that this fact quite explained those criticisms of his which distressed you; you would feel that it was nugatory to argue points of *detail* with one, who, however candid, differed from you in *principle;* and, while you would not quarrel with him for having his own First Principles (seriously as you thought of them theologically), your immediate charge against him would be that he had forgotten that a Catholic has First Principles too, and forgotten also that we have as much right to have our theory of prayer as he to have his own. His surprise and offence constitute no proof even to himself that we are wrong; they only show, that, as we have our First Principles, which we consider true, but which are not capable of proof, so has he his. The previous question remains—Which set of principles is true? He is a theorist, using his theory against our practice, as if our practice might not have its own theory also. But, in fact, he does not dream that we have any intellectual principles whatever as the basis of what we do; he thinks *he* is the only intellectual man; he has mind on his side, it never came into our heads to have it; *we* do not know what mind is. Thus he imagines and determines, knowing nothing whatever of our acute, profound, subtle philosophers, except by name, and ridding himself of the trouble of reading their works by nicknaming them schoolmen or monks.

5.

Now I have come to the point at which the maintenance of private opinion runs into bigotry. As Prejudice is the rejection of reason altogether, so Bigotry is the imposition of private reason,—that is,

of our own views and theories of our own First
Principles, as if they were the absolute truth, and the
standard of all argument, investigation, and judgment.
If there are any men in the world who ought to
abstain from bigotry, it is Protestants. They, whose
very badge is the right of private judgment, should
give as well as take, should allow others what they
claim themselves; but I am sorry to say, as I have
had occasion to say again and again, there is very
little of the spirit of reciprocity among them; they
monopolize a liberty which, when they set out, they
professed was to be for the benefit of all parties.
Not even the intellectual, not even the candid-minded
among them, are free from inconsistency here. They
begin by setting up principles of thought and action
for themselves; then, not content with applying them
to their own thoughts and actions, they make them
the rule for criticizing and condemning our thoughts
and actions too; this, I repeat, is Bigotry. Bigotry
is the infliction of our own unproved First Principles
on others, and the treating others with scorn or hatred
for not accepting them. There are principles, indeed,
as I have already said, such as the First Principles of
morals, not peculiar or proper to the individual, but
the rule of the world, because they come from the
Author of our being, and from no private factory of
man. It is not bigotry to despise intemperance; it is
not bigotry to hate injustice or cruelty; but whatever is
local, or national, or sectional, or personal, or novel, and
nothing more, to make that the standard of judging
all existing opinions, without an attempt at proving
it to be of authority, is mere ridiculous bigotry. "*In
necessariis unitas, in dubiis libertas,*" is ever the rule

of a true philosopher. And though I know in many cases it is very difficult to draw the line, and to decide what principles are, and what are not, independent of individuals, times and places, eternal and divine, yet so far we may safely assert,—that when the very persons who hold certain views, confess, nay, boast, nay, are jealously careful, that those views come of their own private judgment, they at least should be as jealous and as careful to keep them to their own place, and not to use them as if they came distinctly from heaven, or from the nature of things, or from the nature of man. Those persons, surely, are precluded, if they would be consistent, from using their principles as authoritative, who proclaim that they made them for themselves. Protestants, then, if any men alive, are, on their own showing, bigots, if they set up their First Principles as oracles and as standards of all truth.

This being considered, have we not, my Brothers, a curious sight before us? This is what we call an enlightened age: we are to have large views of things; everything is to be put on a philosophical basis; reason is to rule: the world is to begin again; a new and transporting set of views is about to be exhibited to the great human family. Well and good; have them, preach them, enjoy them, but deign to recollect the while, that there have been views in the world before you: that the world has not been going on up to this day without any principles whatever; that the Old Religion was based on principles, and that it is not enough to flourish about your "new lamps," if you would make us give up our "old" ones. Catholicism, I say, had its First Principles before you were born: you say they are false; very well, prove them to be so: they are false, indeed, if yours are true; but not false merely because yours are yours. While yours are yours it is self-evident, indeed, to you, that ours are false; but it is not the common way of carrying on business in the world, to value English goods by French measures, or to pay a debt in paper which was contracted in gold. Catholicism has its First Principles, overthrow them, if you can; endure them, if you cannot. It is not enough to call them effete because they are old, or antiquated because they are ancient. It is not enough to look into our churches, and cry, "It is all a form, *because* divine favour cannot depend on external observances;" or, "It is all a bondage, *because* there is no such thing as sin;" or, "a blasphemy, *because* the Supreme Being cannot be present in ceremonies;" or, "a mummery, *because* prayer cannot move Him;" or, "a tyranny, *because* vows are unnatural;" or, "hypocrisy, *because* no rational man can credit it at all." I say here is endless assumption, unmitigated hypothesis, reckless assertion; prove your "because," "because," "because;" prove your First Principles, and if you cannot, learn philosophic moderation. Why may not my First Principles contest the prize with yours? they have been longer in the world; they have lasted longer, they have done harder work, they have seen rougher service. You sit in your easy-chairs, you dogmatize in your lecture-rooms, you wield your pens: it all looks well on paper: you write exceedingly well: there never was an age in which there was better writing; logical, nervous, eloquent, and pure,—go and carry it all out in the world. Take your First Principles, of which you are so proud, into the crowded streets of our cities, into the formidable classes which make up the bulk of our population; try to work society by them. You think you can; I say you cannot —at least you have not as yet; it is yet to be seen if you can. "Let not him that putteth on his armour boast as he who taketh it off." Do not take it for granted that that is certain which is waiting the test of reason and experiment. Be modest until you are victorious. My principles, which I believe to be eternal, have at least lasted eighteen hundred years; let yours live as many months. That man can sin, that he has duties, that the Divine Being hears prayer, that He gives His favours through visible ordinances, that He is really present in the midst of them, these principles have been the life of nations; they have shown they could be carried out; let any single nation carry out yours, and you will have better claim to speak contemptuously of Catholic rites, of Catholic devotions, of Catholic belief.

What is all this but the very state of mind which we ridicule, and call narrowness, in the case of those who have never travelled? We call them, and rightly, men of contracted ideas, who cannot fancy things going on differently from what they have themselves witnessed at home, and laugh at everything because it is strange. They themselves are the pattern men; their height, their dress, their manners, their food, their language, are all founded in the nature of things; and everything else is good or bad, just in that very degree in which it partakes, or does not partake, of them. All men ought to get up at half-past eight, breakfast between nine and ten, read the newspapers, lunch, take a ride or drive, dine. Here is the great principle of the day—dine; no one is a man who does not dine; yes, dine, and at the right hour; and it must *be* a dinner, with a certain time after dinner, and then, in due time, to bed. Tea and toast, port wine, roast beef, mince-pies at Christmas, lamb at Easter, goose at Michaelmas, these are their great principles. They suspect any one who does otherwise. Figs and maccaroni for the day's fare, or Burgundy and grapes for breakfast!—they are aghast at the atrocity of the notion. And hence you read of some good country gentleman, who, on undertaking a Continental tour, was warned of the privations and mortifications that lay before him from the difference between foreign habits and his own, stretching his imagination to a point of enlargement answerable to the occasion, and making reply that he knew it, that he had dwelt upon the idea, that he had made up his mind to it, and thought himself prepared for anything abroad, provided he could but bargain for a clean table-cloth and a good beef-steak every day.

Here was a man of one idea; there are many men of one idea in the world: your unintellectual machine, who eats, drinks, and sleeps, is a man of one idea. Such, too, is your man of genius, who strikes out some new, or revives some old view in science or in art, and would apply it as a sort of specific or as a key to all possible subjects; and who will not let the world alone, but loads it with bad names if it will not run after him and his darling fancy, if it will not cure all its complaints by chemistry or galvanism, by little doses or great, if it will not adopt the peaked shoes of Edward III., or the steeple hats of the Puritans. Such again are those benevolent persons who, with right intentions, but yet, I think, narrow views, wish to introduce the British constitution and British ideas into every nation and tribe upon earth; differing, how much! from the wise man in the Greek epic, whose characteristic was that he was "versatile,"[1] for he had known "the cities and the *mind* of many men." History and travel expand our views of man and of society; they teach us that distinct principles rule in different countries and in distinct periods; and, though they do *not* teach us that all principles are equally true, or, which is the same thing, that none are either true or false, yet they do teach us, that all are to be regarded with attention and examined with patience, which have prevailed to any great extent among mankind. Such is the temper of a man of the world, of a philosopher. He may hold principles to be false and dangerous, but he will try to enter into them, to enter into the minds of those who hold them; he will consider in what their strength lies, and what can be said for them; he will do his best to analyze and dissect them; he will compare them with others; and he will apply himself to the task of exposing and disproving them. He will not ignore them;—now, what I desiderate at the present day in so many even candid men, and of course much more in the multitude which is uncandid, is a recognition that Catholics *have* principles of their own; I desiderate a study of those principles, a fair representation, a refutation. It is not enough,

[1] Πολύτροπος.

that this age has its principles too; this does not prove them true; it has no right to put ours on one side, and proceed to make its own the immediate touchstones and the sufficient tribunals of our creed, our worship, our ecclesiastical proceedings, and our moral teaching.

6.

To show in how very many instances these remarks apply to the criticisms and judgments passed by Protestants upon the details of Catholic teaching and belief, is simply impossible, on such an occasion as this.—It would be to write a book. I will take one instance, but even to that I cannot hope to do full justice; but it will be something to have drawn your attention to what seems to me an important line of thought, and to the mode of using it in the controversy in which we are engaged.

I will take, then, one of those subjects, of which I spoke in the opening of this Lecture as offensive to Protestants—viz., our belief in the miracles wrought by the relics and the prayers of the saints, which has given both occasion and scope to so many reports and narratives to their honour, true, doubtful, or unfounded, in the Catholic Church. I suppose there is nothing which prejudices us more in the minds of Protestants of all classes than this belief. They inspect our churches, or they attend to our devotions, or they hear our sermons, or they open our books, or they read paragraphs in the newspapers; and it is one and the same story—relics and miracles. Such a belief, such a claim, they consider a self-evident absurdity; they are too indignant even to laugh; they toss the book from them in the fulness of anger and contempt, and they think it superfluous to make one remark in order to convict us of audacious imposture, and to fix upon us the brand of indelible shame. I shall show, then, that this strong feeling arises simply from their assumption of a First Principle, which ought to be proved, if they would be honest reasoners, before it is used to our disadvantage.

You observe, my Brothers, we are now upon a certain question of controversy, in which the argument is *not* directly about *fact*. This is what I noticed in the opening of this Lecture. We accuse our enemies of untruth in most cases; we do not accuse them, on the whole, of untruth here. I know it is very difficult for prejudice such as theirs to open its mouth at all without some mis-statement or exaggeration; still, on the whole, they do bear true, not false witness in the matter of miracles. We do certainly abound, we are exuberant, we overflow with stories which cause our enemies, from no fault of ours, the keenest irritation, and kindle in them the most lively resentment against us. Certainly the Catholic Church, from east to west, from north to south, is, according to our conceptions, hung with miracles. The store of relics is inexhaustible; they are multiplied through all lands, and each particle of each has in it at least a dormant, perhaps an energetic virtue of supernatural operation. At Rome there is the True Cross, the Crib of Bethlehem, and the Chair of St. Peter; portions of the Crown of Thorns are kept at Paris; the Holy Coat is shown at Trèves; the Winding-Sheet at Turin; at Monza, the iron crown is formed out of a Nail of the Cross; and another Nail is claimed for the Duomo of Milan; and pieces of our Lady's Habit are to be seen in the Escurial. The Agnus Dei, blessed medals, the scapular, the cord of St. Francis, all are the medium of divine manifestations and graces. Crucifixes have bowed the head to the suppliant, and Madonnas have bent their eyes upon assembled crowds St. Januarius's blood liquefies periodically at Naples, and St. Winifred's well is the scene of wonders even in an unbelieving country. Women are marked with the sacred stigmata; blood has flowed on Fridays from their five wounds, and their heads are crowned with a circle of lacerations. Relics are ever touching the sick, the diseased, the wounded, sometimes with no result at all, at other times with marked and undeniable efficacy. Who has not heard of the abundant favours gained by the intercession of the Blessed Virgin, and of the marvellous consequences which have attended the invocation of St. Antony of Padua? These phenomena are sometimes reported of Saints in their life-time, as well as after death, especially if they were evangelists or martyrs. The wild beasts crouched before their victims in the Roman amphitheatre; the axe-man was unable to sever St. Cecilia's head from her body, and St. Peter elicited a spring of water for his jailor's baptism in the Mamertine. St. Francis Xavier turned salt water into fresh for five hundred travellers; St. Raymond was transported over the sea on his cloak; St. Andrew shone brightly in the dark; St. Scholastica gained by her prayers a pouring rain; St. Paul was fed by ravens; and St. Frances saw her guardian Angel. I need not continue the catalogue; here what one party urges, the other admits; they join issue over a fact; that fact is the claim of miracles on the part of the Catholic Church; it is the Protestants' charge, and it is our glory.

Observe then, we affirm that the Supreme Being has wrought miracles on earth ever since the time of the Apostles: Protestants deny it. Why do we affirm, why do they deny? we affirm it on a First Principle, they deny it on a First Principle; and on either side the First Principle is made to be decisive of the question. Our First Principle is contradictory of theirs; if theirs be true, we are mistaken; if ours be true, they are mistaken. They take for granted that their First Principle is true; we take for granted that our First Principle is true. Till ours is disproved, we have as much right to consider it true as they to consider theirs true; till theirs is proved, they have as little ground for saying that we go against reason, as for boasting that they go according to it. For our First Principle is our reason, in the same sense in which theirs is their reason, and it is quite as good a reason. Both they and we start with the miracles of the Apostles;[2] and then their First Principle or presumption, against our miracles, is this, "What God did once, He is *not* likely to do again;" while our First Principle or presumption, for our miracles, is this, "What God did once, He *is* likely to do again." They say, It cannot be supposed He will work *many* miracles; we, It cannot be supposed He will work *few*.

I am not aiming at any mere sharp or clever stroke

---

[2] I am arguing with Protestants; if unbelievers are supposed, then they use virtually Hume's celebrated argument, which still is a Presumption or First Principle—viz., it is impossible to fancy the order of nature interrupted.

against them; I wish to be serious and to investigate the real state of the case, and I feel what I am saying very strongly. Protestants say, miracles are *not* likely to occur often; we say they *are* likely to occur often. The two parties, you see, start with contradictory principles, and they determine the particular miracles, which are the subject of dispute, by their respective principles, without looking to such testimony as may be brought in their favour. They do not say, "St. Francis, or St. Antony, or St. Philip Neri did no miracles, for the *evidence* for them is worth nothing," or "because what *looked* like a miracle was not a miracle;" no, but they say, "It is *impossible* they should have wrought miracles." Bring before the Protestant the largest mass of evidence and testimony in proof of the miraculous liquefaction of St. Januarius's blood at Naples, let him be urged by witnesses of the highest character, chemists of the first fame, circumstances the most favourable for the detection of imposture, coincidences, and confirmations the most close and minute and indirect, he will not believe it; his First Principle *blocks* belief. On the other hand, diminish the evidence ever so much, provided you leave some, and reduce the number of witnesses and circumstantial proof; yet you would not altogether wean the Catholic's mind from belief in it; for his First Principle *encourages* such belief. Would any amount of evidence convince the Protestant of the miraculous motion of a Madonna's eyes? is it not to him in itself, prior to proof, simply incredible? would he even listen to the proof? His First Principle settles the matter; no wonder then that the whole history of Catholicism finds so little response in his

Ground of the Protestant View. 303

intellect or sympathy in his heart. It is as impossible that the notion of the miracle should gain admittance into his imagination, as for a lighted candle to remain burning, when dipped into a vessel of water. The water puts it out.

7.

The Protestant, I say, laughs at the very idea of miracles or supernatural acts as occurring at this day; his First Principle is rooted in him; he repels from him the idea of miracles; he laughs at the notion of evidence for them; one is just as likely as another; they are all false. Why? Because of his First Principle: there are no miracles since the Apostles. Here, indeed, is a short and easy way of getting rid of the whole subject, not by reason, but by a First Principle which he calls reason. Yes, it *is* reason, granting his First Principle is true; it is *not* reason, supposing his First Principle is false. It is reason, if the private judgment of an individual, or of a sect, or of a philosophy, or of a nation, be synonymous with reason; it is not reason, if reason is something not local, nor temporal, but universal. Before he advances a step in his argument, he ought to prove his First Principle true; he does not attempt to do so, he takes it for granted; and he proceeds to apply it, gratuitous, personal, peculiar as it is, to all our accounts of miracles taken together, and thereupon and thereby triumphantly rejects them all. This, forsooth, is his spontaneous judgment, his instinctive feeling, his common sense,—a mere private opinion of his own, a Protestant opinion; a lecture-room opinion; not a world-wide opinion, not an instinct ranging through time and space, but an assumption and presumption, which, by education and habit, he has got to think as certain, as much of an axiom, as that two and two make four; and he looks down upon us, and bids us consider ourselves beaten, all because the savour of our statements and narratives and reports and legends is inconsistent with his delicate Protestant sense,—all because our conclusions are different, not from our principles and premisses, but from his.

And now for the structure he proceeds to raise on this foundation of sand. If, he argues, in matter of fact, there be a host of stories about relics and miracles circulated in the Catholic Church, which, as a matter of First Principle, cannot be true; to what must we attribute them? indubitably to enormous stupidity on the one hand, and enormous roguery on the other. This, observe, is an immediate and close inference:—clever men must see through the superstition; those who do not see through it must be dolts. Further, since religion is the subject-matter of the alleged fictions, they must be what are called pious frauds, for the sake of gain and power. Observe, my Brothers, there is in the Church a vast tradition and testimony about miracles: how is it to be accounted for? If miracles *can* take place, then the *truth* of the miracle will be a natural explanation of the *report*, just as the *fact* of a man dying satisfactorily accounts for the *news* that he is dead; but the Protestant cannot so explain it, because he thinks miracles cannot take place; so he is necessarily driven, by way of accounting for the report of them, to impute that report to fraud. He cannot help himself. I repeat it; the whole mass of accusations which Protestants bring against us under this head, Catholic credulity, imposture, pious frauds, hypocrisy, priestcraft, this vast and varied superstructure of imputation, you see, all rests on an assumption, on an opinion of theirs, for which they offer no kind of proof. What then, in fact, do they say more than this, *If* Protestantism be true, you Catholics are a most awful set of knaves?—Here, at least, is a most intelligible and undeniable position.

Now, on the other hand, let me take our own side of the question, and consider how we ourselves stand relatively to the charge made against us. Catholics, then, hold the mystery of the Incarnation; and the Incarnation is the most stupendous event which ever can take place on earth; and after it and henceforth, I do not see how we can scruple at any miracle on the mere ground of its being unlikely to happen. No miracle can be so great as that which took place in the Holy House of Nazareth; it is indefinitely more difficult to believe than all the miracles of the Breviary, of the Martyrology, of Saints' lives, of legends, of local traditions, put together; and there is the grossest inconsistency on the very face of the matter, for any one so to strain out the gnat and to swallow the camel, as to profess what is inconceivable, yet to protest against what is surely within the limits of intelligible hypothesis. If, through divine grace, we once are able to accept the solemn truth that the Supreme Being was born of a mortal woman, what is there to be imagined which can offend us on the ground of its marvellousness? Thus, you see, it happens that, though First Principles are commonly assumed, not proved, ours in this case

X

admits, if not of proof, yet of recommendation, by means of that fundamental truth which Protestants profess as well as we. When we start with assuming that miracles are not unlikely, we are putting forth a position which lies imbedded, as it were, and involved, in the great revealed fact of the Incarnation.

So much is plain on starting; but more is plain too. Miracles are not only not unlikely, they are positively likely; and for this simple reason, because, for the most part, when God begins He goes on. We conceive that when He first did a miracle, He began a series; what He commenced, He continued: what has been, will be. Surely this is good and clear reasoning. To my own mind, certainly, it is incomparably more difficult to believe that the Divine Being should do one miracle and no more, than that He should do a thousand; that He should do one great miracle only, than that He should do a multitude of less besides. This beautiful world of nature, His own work, He broke its harmony; He broke through His own laws which He had imposed on it; He worked out His purposes, not simply through it, but in violation of it. If He did this only in the lifetime of the Apostles, if He did it but once, eighteen hundred years ago and more, that isolated infringement looks as the mere infringement of a rule: if Divine Wisdom would not leave an infringement, an anomaly, a solecism on His work, He might be expected to introduce a series of miracles, and turn the apparent exception into an additional law of His providence. If the Divine Being does a thing once, He is, judging by human reason, likely to do it again. This surely is common sense. If a beggar gets food at a gentleman's house once, does he not send others thither after him? If you are attacked by thieves once, do you forthwith leave your windows open at night? If an acquaintance were convicted of a fraud, would you let that be the signal for reposing confidence in him, as a man who could not possibly deceive you? Nay, suppose you yourselves were once to see a miracle, would you not feel that experience to be like passing a line? should you, in consequence of it, declare, "I never will believe another if I hear of one?" would it not, on the contrary, predispose you to listen to a new report? would you scoff at it and call it priestcraft for the reason that you had actually seen one with your own eyes? I think you would not; then I ask what is the difference of the argument, whether you have seen one or believe one? You believe the Apostolic miracles, therefore be inclined beforehand to believe later ones. Thus you see, our First Principle, that miracles are not unlikely now, is not at all a strange one in the mouths of those who believe that the Supreme Being came miraculously into this world, miraculously united Himself to man's nature, passed a life of miracles, and then gave His Apostles a greater gift of miracles than He exercised Himself. So far on the principle itself; and now, in the next place, see what comes of it.

This comes of it,—that there are two systems going on in the world, one of nature, and one above nature; and two histories, one of common events, and one of miracles; and each system and each history has its own order. When I hear of the miracle of a Saint, my first feeling would be of the same kind as if it were a report of any natural exploit or event. Supposing, for instance, I heard a report of the death of some public man; it would not startle me, even if I did not at once credit it, for all men must die. Did I read of any great feat of valour, I should believe it, if imputed to Alexander or Cœur de Lion. Did I hear of any act of baseness, I should disbelieve it, if imputed to a friend whom I knew and loved. And so, in like manner, were a miracle reported to me as wrought by a member of Parliament, or a Bishop of the Establishment, or a Wesleyan preacher, I should repudiate the notion: were it referred to a saint, or the relic of a saint, or the intercession of a saint, I should not be startled at it, though I might not at once believe it. And I certainly should be right in this conduct, supposing my First Principle be true. Miracles to the Catholic are facts of history and biography, and nothing else; and they are to be regarded and dealt with as other facts; and as natural facts, under circumstances, do not startle Protestants, so supernatural, under circumstances, do not startle the Catholic.[3] They may or may not have taken place in particular cases; he may be unable to determine which; he may have no distinct evidence; he may suspend his judgment, but he will say, "It is very possible;" he never will say, "I cannot believe it."

[3] Douglas, succeeding Middleton, lays down the sceptical and Protestant First Principle thus: "The history of miracles (to make use of the words of an author, whose authority you will think of some weight) is of a kind totally *different* from that of common events; the one to be *suspected always of course*, without the *strongest* evidence to *confirm* it; the other to be *admitted of course*, without *as strong* reason to *suspect* it," &c.—*Criterion*, p. 26.

Take the history of Alfred: you know his wise, mild, beneficent, yet daring character, and his romantic vicissitudes of fortune. This great king has a number of stories, or, as you may call them, legends, told of him. Do you believe them all? no. Do you, on the other hand, think them incredible? no. Do you call a man a dupe or a blockhead for believing them? no. Do you call an author a knave and a cheat who records them? no. You go into neither extreme, whether of implicit faith or of violent reprobation. You are not so extravagant; you see that they suit his character, they *may* have been; yet this is so romantic, that has so little evidence, a third is so confused in dates or in geography, that you are in matter of fact indisposed towards them. Others are probably true, others certainly. Nor do you force every one to take your own view of particular stories; you and your neighbours think differently about this or that in detail and agree to differ. There is in the Museum at Oxford, a jewel or trinket said to be Alfred's; it is shown to all comers: I never heard the keeper of the Museum accused of hypocrisy or fraud for showing, with Alfred's name appended, what he might or might not himself believe to have belonged to that great king: nor did I ever see any party of strangers, who were looking at it with awe, regarded by any self-complacent bystander with scornful compassion. Yet the relic is not to a certainty Alfred's. The world pays civil honour to it on the probability; we pay religious honour to relics, if so be, on the probability. Is the Tower of London shut against sightseers, because the coats of mail or pikes there may have half legendary tales connected with them?

why then may not the country people come up in joyous companies, singing and piping, to see the Holy Coat at Trèves? There is our Queen again, who is so truly and justly popular; she roves about in the midst of tradition and romance; she scatters myths and legends from her as she goes along; she is a being of poetry, and you might fairly be sceptical whether she had any personal existence. She is always at some beautiful, noble, bounteous work or other, if you trust the papers. She is doing alms-deeds in the Highlands; she meets beggars in her rides at Windsor; she writes verses in albums, or draws sketches, or is mistaken for the housekeeper by some blind old woman, or she runs up a hill, as if she were a child. Who finds fault with these things? he would be a cynic, he would be white-livered, and would have gall for blood, who was not struck with this graceful, touching evidence of the love which her subjects bear her. Who could have the head, even if he had the heart, who could be so cross and peevish, who could be so solemn and perverse, as to say that some of the stories *may* be simple lies, and all of them might have stronger evidence than they carry with them? Do you think she is displeased at them? Why, then, should He, the Great Father, who once walked the earth, look sternly on the unavoidable mistakes of His own subjects and children in their devotion to Him and His? Even granting they mistake some cases in particular, from the infirmity of human nature, and the contingencies of evidence, and fancy there is or has been a miracle here or there when there is not;—though a tradition, attached to a picture, or to a shrine, or to a well, be very doubtful; —though one relic be sometimes mistaken for another, and St. Theodore stands for St. Eugenius, or St. Agathocles;—still, once take into account our First Principle, that He is likely to continue miracles among us, which is as good as the Protestant's, and I do not see why He should feel much displeasure with us on account of this error, or should cease to work wonders in our behalf. In the Protestant's view, indeed, who assumes that miracles never are, our thaumatology is one great falsehood; but that is *his* First Principle, as I have said so often, which he does not prove but assume. If *he*, indeed, upheld *our* system, or *we* held *his* principle, in either case he or we should be impostors; but though we should be partners to a fraud, if we thought like Protestants, we surely are not, because we think like Catholics.

8.

Such, then, is the answer which I make to those who would urge against us the multitude of miracles recorded in our Saints' Lives and devotional works, for many of which there is little evidence, and for some next to none. We think them true in the sense in which Protestants think the details of English history true. When they say that, they do not mean to say there are no mistakes in it, but no mistakes of consequence, none which alter the general course of history. Nor do they mean they are equally sure of every part; for evidence is fuller and better for some things than for others. They do not stake their credit on the truth of Froissart or Sully, they do not pledge themselves for the accuracy of Doddington or Walpole, they do not embrace as an Evangelist, Hume, Sharon Turner, or Macaulay. And yet they do not think it necessary, on the other hand, to commence a religious war against **all our** historical catechisms, and abstracts, and dictionaries, and tales and biographies, through the country; they have no call on them to amend and expurgate books of archeology, antiquities, heraldry, architecture, geography, and statistics, to rewrite our inscriptions, and to establish a censorship on **all new** publications for the time to come. And so as regards the miracles of the Catholic Church; if, indeed, miracles never can occur, then, indeed, impute the narratives to fraud; but till you prove they are not likely, we shall consider the histories which have come down to us true on the whole, though in particular cases they may be exaggerated or unfounded. Where, indeed, they can certainly be proved to be false, **there** we shall be bound to do our best to get rid of them; but till that is clear, we shall be liberal enough to allow others to use their private judgment in their favour, as we use ours in their disparagement. For myself, lest I appear in any way to be shrinking from a determinate judgment on the claims of some of those miracles and relics, which Protestants are so startled at, and to be hiding particular questions in what is vague and general, I will avow distinctly, that, putting out of the question the hypothesis of unknown laws of nature (that is, of the professed miracle being not miraculous), I think it impossible to withstand the evidence which is brought for the liquefaction of the blood of St. Januarius at Naples, and for the motion of the eyes of the pictures of the Madonna in the Roman States. I see no reason to doubt the material of the Lombard crown at Monza; and I do not see why the Holy Coat at Trèves may not have been what it professes to be. I firmly believe that portions of the True

Cross are at Rome and elsewhere, that the Crib of Bethlehem is at Rome, and the bodies of St. Peter and St. Paul also. I believe that at Rome too lies St. Stephen, that St. Matthew lies at Salerno, and St. Andrew at Amalfi. I firmly believe that the relics of the saints are doing innumerable miracles and graces daily, and that it needs only for a Catholic to show devotion to any saint in order to receive special benefits from his intercession. I firmly believe that saints in their life-time have before now raised the dead to life, crossed the sea without vessels, multiplied grain and bread, cured incurable diseases, and superseded the operation of the laws of the universe in a multitude of ways. Many men, when they hear an educated man so speak, will at once impute the avowal to insanity, or to an idiosyncrasy, or to imbecility of mind, or to decrepitude of powers, or to fanaticism, or to hypocrisy. They have a right to say so, if they will; and we have a right to ask them why they do not say it of those who bow down before the Mystery of mysteries, the Divine Incarnation. If they do not believe this, they are not yet Protestants; if they do, let them grant that He who has done the greater may do the less.[4]

9.

And now, Brothers of the Oratory, I have come to the end of a somewhat uninteresting, but a necessary discussion. Your lot is cast in the world; you are not gathered together, as we are, into the home and under the shadow of St. Philip; you mix with men of all opinions. Where you see prejudice, there, indeed, it is no use to argue; prejudice thinks its first

[4] *Vide* Note 2 at the end of the volume.

principles self-evident. It can tell falsehoods to our dishonour by the score, yet suddenly it is so jealous of truth, as to be shocked at legends in honour of the saints. With prejudiced persons then, you will make no way; they will not look the question in the face; if they condescend to listen for a moment to your arguments it is in order to pick holes in them, not to ascertain their drift or to estimate their weight. But there are others of a different stamp of whom I spoke in the opening of this Lecture, candid, amiable minds, who wish to think well of our doctrines and devotions, but stumble at them. When you meet with such, ask them whether they are not taking their own principles and opinions for granted, and whether all they have to say against us is not contained in the proposition with which they start. Entreat them to consider how they know their existing opinions to be true; whether they are innate and necessary; whether they are not local, national, or temporary; whether they have ever spread over the earth, ever held nations together; whether they have ever or often done a great thing. If they say that penances are absurd, or images superstitious, or infallibility impossible, or sacraments mere charms, or a priesthood priestcraft, get them to put their ideas into shape and to tell you their reasons for them. Trace up their philosophy for them, as you have traced up their tradition; the fault lies in the root; every step of it is easy but the first. Perhaps you will make them Catholics by this process; at least you will make them perceive what they believe and what they do not, and will teach them to be more tolerant of a Religion which unhappily they do not see their way to embrace.

LECTURE VIII.

IGNORANCE CONCERNING CATHOLICS THE PROTECTION OF THE PROTESTANT VIEW.

I.

You may have asked yourselves, Brothers of the Oratory, why it was that, in exposing, as I did last week, the shallowness of the philosophy on which our opponents erect their structure of argument against us, I did not take, as my illustration, an instance far more simple and ready to my hand than that to which I actually directed your attention. It was my object, on that occasion, to show that Protestants virtually assume the point in debate between them and us, in any particular controversy, in the very principles with which they set out; that those first principles, for which they offer no proof, involve their conclusions; so that, if we are betrayed into the inadvertence of passing them over without remark, we are forthwith defeated and routed, even before we have begun to move forward to the attack, as might happen to cavalry who manœuvred on a swamp, or to a guerilla force which ventured on the open plain. Protestants and Catholics each have their own ground, and cannot engage on any other; the question in dispute between them is more elementary than men commonly suppose; it relates to the ground itself, on which the battle is legitimately and rightfully to be fought; the first principles assumed in the starting of the controversy determine the issue. Protestants in fact do but say that we are superstitious, because it is superstitious to do as we do; that we are deluded, because it is a delusion to believe what we believe; that we are knaves, because it must be knavery to teach what we teach. A short and pleasant argument, easier even and safer than that extempore and improvisatore mode of fabricating and fabling against us, of which I have said so much in former Lectures; easier and safer, inasmuch as, according to the proverb, "great wits ought to have long memories," when they deal with facts. In arguments about facts, there must be consistency, and speciousness, and proof, and circumstantial evidence; private judgment in short becomes subject to sundry and serious liabilities when it deals with history and testimony, from which it is comparatively free when it expatiates in opinions and views. Now of this high *à priori* mode of deciding the question, the specimen I actually took was the Protestant argument against relics and miracles; and I selected this instance for its own sake, because I wished to bring out what I thought an important truth as regarded them; but a more obvious instance certainly would have been the surprising obtuseness, for I can use no other word, with which the Protestant Rule of Faith, which Catholics disown, is so often obtruded on us, as a necessary basis of discussion, which it is thought absurd and self-destructive not to accept, in any controversy about doctrine.

All the world knows that Catholics hold that the Apostles made over the Divine Revelation to the generation after them, not only in writing, but by word of mouth, and in the ritual of the Church. We consider that the New Testament is not the whole of what they left us; that they left us a number of doctrines, not in writing at all, but living in the minds and mouths of the faithful; Protestants deny this. They have a right to deny it; but they have no right to assume their denial to be true without proof, and to use it as self-evident, and to triumph over us as beaten, merely because we will not admit it. Yet this they actually do; can anything be more preposterous? however, they do this as innocently and naturally as if it were the most logical of processes, and the fairest and most unexceptionable of proceedings. For instance there was a country gentleman in this neighbourhood in the course of last year, who, having made some essays in theology among his tenantry in his walks over his estate, challenged me to prove some point, I am not clear what, but I think it was the infallibility of the Holy See, or of the Church. Were my time my own, I should never shrink from any controversy, having the experience of twenty years, that the more Catholicism and its doctrines are sifted, the more distinct and luminous will its truth ever come out into view; and in the instance in question I did not decline the invitation. However, it soon turned out that it was a new idea to the gentleman in question, that I was not bound to prove the point in debate simply by Scripture; he considered that Scripture was to be the sole basis of the discussion. This was quite another thing. For myself, I firmly believe that in Scripture the Catholic doctrine on the subject *is* contained; but had I accepted this gratuitous and officious proposition, you see I should have been simply recognising a Protestant principle, which I disown. He would not controvert with me at all, unless I subscribed to a doctrine which I believe to be, not only a dangerous, but an absurd error; and, because I would not allow him to assume what it was his business to prove, before he brought it forward, and because I challenged him to prove that Scripture was, as he assumed, the Rule of Faith, he turned away as happy and self-satisfied as if he had gained a victory. That all truth is contained in Scripture was his first principle; he thought none but an idiot could doubt it; none but a Jesuit could deny it; he thought it axiomatic; he thought that to offer proof was even a profanation of so self-evident a point, and that to demand it was a *reductio ad absurdum* of the person demanding;—but this, I repeat, was no extraordinary instance of Protestant argumentation; it occurs every other day.

The instance in controversy, to which I have been alluding, leads by no very difficult nor circuitous transition to the subject to which I mean to devote the present Lecture. Let it be observed, that the fallacy involved in the Protestant Rule of Faith is this,—that its upholders fancy, most unnaturally, that the accidental and occasional writings of an Apostle convey to them of necessity his whole mind. It does not occur to them to ask themselves, whether, as he has in part committed his teaching to writing so possibly he may not have expressed it in part through other channels also. Very different this from their mode of acting in matters of this world, in which nothing are they more distrustful of, or discontented with, than mere letter-writing, when they would arrive at the real state of a case in which they are interested. When a government, or the proprietors of a newspaper, would gain accurate information on any subject, they send some one to the spot, to see with his eyes. When a man of business would bring a negotiation to a safe and satisfactory conclusion, he exclaims that letters are endless, and forthwith despatches a confidential person to transact the matter with the parties with whom he is treating. We know how unwilling heads of families are to take servants by written characters, considering that writing is not minute and real enough for their purpose. Writing, of course, has special advantages, but it has its defects; and other methods of information compensate for them. It must be recollected, too, as regards the New Testament, that it is not a technical document, like an act of Parliament, or a legal instrument, but is made up of various portions, exhibiting, more or less, the free and flowing course of thought of their respective writers. It is not worded with the scientific precision of a formal treatise, a creed, or a last will and testament. Now, works written in this natural style are especially liable to receive an interpretation, and to make an impression, not in correspondence with the writer's intention, but according to the private principles and feelings of the reader. The imagination draws the unknown or absent author in lineaments altogether different from the original. Did we suddenly see St. Peter or St.

Paul, and hear him converse, most of us would not recognise, or even suspect him to be the Apostle. How surprised we sometimes are by the sight of those of whom we have often heard speak, or whose writings we have often read! We cannot believe we have the living author before us. Hence it is common to hear it said in favour of intemperate partisans by their friends, "If you knew him, you really would like him; he is so different from his mode of writing or speaking"; others, on the other hand, meet with a person whom they have long admired through the medium of his works, and are quite mortified and annoyed that they like his conversation and his manners so little.

Unless my memory fails me of what I read years ago, a well-known authoress, lately deceased, supplies in her tales one or two instances in point. I recollect the description of an old-fashioned, straightforward East Indian, who had for years corresponded with the widow of a friend in England, and from her letters had conceived a high opinion of her good sense and propriety of feeling. Then, as the story goes on to tell, he comes back to England, becomes acquainted with her, and, to his disappointment, is gradually made aware that she is nothing else than a worldly, heartless, and manœuvring woman. The same writer draws elsewhere a very young lady, who, in a spirit of romance, has carried on a correspondence with another female whom she never saw; on the strength of which, from a conviction of the sympathy which must exist between them, she runs from home to join her, with the view of retiring with her for life to some secluded valley in Wales; but is shocked to find, on meeting her, that after all she is vulgar, unattractive, and middle-aged. Were it necessary, numberless instances might be given to the purpose; of mistakes, too, of every kind; of persons, when seen, turning out different from their writings, for the better as well as for the worse, or neither for the better nor the worse, but still so different as to surprise us and make us muse; different in opinion, or in principle, or in conduct, or in impression and effect. And thus Scripture, in like manner, though written under a supernatural guidance, is, from the nature of the case, from the defect of human language, and the infirmity of the recipient, unable by itself to convey the real mind of its writers to all who read it. Instead of its forcing its meaning upon the reader, the reader forces his own meaning upon it, colours it with his own thoughts and distorts it to his own purposes; so that something is evidently needed besides it, such as the teaching of the Church, to protect it from the false private judgment of the individual. And if this be true when the New Testament, as a whole, is contemplated, how much more certainly will it take place when Protestants contract their reading professedly to only a part of it, as to St. Paul's Epistles; and then again out of St. Paul, select the two Epistles to the Romans and Galatians; and still further, as is so common, confine themselves to one or two sentences, which constitute practically the whole of the Protestant written word! Why, of course, it is very easy to put what sense they please on one or two verses; and thus the Religion of the Apostles may come in the event to mean anything or nothing.

2.

Here, then, we are arrived at the subject on which I mean to remark this evening. Protestants judge of the Apostles' doctrine by "texts," as they are commonly called, taken from Scripture, and nothing more; and they judge of our doctrine too by "texts" taken from our writings, and nothing more. Picked verses, bits torn from the context, half sentences, are the warrant of the Protestant Idea, of what is Apostolic truth, on the one hand, and, on the other, of what is Catholic falsehood. As they have their chips and fragments of St. Paul and St. John, so have they their chips and fragments of Suarez and Bellarmine; and out of the former they make to themselves their own Christian religion, and out of the latter our Antichristian superstition. They do not ask themselves sincerely, as a matter of fact and history, *What* did the Apostles teach then? nor do they ask sincerely, and as a matter of fact, *What* do Catholics teach now? they judge of the Apostles and they judge of us by scraps, and on these scraps they exercise their private judgment,—that is, their Prejudice, as I described two Lectures back, and their Assumed Principles, as I described in my foregoing Lecture; and the process ends in their bringing forth, out of their scraps from the Apostles, what they call "Scriptural Religion," and out of their scraps from our theologians, what they call Popery.

The first Christians were a living body; they were thousands of zealous, energetic men, who preached, disputed, catechized, and conversed from year's end to year's end. They spoke by innumerable tongues, with one heart and one soul, all saying the same thing; all this multitudinous testimony about the truths of Revelation, Protestants narrow down into one or two meagre sentences, which at their own will and pleasure they select from St. Paul, and at their own will and pleasure they explain, and call the Gospel. They do just the same thing with us; Catholics, at least, have a lively illustration and evidence of the absurdity of Protestant private judgment as exercised on the Apostolic writings, in the visible fact of its absurdity as exercised on themselves. They, as their forefathers, the first Christians, are a living body; they, too, preach, dispute, catechize, converse with innumerable tongues, saying the same thing as our adversaries confess, all over the earth. Well, then, you would think the obvious way was, if they would know what we really teach, to come and ask us, to talk with us, to try to enter into our views, and to attend to our teaching. Not at all; they do not dream of doing so; they take their "texts;" they have got their cut-and-dried specimens from our divines, which the Protestant Tradition hands down from generation to generation; and, as by the aid of their verses from Scripture, they think they understand the Gospel better than the first Christians, so, by the help of these choice extracts from our works, they think they understand our doctrine better than we do ourselves. They will not allow us to explain our own books. So sure are they of their knowledge, and so superior to us, that they have no difficulty in setting us right, and in accounting for our contradicting them. Sometimes Catholics are "evasive and shuffling," which, of course, will explain everything;

sometimes they simply "have never been told what their creed really is;" the priest keeps it from them, and cheats them; as yet, too, perhaps they are "recent converts," and do not know the actual state of things, though they will know in time. Thus Protestants judge us by their "texts;" and by "texts" I do not mean only passages from our writers, but all those samples of whatever kind, historical, ecclesiastical, biographical, or political, carefully prepared, improved, and finished off by successive artists for the occasion, which they think so much more worthy of credit and reliance as to facts, than us and our word, who are in the very communion to which those texts relate. Some good personal knowledge of us, and intercourse with us, not in the way of controversy or criticism, but what is prior—viz., in the way of sincere inquiry, in order to ascertain how things really lie, such knowledge and intercourse would be worth all the conclusions, however elaborate and subtle, from rumours, false witnessings, suspicions, romantic scenes, morsels of history, morsels of theology, morsels of our miraculous legends, morsels of our devotional writers, morsels from our individual members, whether unlearned or intemperate, which are the "text" of the traditional Protestant view against us. This, then, is the last of the causes, which in the course of these Lectures I shall assign, and on which this evening I shall insist, by way of accounting for the hatred and contempt shown towards the Catholics of England by their fellow-countrymen— viz., that the Catholics of England, as a body, are not personally known.

3.

I have already observed, that in matters of this world, when a man would really get information on a subject, he eschews reports, and mistrusts understandings, and betakes himself to head-quarters. The best letters and travels about a foreign people are tame and dead compared with the view he gains by residence among them; and when that has continued for a sufficient time, he perceives how unreal were even those first impressions, which, on his arriving, were made upon him by the successive accidents of the hour. Knowledge thus obtained cannot be communicated to others; it is imbibed and appropriated by the mind as a personal possession; an idea of the people among whom he lives is set up within him; he may like them or not, but his perception is real, and, if any one questions it, he need but appeal to the circumstance of his long residence in the country, and say he has a right to an opinion, which, nevertheless, he can perhaps but poorly and partially defend. He can but give his testimony, and must be believed on his reputation. And surely, if he has a fair name for powers of observation and good sense, he may be believed without proof. He has witnessed what others argue about. He has contemplated the national character in life and in action, as it is brought out in its opinions, aims, sentiments, and dispositions in the course of the day and the year; he has heard the words, seen the deeds, watched the manners, breathed the atmosphere, and so caught the true idea of the people;—in other words, he has mastered their Tradition. This is what Catholics mean by Tradition, and why they go so much by it. It does not *prove* our doctrines to the man in question, but it will tell him, in a way no other informant can tell him, *what* our doctrines are. It has a substance and a reality peculiar to itself; for it is not a sample or specimen of us merely, but it is we, our thinking, speaking, acting self; our principles, our judgments, our proceedings. What we hold, what we do not hold, what we like, what we hate, cannot all be written down, whether by us or by others; you can have no daguerreotype of intellect, affection, and will; at best you have but a few bold strokes recorded for the benefit of others, according to the skill of the individual artist. Those who write books about a people or a school of men are hardly more than extempore sketchers; or they paint from memory; if you would have the real thing, what the men are, what they think, what they do, close your books, take a ticket by the first train, cross the Channel, plunge in among them, drink them in. This is what is called painting from the life; and what is here called life the Catholic calls Tradition, which eclipses and supersedes, when and where it can be had, the amplest collection of "texts" and extracts about our doctrine and polity which was ever put together by the ablest of compilers.

Now let me quote some words of my own on this subject, when I was a Protestant. As they are written in controversy with Catholics, they are so much more to my present purpose; especially as I did not when I wrote them, see their bearing on the point I am now insisting on. The passage is long, but its appositeness may excuse it.

"We hear it said," I then observed, "that they [the

Catholics] go by Tradition; and we fancy in consequence that there are a *certain definite number of statements ready framed and compiled*, which they profess to have received from the Apostles. One may hear the question sometimes asked, for instance, *where* their professed Traditions are to be found, whether there is any *collection* of them, and whether they are printed and published. Now, though they would allow that the Traditions of the Church are, in fact, contained in the writings of her Doctors, still this question proceeds on somewhat of a misconception of their real theory, which seems to be as follows :—By tradition they mean the whole system of faith and ordinances, which they have received from the generation before them, and that generation again from the generation before itself. And in this sense undoubtedly we all go by Tradition in matters of this world. Where is the corporation, society, or fraternity of any kind, but has certain received rules and understood practices, which are nowhere put down in writing? How often do we hear it said, that this or that person has 'acted unusually;' that so and so 'was never done before;' that it is 'against rule,' and the like; and then, perhaps, to avoid the inconvenience of such irregularity in future, what was before a tacit engagement is turned into a formal and explicit order or principle. The need of a regulation must be discovered before it is supplied; and the virtual transgression of it goes before its imposition. At this very time, great part of the law of the land is administered under the sanction of such a Tradition: it is not contained in any formal or authoritative code, it depends on custom or precedent. There is no explicit written law, for instance, simply declaring murder to be a capital offence, unless, indeed, we have recourse to the divine command in the ninth chapter of the book of Genesis. Murderers are hanged by *custom*. Such as this is the Tradition of the Church; Tradition is uniform custom. . It is silent, but it lives. It is silent like the rapids of a river, before the rocks intercept it. It is the Church's . . habit of opinion and feeling, which she reflects upon, masters and expresses, according to the emergency. We see, then, the mistake of asking for a complete collection of the Roman traditions; as well might we ask for a collection of a man's tastes and opinions on a given subject. Tradition in its fulness is necessarily unwritten; it is the mode in which a society has felt or acted, during a certain period, and it cannot be circumscribed, any more than a man's countenance and manner can be conveyed to strangers in any set of propositions."[1]

I see nothing to alter in these remarks, written many years before I became a Catholic; and you see with what force they tell against the system of judging any body of men by extracts, passages, specimens, and sayings—nay, even by their documents, if these are taken by us to be sufficient informants, instead of our studying the living body itself. For instance, there has been lately a good deal of surprise expressed in some quarters, though it is not likely to have attracted your attention, that the infallibility of the Church has never been decreed, whether in General Council or by other ecclesiastical authority, to be a Catholic doctrine. This has been put about as a discovery, and an important one: and Catholics have been triumphantly asked, how it is that the tenet which is at the bottom of their whole

[1] Prophetical Office, Lecture I. pp. 38—41.

system is nowhere set down in writing and propounded for belief. But, in truth, there is neither novelty nor importance in the remark: on the one hand, it has been made again and again;[2] and on the other, whenever it has been urged against us, it has been simply urged from ignorance, as I have already shown you, of the real state of the case. Is nothing true but what has been written down? on the contrary, the whole Catholic truth has ever lived, and only lived, in the hearts and on the tongues of the Catholic people; and, while it is one mistake in the objectors in question, to think that they know the Catholic faith, it is a second, to think that they can teach it to Catholics. Which party is more likely to be in possession of what Catholics believe, they or we? There is a maxim commonly accepted, that "Every one is to be trusted in his own art;" from which it would follow, that, as Frenchmen are the best masters of French, and pilots the best steersmen on the river, Catholics ought to know Catholicism better than other men. Military men do not show particular respect for the criticisms of civilians. As for amateur physicians, I suppose most of us would rather be doctored by the village nurse, who blindly goes by tradition and teaching, than by a clever person, who, among other things, has dabbled in family vade-mecums and materia-medicas, abounds in theories and views, and has a taste for experiments. Again, I have heard able men, who were not lawyers, impugn the institution of Trial by Jury; and the answer to them has been, "You are not learned in the law, it works

---

[2] *E.g.* By myself, though not in objection, in the work above quoted, Lecture X. p. 293. By Cressy, in Dr. Hammond's Works, vol. ii. p. 635, two centuries ago.

well." In like manner, a great statesman says of Protestant Clergymen, that they "understand least and take the worst measure of human affairs, of all mankind that can write and read." Yet any one is thought qualified to attack or to instruct a Catholic in matters of his religion; a country gentleman, a navy captain, a half-pay officer, with time on his hands, never having seen a Catholic, or a Catholic ceremonial, or a Catholic treatise, in his life, is competent, by means of one or two periodicals and tracts, and a set of Protestant extracts against Popery, to teach the Pope in his own religion, and refute a Council.

4.

Suarez, Vasquez, de Lugo, Lambertini, St. Thomas, St. Buonaventura, a goodly succession of folios on our shelves! You would think the doctrine would take some time to master, which has occupied the lives and elicited the genius of some of the greatest masters of thought whom the world has known. Our Protestant, however, is sure there must be very little in such works, because they are so voluminous. He has not studied our doctrines, he has not learned our terms; he calls our theological language jargon, and he thinks the whole matter lies in a nutshell. He is ever mistaking one thing for another, and thinks it does not signify Ignorance in his case is the mother, not certainly of devotion, but of inconceivable conceit and preternatural injustice. If he is to attack or reply, up he takes the first specimen or sample of our doctrine, which the Reformation Society has provided, some dreadful sentiment of the Jesuit Bellarmine, or the Schoolman Scotus. He has never turned to the passage in the original work, never verified it, never consulted the context, never construed its wording; he blindly puts his own sense upon it, or the "authorized version" given to it by the Society in question, and boldly presents it to the British public, which is forthwith just as much shocked at it as he is. Now, anything is startling and grotesque, if taken out of its place, and surveyed without reference to the whole to which it belongs. The perfection of the parts lies in their subserviency to a whole; and they often have no meaning except in their bearing upon each other. How can you tell whether a thing is good or bad, unless you know what it is intended for? Protestants, however, separate our statements from their occasions and their objects, and then ask what in the world can be their meaning or their use. This is evident to any one whose intellect is not fettered to his particular party, and who does but take the trouble to consider Catholic doctrines, not as they stand in Reformation Tracts, torn up by the roots or planted head-downwards, but as they are found in our own gardens. I am tempted to quote a passage on the subject from a recent Review, which is as far as possible from showing any leaning to Catholicism. You will see how fully an impartial writer, neither Catholic nor Protestant, bears me out in what I have said:—

"A true British Protestant," he says, "whose notions of 'Popery' are limited to what he hears from an Evangelical curate, or has seen at the opening of a Jesuit church, looks on the whole system as an obsolete mummery, and no more believes that men of sense can seriously adopt it, than that they will be converted to the practice of eating their dinner with a Chinaman's chopsticks instead of the knife and fork. . . . . Few even of educated Englishmen have any suspicion of the depth and solidity of the Catholic dogma, its wide and various adaptation to wants ineffaceable from the human heart, its wonderful fusion of the supernatural into the natural life, its vast resources for a powerful hold upon the conscience. . . . . Into this interior view, however, the popular polemics neither give, nor have the slightest insight. . . . . It is not among the ignorant and vulgar, but among the intellectual and imaginative; not by appeals to the senses in worship, but by consistency and subtlety of thought, that in our days converts will be made to the ancient Church. . . . . When a thoughtful man, accustomed to defer to historical authority, and competent to estimate moral theories as a whole, is led to penetrate beneath the surface, he is unprepared for the sight of so much speculative grandeur; and if he has been a mere Anglican or Lutheran, is perhaps astonished into the conclusion that the elder system has the advantage in philosophy and antiquity alike."[3]

You see how entirely this able writer, with no sort of belief in Catholicism, justifies what I have been saying. Fragments, extracts, specimens, convey no idea to the world of what we are; he who wishes to know us must condescend to study us. The Catholic doctrine is after all too great to be comfortably accommodated in a Protestant nutshell; it cannot be surveyed at a glance, or refuted by a syllogism:—and what this author says of Catholic doctrine applies to Catholic devotion also. Last week I made some observations on our miracles; and I then said that they would be scorned and rejected, or not, according as this or that

[3] Westminster Review, Jan. 1851.

First Principle concerning them was taken for granted but now I am going to advance a step further. I really think then, that, even putting aside First Principles, no one can read the lives of certain of our Saints, as St. Francis Xavier, or St. Philip Neri, with seriousness and attention, without rising up from the perusal,—I do not say converted to Catholicism (that is a distinct matter, which I have kept apart throughout these Lectures),— but indisposed to renew the ridicule and scorn in which he has indulged previously. One isolated miracle looks strange, but many interpret each other: this or that, separated from the system of which they are a part, may be perfectly incredible; but when they are viewed as portions of a whole, they press upon the inquirer a feeling, I do not say absolutely of conviction, but at least of wonder, of perplexity, and almost of awe. When you consider the vast number which are recorded, for instance, in the Life of St. Philip, their variety, their exuberance in a short space of time, the circumstantial exactness with which they are recorded, the diversity and multitude of witnesses and attestations which occur in the course of the narrative, the thought will possess you, even though you are not yet able to receive them, that after all fraud or credulity is no sufficient account of them. No skill could invent so many, so rapidly, so consistently, and so naturally; and you are sensible, and you confess, that, whatever be the truth of the matter, you have not got to the bottom of it. You have ceased to contemn, you have learned to respect.

5.

And so again I would say of any book which lets you into the private life of personages who have had any great deal to do with the government of the Church; which brings you, so to say behind the scenes, where all pretence is impossible, and where men appear what they are: it is simply impossible, or at least it would be as good as a miracle, for any one to study such works, and still consider that the Pope was the man of sin, and the Mother of Saints a Jezebel. You see that Popes and Cardinals and Prelates are not griffins and wiverns, but men; good men, or bad men, or neither one nor the other, as the case may be; bold men, or weak men, worldly men or unworldly, but still men. They have human feelings, human affections, human virtues, human anxieties, human hopes and joys, whatever higher than mere human excellence a Catholic of course would ascribe to them. They are no longer, as before, the wild beasts, or the frogs, or the locusts, or the plagues of the Apocalypse; such a notion, if you have ever entertained it, is gone for ever. You feel it to have been a ridiculous illusion, and you laugh at it. For instance, I would take such a book as Cardinal Pacca's Memoirs of Pope Pius the VIIth's captivity. Here is a book of facts: here is a narrative, simple and natural. It does not give you the history of an absolute hero or of a saint; but of a good, religious, holy man, who would have rather died any moment than offend God; who had an overpowering sense of his responsibility, and a diffidence in his own judgment which made him sometimes err in his line of conduct. Here, too, is vividly brought out before you what we mean by Papal infallibility, or rather what we do not mean by it: you see how the Pope was open to any mistake, as others may be, in his own person, true as it is, that whenever he spoke *ex cathedrâ* on subjects of revealed truth, he spoke as its divinely-ordained expounder. It is difficult to bring this home to you by any mere extracts from such a work; and I shall be perhaps falling into the very fault I am exposing if I attempt to do so; yet I cannot refrain asking you candidly, whether passages such as the following can be said to fit in with the received Protestant Tradition of the Pope, as a sort of diabolical automaton, spouting out sin and wickedness by the necessity of his nature.

When Pope Pius and Cardinal Pacca were carried off by the French from Rome, as they sat in the carriage, "The Pope," says the Cardinal, "a few minutes afterwards, asked me whether I had with me any money: to which I replied, 'Your holiness saw that I was arrested in your own apartments, so that I have had no opportunity of providing myself.' We then both of us drew forth our purses, and, notwithstanding the state of affliction we were in at being thus torn away from Rome, and all that was dear to us, we could hardly compose our countenances on finding the contents of each purse to consist, in that of the Pope of one papetto (about 10d.), and in mine three grossi (7$\frac{1}{2}d$.). Thus the Sovereign of Rome and his Prime Minister set forth upon their journey, literally, without figure of speech or metaphor, in true Apostolic style, conformable with the precept of our Saviour addressed to His disciples. 'Take nothing for your journey, neither staves, nor scrip, neither bread, neither money; neither have two coats apiece.' We were without eatables, and we had no clothes except those we wore, not even a shirt; and the habits, such as they were, were most inconvenient for travelling. .... With regard to money, we had precisely thirty-five baiocchi (halfpence) between us. The Pope, extending his hand, showed his papetto to General Radet, saying at the same time, 'Look here; this is all I possess, all that remains of my principality.'"⁴

Or take again the account of the Pontiff's conduct after having been betrayed into signing the unhappy Concordat with Napoleon. "The Pope, so long as the Emperor remained at Fontainebleau, manifested no outward appearance of the feelings that agitated his heart with regard to what had happened; but so soon as Napoleon was gone, he fell into a state of profound despondency, and was attacked by fever. Conversing with the Cardinals . . . and discussing the subject of the articles to which he had just affixed his signature, he at once saw, by the undisguised expression of their countenances, the fatal consequences likely to be the fruit of that ill-advised deed, and became so horror-struck and afflicted in consequence, that for several days he abstained from the celebration of the holy sacrifice, under the impression that he had acted unworthily. .... Perceiving the general disapprobation, and, as it were, shudder of the public mind among all religious, well-conducted persons, he fell into that hopeless state of deep melancholy, which I before attempted to describe, on the occasion of my arrival at Fontainebleau."⁵ "At first sight of the Holy Father, I was thoroughly shocked and astonished to see how pale and emaciated he had become, how his body was bent, how his eyes were fixed and sunk in his head, and how he looked at me

⁴ Head's Pacca, vol. i. p. 157. ⁵ Ibid. vol. ii. p. 143.

with, as it were, the glare of a man grown stupid. . . . The solitude and silence of the place, the expression of sadness that appeared on every countenance, added to the recent spectacle of profound grief I had witnessed in the person of the Pope, and, above all, the unexpectedly cold reception I had experienced from his Holiness, occasioned me a degree of surprise, and a sorrowful compression of heart, that it is far more easy for an indifferent person to imagine than for myself to describe. . . He was . . overwhelmed by a depression of spirits the most profound, so much so, that in the course of speaking to me of what had happened, he frequently broke forth in the most plaintive ejaculations, saying, among many other similarly interjectional expressions, that the thought of what had been done tormented him continually, that he could not get it out of his mind, that he could neither rest by day nor sleep by night; that he could not eat more than barely sufficient to sustain life."[6]

Then observe the difference after he had retracted the deed which distressed him so much, though at the very time he was anticipating the utmost fury of Napoleon in consequence, whose prisoner he was. "There suddenly appeared in his person and countenance an unexpected alteration. Previously, the profound grief in which, as I have before stated, he was continually immersed, was consuming him day by day, and was deeply imprinted on his features, which now, on the contrary, became all at once serene, and, as he gradually recovered his usual gaiety of spirits, were occasionally animated by a smile. Neither did he any longer complain of loss of appe-

[6] Head's Pacca, vol. i. p. 406.

tite, or of the inquietude and agitation that every night, for a considerable time before, had interrupted his repose."[7]

These passages put one in mind of the beautiful legend contained in the Breviary of a far greater fault, the fault of Pope Marcellinus. "In the monstrous Diocletian persecution," says the Lesson, "Marcellinus, overcome with terror, sacrificed to the idols of the gods; for which sin he soon conceived so great repentance, that he came in sackcloth to Sinuessa, to a full council of Bishops, where, with abundant tears, he openly confessed his crime. Whom, however, none dare condemn, but all with one voice cried out, 'Thy own mouth, not our judgment, be thy judge, for the first See is judged by none. Peter, too, by a like infirmity of mind, failed, and by like tears obtained pardon from God.' Then he returned to Rome, went to the Emperor, severely reproached him for tempting him to that impiety, and with three others was beheaded."

Popes, then, though they are infallible in their office, as Prophets and Vicars of the Most High, and though they have generally been men of holy life, and many of them actually saints, have the trials, and incur the risks of other men. Our doctrine of infallibility means something very different from what Protestants think it means. And so again, all the inconsistencies which they think they find in what we teach of the sanctity of the Priesthood compared with the actual conduct of a portion of the members of it, would vanish, if they understood that a priest, in a Catholic sense, as in St. Paul's sense, is one "who can have compassion on the ignorant, and on them that err, *for that he himself also*

[7] Head's Pacca, vol. ii. p. 187.

is encompassed with infirmity." Yet, strange to say, so little are they aware of our real doctrine on the subject, that even since these Lectures began, it has been said to me in reference to them in print, "A vulgar error in your Church is, that the Priests are so divinely protected that one of them can hardly err, can hardly sin. This notion is now at an end, as far as you are concerned." Most marvellous! This writer's idea, and the idea of most Protestants is, that we profess that all Priests are angels, but that really they are all devils. No, neither the one nor the other; if these Protestants came to us and asked, they would find that we taught a far different doctrine—viz., that Priests were mortal men, who were intrusted with high gifts for the good of the people, that they might err as other men, that they would fall if they were not watchful, that in various times and places large numbers had fallen, so much so, that the Priesthood of whole countries had before now apostatized, as happened in great measure in England three centuries ago, and that at all times there was a certain remnant scattered about of priests who did not live up to their faith and their profession; still that, on the whole, they had been, as a body, the salt of the earth and the light of the world, through the power of divine grace, and that thus, in spite of the frailty of human nature, they had fulfilled the blessed purposes of their institution.

But not in one or two points merely, but in everything we think and say and do, as Catholics, were we but known, what a reformation would there not at once follow in the national mind in respect to us! British fair dealing and good sense would then recover their supremacy; and Maria Monks and Teodores would find their occupation gone. We should hear no more of the laity being led blindfold, of their being forced to digest impossibilities under menace of perdition, of their struggles to get loose continually overmastered by their superstition, and of their heart having no part in their profession. The spectres of tyranny, hypocrisy, and fraud would flit away with the morning light. There would be no more dread of being burned alive by Papists, or of the gutters overflowing with Protestant blood. Dungeons, racks, pulleys, and quick-lime would be like the leavings of a yesterday's revel. Nor would the political aims and plots and intrigues, so readily imputed to us, seem more substantial; and though I suppose, there is lying, and littleness, and overreaching, and rivalry, to be found among us as among other sons of Adam, yet the notion that we monopolized these vile qualities, or had more than our share of them, would be an exploded superstition. This indeed would be a short and easy way, not of making Protestants Catholics, but of reversing their ridiculous dreams about us,—I mean, if they actually saw what they so interminably argue about. But it is not to be:—first comes in the way that very love of arguing and of having an opinion, to which my last words have alluded. Men would be sorry indeed that the controversy should be taken from the region of argument and transferred to that of fact. They like to think as they please; and as they would by no means welcome St. Paul, did he come from heaven to instruct them in the actual meaning of his "texts" in Romans iii. or Galatians ii., so they would think it a hardship to be told that they must not go on maintaining and proving, that we were really what their eyes then would testify we were not. And then, too, dear scandal and romancing put in their claim ; how would the world go on, and whence would come its staple food and its cheap luxuries, if Catholicism were taken from the market? Why it would be like the cotton crop failing, or a new tax put upon tea. And then, too, comes prejudice, "like the horseleech, crying, Give, give : " how is prejudice to exist without Catholic iniquities and enormities? prejudice, which could not fast for a day, which would be in torment inexpressible, and call it Popish persecution, to be kept on this sort of meagre for a Lent, and would shake down Queen and Parliament with the violence of its convulsions, rather than it should never suck a Catholic's sweet bones and drink his blood any more.

Prejudice and hatred, political party, animosities of race and country, love of gossip and scandal, private judgments, resentments, sensitive jealousies, these, and a number of bad principles besides, extending through the country, present an almost insuperable obstacle to our obtaining a fair hearing and receiving a careful examination. There are other feelings, too, not wrong, as I would trust, in which before now I have participated myself, but equally drawing a *cordon* between Catholics and the rest of the population. One, for instance, is the motive frequently influencing those who really feel a great drawing towards the Catholic Church, though they are unable to accept her doctrines ; and who, wishing to act, not by affection or liking or fancy, but by reason, are led to dread lest the impulses of love, gratitude, admiration, and devotion which they feel within them, should overcome in their hearts the claims of truth and justice, and decide the matter peremptorily for them, if they subjected themselves to an intercourse with Catholics. And another consideration weighs with such Protestants as are in a responsible situation in their own communion, or are its ministers and functionaries. These persons feel that while they hold office in a body which is at war with Catholics, they are as little at liberty to hold friendly intercourse with them, even with the open avowal of their differing from them in serious matters, as an English officer or a member of Parliament may lawfully correspond with the French Government during a time of hostilities. These various motives, and others besides, better and worse, are, I repeat, almost an insuperable barrier in the way of any real and familiar intercourse between Protestants and ourselves : and they act, in consequence, as the means of perpetuating what may be considered the chief negative cause, and the simplest explanation of the absurdities so commonly entertained about us by all classes of society. Personal intercourse, then, being practically just as much out of the question with us, as with the Apostles themselves or the Jewish prophets, Protestantism has nothing left for it, when it would argue about us, but to have recourse, as in the case of Scripture, to its "texts," its chips, shavings, brickbats, potsherds, and other odds and ends of the Heavenly City, which form the authenticated and ticketed specimens of what the Catholic Religion is in its great national Museum.

6.

I am complaining of nothing which I do not myself wish to avoid in dealing with my opponents. I wish them to be judged by their traditions; and in these Lectures I have steadily kept in view the Elizabethan Tradition, and wished to consider it the centre and the life of all they say and do. If I select their words or their acts, I wish to throw myself into them, and determine what they mean by the light of this informing principle. And I have means of doing so which many others have not, having been a Protestant myself. I have stood on their ground; and would always aim at handling their arguments, not as so many dead words, but as the words of a speaker in a particular state of mind, which must be experienced, or witnessed, or explored, if it is to be understood. Calvin, for instance, somewhere calls his own doctrine, that souls are lost without their own free will by the necessity of divine predestination, horrible; at least, so he is said to do, for I do not know his writings myself. Now I conceive he never can really say this; I conceive he uses the Latin word in the sense of fearful or awful, and that to make him say "horrible" is the mere unfairness of some Lutheran adversary, who will not enter into his meaning. This is to go by the letter, not by the spirit; by the text, not by the tradition. The lawyers, again, as I noticed in my first Lecture, speak of the "Omnipotence of Parliament;" I never will be so unjust to them as to take them literally. I am perfectly sure that it never entered into the head of any Speaker, or Prime Minister, or Serjeant-at-arms, to claim any superhuman prerogative for the Two Houses. Those officials all feel intensely, I am sure, that they are but feeble and fallible creatures, and would laugh at any one who shuddered at their use of a phrase which has a parliamentary sense as well as a theological. Now I only claim to be heard in turn with the same candour which I exemplify so fully, when I speak myself of the omnipotence of the Blessed Virgin. When such an expression is used by a Catholic, he would be as indignant as a member of Parliament to find it perverted by an enemy from the innocent sense in which he used it. Parliament is omnipotent, as having the power to do what it will, not in France, or in Germany, or in Russia, much less all over the earth, much less in heaven, but within the United Kingdom; and in like manner the Blessed Virgin is called omnipotent, as being able to gain from God what she desires by the medium of prayer. Prayer is regarded as omnipotent in Scripture, and she in consequence, as being the chief intercessor among creatures, is considered omnipotent too. And the same remark applies to a great number of other words in Catholic theology. When the Church is called "holy," it is not meant that her authorities are always good men, though nothing is more common with Protestants than so to suppose. "Worship," again, is another term which is commonly misunderstood; "indulgence" is another; "merit," "intention," "scandal," "religion," "obedience," all have their own senses, which our opponents must learn from Catholics, and cannot well find out for themselves.

I have a good old woman in my eye, who, to the great amusement of all hearers, goes about saying that her priest has given her "absolution for a week;" what a horrid story for Exeter Hall! Here is a poor creature, with one foot in the grave, who is actually assured by her confessor, doubtless for some due pecuniary consideration, that for a week to come she may commit any sort of enormity to which she is inclined with impunity. Absolution for a week! then it seems, she has discounted, if I may so speak, her prospective confessions, and may lie, thieve, drink, and swear for a whole seven days with a clear conscience! But now what does she really mean? I defy a Protestant to get the meaning out of the words, even if he wished to be fair; he must come to us for it. She means, then, that she has leave to communicate for a week to come, on her usual days of communion, whatever be their number, without coming to confession before each day. But how can her words have this meaning? in this way, as you know, my Brothers, well. Catholics are not bound to come to confession before communion, unless they have committed some greater sin; nor are they commonly advised by their priests to come every time, though they often do so. When, then, she said she had got absolution for a week, she meant to express, that the priest had told her that her once going to confession would be often enough, for all her days of communion, during a week to come, supposing (which was not to be expected in so pious a woman) she fell into no great sin. You see how many words it takes duly to unfold the meaning of one familiar expression.

This instance of Popish profligacy has not yet got into the Protestant prints; but there are others, not unlike it, which before now have made a great noise in the world. I will give you an instance of a mistake, not, indeed, as to a colloquialism, but as to the force of a technical phrase. When forms are often repeated, at length they are shortened; every schoolboy knows this in learning geometry, where at first every word of the process of proof is supplied with formal exactness, and then, as the treatise advances, the modes of expressions are abbreviated. Many of our familiar words are abbreviations of this sort; such is an "omnibus;" again, a "stage," in the sense of a stage-coach; we talk of the "rail," when we mean the "rail-road;" we speak of "laying the table" for dinner, when we mean "laying the cloth on the table;" and a king's levy properly means his "rising in the morning," but is taken to mean his showing himself to his nobles and others who come to pay him their respects. So again, innkeepers paint up, "Entertainment for man and horse;" they do not add the important words, "to those who can pay for it." Every other private house in our streets has "Ring the bell" upon its door; that is, "if you have business within." And so, again, in Catholicism the word "penance," which properly means repentance, often stands for the punishment annexed to the repentance, as when we talk of the imposition of "penances." Now, in like manner, as to Indulgences, "to absolve from sin" sometimes means one of two things quite distinct from real absolution. First, it may mean nothing else but to remit the *punishment* of sin; and next, it may mean to absolve *externally* or to *reconcile* to the Church, in the sense in which I explained the phrase in a previous Lecture.[8] Here, however, I am going to speak of the phrase in the former of these two senses—viz., as the remission of the *punishment* remaining *after* pardon of the sin. This is an indulgence; indulgence never is *absolution* or pardon itself. At the same time it is quite certain that, as far as words go, Indulgences have sometimes been drawn up in such a form as conveys to a Protestant reader the idea of real absolution, which they always presuppose and never convey. To a person who is not pardoned

---

[8] In Lecture III. This sense, however, is unusual; *vide* Ferraris, Biblioth., art. Indul., App. § 6.

(and pardoned he cannot be without repentance), an Indulgence does no good whatever; an Indulgence supposes the person receiving it to be already absolved and in a state of grace, and then it remits to him the punishment which remains due to his past sins, whatever they are; but that this is really the meaning, a Protestant will as little gather from the form of words in which it has been sometimes drawn up, as he would gather from the good old soul's words cited just now, that "absolution" means "leave to go to communion." If Protestants will not take their information from Catholics on points such as this, but are determined to judge for themselves and to insist on the letter, there is no help for it.

And the same remark in a measure applies to another expression to be found in Indulgences. In Tetzel's famous form at the beginning of the Reformation, we read as follows:—" Shouldest thou not presently die, let this grace remain in full force, and avail thee at the point of death." On this Dr. Waddington, ordinarily a cautious as well as candid writer, observes, "[It cannot] be disputed that it conferred an entire absolution, not only from all past, but also from all future sins. It is impossible with any shadow of *reason* to affix any other meaning to the concluding paragraph,"[9]—which is the one I have quoted. Reason; how can reason help you here? could you have found out that "absolution" meant "leave for communion" by reason? Some things are determined by reason, others by sense, and others by testimony. We go to dictionaries for information of one kind, and to gazetteers for information of another

[9] Reformation, vol. i. p. 27.

kind. No one discovers the price of stocks, ministerial measures, or the fashions of the new year, by reason. Whatever is spontaneous, accidental, variable, self-dependent, whatever is objective, we must go out of ourselves to determine. And such, among other instances, is the force of language, such the use of formulas, such the value of theological terms. You learn pure English by reading classical authors and mixing in good society. Go then to those with whom such terms are familiar, who are masters of the science of them, and they will read the above sentence for you, not by reason, but by the usage of the Church; and they will read it thus:—
"If thou diest not now, but time hence, this Indulgence will then avail thee, in the hour of death, that is, provided thou art then in a state of *grace*."

There is no prospective pardon in these words so explained; an Indulgence has nothing to do with pardon; it presupposes pardon; it is an additional remission upon and after pardon, being the remission of the arrears of suffering due from those who are already pardoned. If on receipt of this Indulgence the recipient rushed into sin, the benefit of the Indulgence would be at least suspended, till he repented, went to confession, gained a new spirit, and was restored to God's favour. If he was found in this state of pardon and grace at the point of death, then it would avail him at the point of death. Then, that pardon which his true repentance would gain him in the sacrament of penance, would be crowned by the further remission of punishment through the Indulgence, certainly not otherwise. If, however, a controversialist says that an ordinary Catholic cannot possibly understand all this, that is a question of fact, not of reason; it does not stand to reason that he cannot: reason does not come in here. I do not say that an ordinary layman *will* express himself with theological accuracy, but he knows perfectly well that an Indulgence is no pardon for prospective sin, that it is no standing pardon for a state of sin. If you think he does not, come and see. That is my keynote from first to last; come and see, instead of remaining afar off, and judging by reason.

7.

There are Protestant books explaining difficult passages of the Old Testament by means of present manners and customs among the Orientals; a very sensible proceeding, and well deserving of imitation by Protestants in the case before us: let *our* obscure words and forms be interpreted by the understandings and habits of the Catholic people. On the other hand, in Dean Swift's well-known tale, you have an account of certain philosophers of Laputa, who carried their head under their arm. These sagacious persons seldom made direct use of their senses, but acted by reason; a tailor for instance, who has to measure for a suit of clothes, I think, is described, not as taking out his measures, but his instruments, quadrant, telescope, and the like. He measured a man as he would measure a mountain or a bog; and he ascertained his build and his carriage as he might determine the right ascension of Sirius or the revolution of a comet. It is but a vulgar way to handle and turn about the living subject who was before him; so our Laputan retreated, pulled out his theodolite instead of his slips of parchment, and made an observation from a distance. It was a grand idea to make a coat by private judgment and a theodolite; and depend upon it, when it came home it did not fit. Our Protestants wield the theodolite too; they keep at a convenient distance from us, take the angles, calculate the sines and cosines, and work out an algebraic process, when common sense would bid them ask us a few questions. They observe latitude and longitude, the dip of the needle, the state of the atmosphere; our path is an orbit, and our locus is expressed by an equation. They communicate with us by gestures, as you talk to the deaf and dumb; and they are more proud of doing something, right or wrong, by a ceremony of this kind which is their own doing, than of having the learning of the Benedictines or the Bollandists, if they are to go to school for it.

Open their tracts or pamphlets at random, and you will not have long to look for instances;—a priest is told one afternoon that a parishioner wishes to go to confession. He breaks off what he is doing, disappointed, perhaps, at the interruption, rushes into church, takes up his stole, and turns his ear towards his penitent. It is altogether a matter of routine work with him, with a lifting up indeed of the heart to his Maker and Lord, but still a matter too familiar to make any great impression on him, beyond that of his knowing he is called to a serious duty, which he must discharge to the best of his ability. A Scripture reader, or some such personage, opens the door, and peeps in; he perceives what is going on, and stands gazing. What is his comment? I wish I had kept the paragraph, as I read it; but it was to this effect,—" I saw a priest with a poor wretch at his feet —how like a god he looked!" Can anything, my Brothers, be more unreal, more fantastic? Yet all this comes of standing gazing at the door.

How many are the souls, in distress, anxiety or loneliness, whose one need is to find a being to whom they can pour out their feelings unheard by the world? Tell them out they must; they cannot tell them out to those whom they see every hour. They want to tell them and not to tell them; and they want to tell them out, yet be as if they be not told; they wish to tell them to one who is strong enough to bear them, yet not too strong to despise them; they wish to tell them to one who can at once advise and can sympathize with them; they wish to relieve themselves of a load, to gain a solace, to receive the assurance that there is one who thinks of them, and one to whom in thought they can recur, to whom they can betake themselves, if necessary, from time to time, while they are in the world. How many a Protestant's heart would leap at the news of such a benefit, putting aside all distinct ideas of a sacramental ordinance, or of a grant of pardon and the conveyance of grace! If there is a heavenly idea in the Catholic Church, looking at it simply as an idea, surely, next after the Blessed Sacrament, Confession is such. And such is it ever found in fact,—the very act of kneeling, the low and contrite voice, the sign of the cross hanging, so to say, over the head bowed low, and the words of peace and blessing. Oh what a soothing charm is there, which the world can neither give nor take away! Oh what piercing, heart-subduing tranquillity, provoking tears of joy, is poured, almost substantially and physically upon the soul, the oil of gladness, as Scripture calls it, when the penitent at length rises, his God reconciled to him, his sins rolled away for ever! This is confession as it is in fact; as those bear witness to it who know it by experience; what is it in the language of the Protestant? His language is, I may say, maniacal; listen to his ravings, as far as I dare quote them, about what he knows just as much of as the blind know of colours: "If I could follow my heart wherever it would go," he cries about the priest, "I would go into his dark and damnable confessional, where my poor Roman Catholic countrymen intrust their wives and daughters to him, under the awful delusion of false religion; and, while the tyrant is pressing his . . infernal investigation, putting the heart and feeling of the helpless creature on the moral rack, till she sink enslaved and powerless at his feet, I would drag the victim forth in triumph from his grasp, and ring in the monster's ear, No Popery!"

These are the words of a fanatic; but grave, sober men can in their own way say things quite as absurd, quite as opprobrious. There is a gentleman,[1] who, since these Lectures began, has opened a public correspondence with me; I quoted from him just now.[2] One of his principal points, to which he gave his confident adhesion, was this, that at least one in twelve of our Priests in large towns doubts or disbelieves. How did he prove it? A conscientious person does

[1] Mr. Seely, the reputed author of several able works. The wider his name and his charge against us are circulated, the better for the cause of truth. Neither the one nor the other should be hushed up.

[2] P. 339.

not advance grave charges against others, much less the gravest possible, without the best of reasons. Even to think ill of others, without sufficient cause, is in a Catholic's estimation, an offence: but to speak out to the world a proposition such as this, distinctly to accuse his neighbour of the worst of crimes, is either a great duty or a great sin. The proof, too, should be proportionate to the imputation. And that the more, because he went further than I have yet said: he actually singled out a place; he named Birmingham, and he insinuated that such infidels or sceptics were found among the priests of this very town. Well, then, we must suppose he speaks on the best authority; he has come to Birmingham, he knows the priests, he has some distinct evidence. He accuses us of a sin which includes blasphemy, sacrilege, hypocrisy, fraud, and virtually immorality, besides its own proper heinousness, which is of the first order, and he must have, of course, reason for what he says. What then is his method of proof? simply the Laputan. He brandishes his theodolite, he proves us to be proud rebels against our God, and odious impostors toward men, by mathematics; he draws out a rule of three sum on paper, and leaves us to settle with it as we may. He argues, that, because France had a body of infidel priests in last century, who did *not* disguise themselves, because Spain had a knot of infidels who, for *fear* of the Inquisition, did, therefore now in England, where nothing is heard of infidelity, and where there is nothing to frighten it into *silence*, it exists in every large town. Moreover, because there were infidel priests in the special 18th century, therefore there are infidel priests in the 19th.

Further, because there were in France fifty or sixty or a hundred infidels among 380,000 ecclesiastics, and a sprinkling in Spain among 125,000, that there are in England infidels now in the proportion of one to twelve. To this antecedent proof he added a few cases true or false, at home or abroad, which it was impossible to examine or refute, of a professedly recent date; and on these grounds he ventured forth with his definite assertion, simply satisfied of its truth, its equity, and its charitableness.

And now for something, if not more wonderful, at least more observable still. After thus speaking, he was surprised I should consider it a "*charge*," and a charge against the priests of Birmingham. He complains, that is, that I have given a *personal* turn to his assertion. Ah, true, I ought to have remembered that Catholic priests, in the judgment of a good Protestant, are not persons at all. I had forgotten what I have already said in the First of these Lectures; we are not men, we have not characters to lose, we have not feelings to be wounded, we have not friends, we have not penitents, we have not congregations; we have nothing personal about us, we are not the fellow-creatures of our accusers, we are not gentlemen, we are not Christians, we are abstractions, we are shadows, we are heraldic emblazonments, we are the griffins and wiverns of the old family picture, we are stage characters with a mask and a dagger, we are mummies from Egypt or antediluvian ornithorhynchi, we are unresisting ninepins, to be set up and knocked down by every mischievous boy; we are the John Doe and Richard Roe of the lawyers, the Titius and Bertha of the canonists, who come forth for every occasion, and are to endure any amount of abuse or misfortune. Did the figures come down from some old piece of tapestry, or were a lion rampant from an inn door suddenly to walk the streets, a Protestant would not be more surprised than at the notion that we have nerves, that we have hearts, that we have sensibilities. For we are but the frogs in the fable; "What is your sport," they said to the truant who was pelting them, "is our destruction;" yes, it is our portion from the beginning, it is our birthright, though not quite our destruction, to be the helots of the pride of the world.

8.

But more remains to be said. It often may happen in matters of research, not indeed when the rule of charity comes in, but in philosophical subjects and the like, that men are obliged to make use of indirect reasonings, in default of testimony and fact. That was not so here. There was evidence, to a considerable extent, the other way. Now observe this, my Brothers. You know how anxious the Protestant world is to get hold of any priest who has left the Catholic body. Why? because he would tell them *facts* about it; certainly Protestants are not always indifferent about facts: that is, when they hope they will tell against us. Well, they go to this priest or that monk, who has transferred himself to Protestantism, in order to get all the information about us they can. Now are Protestantizing priests and monks the only evidence of the kind which they could obtain on the subject? Frenchmen who come from France are evidence about France; but are not Englishmen who go to France evidence too? If some persons come from Rome, have none gone to Rome? and have not they too something to offer in the way of evidence? Yes, surely, they have much to say about Catholic priests. It was offered by myself to the gentleman of whom I have been speaking; it was offered, and it was not accepted. He who could argue by wholesale from some mere instance of a Catholic priest who had become a Protestant, would learn nothing from the direct avowals of a Protestant who had become a Catholic Priest. The one was the pregnant germ of an arbitrary deduction, the other was no credible testimony to a matter of fact.

Now, my Brothers, I should not insist on all this, if it merely related to any personal matter of mine; but you see, it affords a very observable illustration of the point on which I am insisting—viz., that to know Catholics is the best refutation of what is said against them. You are aware, then, that a number of highly educated Protestants have of late years joined the Catholic Church. If their former co-religionists desired to have some real and good information what Catholics are like, they could not have better than that which these persons had to offer. They had belonged to a system which allowed of the largest private judgment, and they had made use of their liberty. They had made use of it first to reject the Protestantism of the day, and to recur back to another form of Protestantism which was in some repute two hundred years ago. Further, they used their liberty to attack the See of Rome, so firmly were they persuaded that the Popedom was not a divine institution. No one can say they did not enter into the feelings of suspicion and jealousy which Protestants entertain towards Rome. For myself, though I never, as I believe, spoke against individuals, I felt and expressed this deep suspicion about the system; and it would be well indeed for Catholicism in this country, if every Protestant but studied it with a tenth part of the care which I have bestowed on the examination and expression of Protestant arguments and views. Well, the private judgment of these men went on acting, for a Protestant can have no guide but it; and to their surprise, as time proceeded, they found it bringing them nearer to the Catholic Church, and at length it fairly brought them into it. What did Protestants say then? Why, they said that the same private judgment which had led them into the Catholic Church, would, in course of time, lead them out of it. They said, too, that these new Catholics, when they came to see what Catholics were like, would be unable to stop among them. Mind, they put it to this test; this was their issue; they left the decision of the question to the event; they knew that the persons of whom they spoke were honest men; they knew that they had given up a great deal to become Catholics; they were sure that they would not take part in an imposition: and therefore they said, " Let them go, they will soon come back; let them go to Rome itself, they are sure to be disgusted; they will meet at Rome, and in France, and in England, and everywhere, infidel priests by the bushel, and will tire of their new religion. And besides, they will soon begin to doubt about it themselves; their private judgment will not submit to all they will have to believe, and they will go out of Catholicism as they came into it."

You observe, then, my Brothers, that our testimony is not a common one, it has a claim to be heard; it has been appealed to by anticipation, let it then be heard after the event. There is no doubt that the whole Protestant world would have made a great deal of our dropping off from the Catholic body; why, then, ought it not to be struck by the fact of our continuing in it, being dutiful and loyal to it, and finding our rest in it? You know perfectly well Protestants would have listened greedily, if we had left and borne witness against it; why, then, ought they not in consistency to listen seriously when we glory in it, and bear witness for it? Who in the whole world are likely to be more trustworthy witnesses of the fact, whether or not one in twelve of our town priests disbelieves or doubts, than these converts, men of education, of intelligence, of independent minds, who have their eyes about them, who are scattered to and fro through all the country, who are, some of them, priests themselves? Is there anyone who knows us personally who will dare to say we are not to be believed, not to be trusted? no: only those who know us not. But so it is to be; our evidence is to be put aside, and the Laputan method to carry the day. Catholics are to be surveyed from without, not inspected from within: texts and formulas are to prevail over broad and luminous facts. There is a story of a logician at some place of learning, who, as he was walking one evening past the public library, was hailed by an unfortunate person from one of its windows, who told him he had been locked in by mistake when it closed, and begged him to send to his relief the official who kept the keys. Our logician is said to have looked at him attentively, pronounced the following syllogism, and walked away: "No man can be in the library after 4 o'clock P.M. You are a man: therefore you are not in the library."

And thus Catholic priests are left duly locked up by Barbara or Celarent, because, forsooth, one grain of Protestant logic is to weigh more than cartloads of Catholic testimony.

9.

No, if our opponents would decide the matter by testimony, if they would submit their assertions to the ordeal of facts, their cause is lost; so they prefer much to go by prejudices, arbitrary principles, and texts. Evidence they can have to satisfy for the asking; but what boots it to pipe and sing to the deaf, or to convince the self-satisfied heart against its will? One there was who left the Protestant religion under circumstances different from any to which I have hitherto alluded. He never joined in the religious movement which has brought so many to the Church; nay, he wrote against that movement; he wrote, not in bitterness and contempt, as many have done, and do, but as a gentleman and a man of serious principle; he wrote against myself. But, though he started from so different a point, he, too, came near the Church, he, too, entered it. He did so at a great sacrifice; he had devoted a great part of his fortune to the building of a Protestant church. It was all but finished when the call came; he rose and obeyed it, and had to leave his means of subsistence behind him, turned into stone. He came into the Catholic Church, and he remains a layman in it. See, then, here is a witness altogether different: ought not this to content our enemies? or are the boys in the market-place still to cry to them, "We have piped to you, and you have not danced; we have lamented, and you have not mourned"? Are they suspicious of those who belonged to a certain movement before they became Catholics? here is one who opposed it: are they suspicious of a convert priest? here is a convert layman. Now, he happens, some years after his conversion, to have written an account of his experience of the Catholic Religion; how many of our enemies have had the grace—I can use no lighter term—have had the grace to look into it? Yet what possible reason can they give for having neglected to study and to profit by it? It is the grave testimony of one, in whom, as in that illustrious witness of old in the heathen country, "no cause nor suspicion" can be found, "unless concerning the law of his God."

"I came," he says, and he shall conclude this Lecture for me, "forced by my convictions, and almost against my will, into this mighty community whose embrace I had all my life dreaded as something paralyzing, enslaving, and torturing. No sooner, however, could I look around me, and mark what presented itself to my eyes, than I saw that I was in a world where all was as satisfying as it was new. For the first time I met with a body of men and women who could talk and act as Christians, without cant, without restraint, without formality, without hypocrisy. After years and years of disappointment, in which the more deeply I saw into the hearts and lives of Protestants of every class, the more clearly I perceived that the religion they professed had *not* become their second nature, but was a thing put on, which did not fit them, which confined their movements, and gave them an outward look, while it was not wrought into the depth of their being,—after years and years of this disappointment, in which the contrast between the Bible, which they praised, and the spirit of their own lives, and the doctrines they preached, struck me more bitterly each succeeding day, at length I found myself in the midst of a race, with whom Christianity was not a rule, but a principle; not a restraint, but a second nature; not a bondage, but a freedom; in which it had precisely that effect which it claims to produce upon man; in which not a few hours, or an occasional day, was set apart for religion, but in which *life* was religious; in which men spoke at all hours, and in all occupations, of religious things, naturally, as men speak of secular things in which they are deeply interested; in which religious thoughts and short prayers were found not incompatible with the necessary duties and pleasures which fill up the road of existence; and in which, the more deeply I was enabled to penetrate below the surface, the more genuine was the goodness which I found, and the more inexhaustible I perceived to be those treasures of grace, which Divine Goodness places at the disposal (so to say) of every soul that seeks them within this favoured communion.

"And now, when so long a period has elapsed since my first submission to the Church, that everything like a sense of novelty has long passed away, and I have tested experimentally the value of all that she has to offer; now that I can employ her means of grace, and take a part in the working of her system, with all that ease and readiness which long practice alone can bestow; the more profound is my sense of her divine origin, of the divine power which resides in her, and of the boundless variety and perfection of the blessings she has to bestow. The more I know her, the more complete do I perceive to be her correspondence to what she professes to be. She is exactly what the one Church of Christ is proclaimed to be in Scripture, and nothing less, and nothing more. . . . . Truly can I say with the patriarch, 'The Lord is in this place, and I knew it not. This is no other than the house of God, and the gate of heaven.' The Catholic Church *can* be nothing less than the spiritual body of Jesus Christ. Nothing less than that adorable Presence, before which the Angels veil their faces, can make her what she is to those who are within her fold. Argument is needed no longer. The scoffings of the infidel, the objections of the Protestant, the sneers of the man of the world, pass over their heads, as clouds over a mountain peak, and leave them calm and undisturbed, with their feet resting upon the Rock of ages. They *know* in whom they have believed. They have passed from speculation to action, and found that all is real, genuine, life-giving, and enduring. . . . . I know only one fear—the fear that my heart may be faithless to Him who has bestowed on me this unspeakable blessing ; I know only one mystery, which the more I think upon it, the more incomprehensible does it appear,—the mystery of that calling which brought *me* into this house of rest, while millions and millions are still driven to and fro in the turbulent ocean of the world, without rudder, and without compass, without helmsman and without anchor, to drift before the gale upon the fatal shore."[3]

[3] Capes's "Four Years' Experience of the Catholic Religion : Burns, London, 1849," pp. 92-95. Mr. Capes returned to the Anglican Church in 1870, on occasion, I believe, of the definition by the Vatican Council of the Pope's Infallibility, but that change does not invalidate his testimony to matters of fact [Ed. 1872].

LECTURE IX.[1]

DUTIES OF CATHOLICS TOWARDS THE PROTESTANT VIEW.

IN this concluding Lecture, my Brothers of the Oratory, I shall attempt, in as few words as possible, to sum up what I have been showing in those which preceded it, and to set before you what I have proposed to myself in the investigation.

You know, then, that at this time we are all in considerable anxiety, and some risk, as regards the future prospects of Catholicism in England. Open threats in the most influential quarters are put forward, as if we might even lose the rights of British subjects, and be deprived of the free exercise of our religion. There has been an attempt to put our convents, in the eye of the law, on a level with madhouses; and one of the Anglican Prelates in Parliament has constituted himself judge whether the dimensions of our churches were sufficient or too large for the "accommodation," to use the Protestant word, of our people. A bill, too, has been passed, about which all of us know enough, without my having the trouble to give it any designation.

The duty of the Catholic Church is to preach to the

[1] Written in 1851 apropos of the events of that year.

world; and her promise and prerogative is success in preaching; but this is a subject which has not come into the scope of our discussions in this place. What I have been saying has no direct reference to any such end. I have not urged it on you, as I well might, in the case of those who, like you, love their religion so well that they wish others to enjoy the benefit of it with them. What I have said, however, does not presuppose this; it has not sprung out of any duty that we have of extending the limits of the Catholic pale; it would not have been superseded, if we had no such duty. I have not been aiming at the conversion of any persons, who are not Catholics, who have heard me: I have not been defending Catholic, or attacking Protestant doctrines, except indirectly and incidentally. The condition or hypothesis with which I have been entering into the discussion has been the present anti-Catholic agitation; and my object has been that of self-defence with reference to it. In the present state of things Catholics must, from the mere instinct of self-preservation, look about them; they are assailed by a very formidable party, or power, as I should rather call it, in this country, by its Protestantism. In the Protestantism of the country I do not include, of course, all who are not Catholics. By Protestants I mean the heirs of the Traditions of Elizabeth; I mean the country gentlemen, the Whig political party, the Church Establishment, and the Wesleyan Conference. I cannot over-estimate their power: they and their principles are established: yet I should be unjust, on the other hand, to all classes in the community if I made this Elizabethan Protestantism synonymous with the mind and the philosophy of the whole country. However, it is a tremendous power, and we are menaced by it; this is the condition of things; what must we do? put ourselves on the defensive; this, then, has been my scope. I have not been aggressive, but on the defensive; and what is the first step of those who are getting ready for their defence against a foe? to reconnoitre him. It is simply this that I have been engaged upon in these Lectures.

This, I say, has been my object, a reconnoitring or survey of a strong and furious enemy, undertaken with a view to self-defence. And I report as follows:—

1.

I find he is in a very strong position, but that he takes a very incorrect view of us, and that this is his strength and our danger. Different from the case of actual warfare, in which ignorance is weakness, here ignorance is power; and in truth he does know as little about us as well can be conceived. He has got old pictures and old maps made years and years ago, which have come down to him from his fathers; and instead of deigning to look at us, and learn anything about us, he adheres to them as if it were a point of faith to do so. This was the subject of my first Lecture; I showed that the English Elizabethan Protestant had a view of our monks, Jesuits, and Church, quite his own, unlike that of his more learned brethren abroad: and moreover, that he was apparently ignorant of the existence of any view besides it, or that it was possible for any sane man to doubt it, or any honest man to deny it. Next came the cause of this phenomenon, and it was this:—Protestantism is established in the widest sense of the word; its doctrine, religious, political, ecclesiastical, moral, is

placed in exclusive possession of all the high places of
the land. It is forced upon all persons in station and
office, or almost all, under sanction of an oath ; it is
endowed with the amplest estates, and with revenues
supplied by Government and by chartered and other
bodies. It has innumerable fine churches, planted up
and down in every town, and village, and hamlet in the
land. In consequence, everyone speaks Protestantism,
even those who do not in their hearts love it ; it is the
current coin of the realm. As English is the natural
tongue, so Protestantism is the intellectual and moral
language of the body politic. The Queen *ex officio*
speaks Protestantism ; so does the court, so do her
ministers. All but a small portion of the two Houses of
Parliament; and those who do not are forced to apologize
for not speaking it, and to speak as much of it as they
conscientiously can. The Law speaks Protestantism,
and the Lawyers ; and the State Bishops and clergy of
course. All the great authors of the nation, the multitudinous literature of the day, the public press, speak
Protestantism. Protestantism the Universities ; Protestantism the schools, high, and low, and middle.
Thus there is an incessant, unwearied circulation of
Protestantism all over the whole country, for 365 days
in the year from morning till night ; and this, for
nearly three centuries, has been almost one of the
functions of national life. As the pulse, the lungs, the
absorbents, the nerves, the pores of the animal body,
are ever at their work, as that motion is its life, so in
the political structure of the country there is an action
of the life of Protestantism, constant and regular. It
is a vocal life ; and in this consists its perpetuation, its
reproduction. What it utters, it teaches, it propagates

by uttering; it is ever impressing itself, diffusing itself all around; it is ever transmitting itself to the rising, generation; it is ever keeping itself fresh, and young, and vigorous, by the process of a restless agitation. This, then, is the elementary cause of the view which Englishmen are accustomed to take of Catholicism and its professors. They survey us in the light of their Tradition; and this was the subject of my second Lecture.

Well, but you will ask, Have Catholics nothing to say for themselves? yes, a great deal, but we have no opportunity of saying it. The public will not recognize us; it interrupts and puts us down. Men close their ears and throw up dust in the air when we begin to speak: they close their eyes when we come forward, and begin pelting us at randon. Far less will they come near us, and ask us questions, and listen to our answers. This was the subject of my foregoing or eighth Lecture, in which I had not time to say nearly as much as I had intended. I could have shown you, how first, Protestants got rid of Catholicism from the kingdom as a worship; how next the Catholics who remained they put under crushing laws; how every priest who said mass or exercised any function on English ground was liable to perpetual imprisonment, and any foreign priest, who was subject to the crown of England, coming into England, was guilty of high treason, and all who harboured him, of felony. I could have told you how that converting or being converted to Catholicism was high treason; how no Catholic was allowed to inherit or purchase land; no Catholic could hear mass without fine and imprisonment; no Catholic might keep school under pain of imprisonment for life ; nor might, in default of schools at home, send a child abroad for education, without forfeiting all his estates, goods, and chattels, and incurring a civil outlawry ; moreover, how, if a Catholic did not attend the established worship, he was not allowed to come within ten miles of London, nor could travel five miles from home, or bring any action at law ; and how he might not be married or buried, or have his children baptized, by any but ministers of the Established Church. I am not quoting these laws with a view to expose their wholesale cruelty and tyranny, though I might well do so ; but in order to show you how impossible it was for Catholics to defend themselves, when they were denied even to speak. You see, the Protestant Tradition had it all its own way ; Elizabeth, and her great men, and her preachers, killed and drove away all the Catholics they could ; knocked down the remainder, and then at their leisure proved unanswerably and triumphantly the absurdity of Popery, and the heavenly beauty and perfection of Protestantism. Never did we undergo so utter and complete a refutation ; we had not one word to utter in our defence. When she had thus beaten the breath out of us, and made us simply ridiculous, she put us on our feet again, thrust us into a chair, hoisted us up aloft, and carried us about as a sort of Guy Faux, to show to all the boys and riff-raff of the towns what a Papist was like. Then, as if this were not enough, lest anyone should come and ask us anything about our religion, she and her preachers put it about that we had the plague, so that, for fear of a moral infection, scarce a soul had the courage to look at us, or breathe the same air with us.

This was a fair beginning for the Protestantizing

of the people, and everything else that was needed followed in due time, as a matter of course. Protestantism being taught everywhere, Protestant principles were taught with it, which are necessarily the very reverse of Catholic principles. The consequence was plain—viz., that even before the people heard a Catholic open his mouth, they were forearmed against what he would say, for they had been taught this or that as if a precious truth, belief in which was *ipso facto* the disbelief and condemnation of some Catholic doctrine or other. When a person goes to a fever ward, he takes some essence with him to prevent his catching the disorder; and of this kind are the anti-Catholic principles in which Protestants are instructed from the cradle. For instance, they are taught to get by heart without any sort of proof, as a kind of alphabet or spelling lesson, such propositions as these:—"miracles have ceased long ago;" "all truth is in the Bible;" "any one can understand the Bible;" "all penance is absurd;" "a priesthood is pagan, not Christian," and a multitude of others. These are universally taught and accepted, as if equally true and equally important, just as are the principles "it is wrong to murder or thieve," or "there is a judgment to come." When then a person sets out in life with these maxims as a sort of stock in trade in all religious speculations, and encounters Catholics, whose opinions hitherto he had known nothing at all about, you see he has been made quite proof against them, and unsusceptible of their doctrines, their worship, and their reasoning, by the preparation to which he has been subjected. He feels an instinctive repugnance to everything Catholic, by reason of these arbitrary principles, which he has been taught to hold, and which he thinks identical with reason. "What? you have priests in your religion," he says; "but do you not know, are you so behind the world as not to know, that priests are pagan, not Christian?" And sometimes he thinks that, directly he has uttered some such great maxim, the Catholic will turn Protestant at once, or, at least, ought to do so, and if he does not, is either dull or hypocritical. And so again, "You hold saints are to be invoked, but the practice is not in the Bible, and nothing is true that is not there." And again, "They say that in Ireland and elsewhere the priests impose heavy penances; but this is against common sense, for all penances are absurd." Thus the Protestant takes the whole question for granted on starting;—and this was the subject of my seventh Lecture.

This fault of mind I called Assumption or Theorizing; and another quite as great, and far more odious, is Prejudice; and this came into discussion in the sixth Lecture. The perpetual talk against Catholicism, which goes on everywhere, in the higher classes, in literary circles, in the public press, and in the Protestant Church and its various dependencies, makes an impression, or fixes a stain, which it is continually deepening, on the minds which are exposed to its influence; and thus, quite independent of any distinct reasons and facts for thinking so, the multitude of men are quite certain that something very horrible is going on among Catholics. They are convinced that we are all but fiends, so that there is no doubt at all, even before going into the matter, that all that is said against us is true, and all that is said for us is false.

These, then, are the two special daughters, as they

may be called, of the Protestant Tradition, Theory or Assumption on the one hand, and Prejudice on the other,—Theory which scorns us, and Prejudice which hates us; yet, though coming of one stock, they are very different in their constitution, for Theory is of so ethereal a nature, that it needs nothing to feed upon; it lives on its own thoughts, and in a world of its own, whereas Prejudice is ever craving for food, victuals are in constant request for its consumption every day; and accordingly they are served up in unceasing succession, Titus Oates, Maria Monk, and Jeffreys, being the purveyors, and platform and pulpit speakers being the cooks. And this formed the subject of the third, fourth, and fifth Lectures.

Such, then, is Popular Protestantism, considered in its opposition to Catholics. Its truth is Establishment by law; its philosophy is Theory; its faith is Prejudice; its facts are Fictions; its reasonings Fallacies; and its security is Ignorance about those whom it is opposing. The Law says that white is black; Ignorance says, why not? Theory says it ought to be, Fallacy says it must be, Fiction says it is, and Prejudice says it shall be.

2.

And now, what are our duties at this moment towards this enemy of ours? How are we to bear ourselves towards it? what are we to do with it? what is to come of the survey we have taken of it? with what practical remark and seasonable advice am I to conclude this attempt to determine our relation to it? The lesson we gain is obvious and simple, but as difficult, you will say, as it is simple; for the means and the end are almost identical, and in executing the one we have already reached the other. Protestantism is fierce, because it does not know you; ignorance is its strength; error is its life. Therefore bring yourselves before it, press yourselves upon it, force yourselves into notice against its will. Oblige men to know you; persuade them, importune them, shame them into knowing you. Make it so clear what you are, that they cannot affect not to see you, nor refuse to justify you. Do not even let them off with silence, but give them no escape from confessing that you are not what they have thought you were. They will look down, they will look aside, they will look in the air, they will shut their eyes, they will keep them shut. They will do all in their power not to see you; the nearer you come, they will close their eyelids all the tighter; they will be very angry and frightened, and give the alarm as if you were going to murder them. They will do anything but look at you. They are, many of them, half conscious they have been wrong, but fear the consequences of becoming sure of it; they will think it best to let things alone, and to persist in injustice for good and all, since they have been for so long a time committed to it; they will be too proud to confess themselves mistaken; they prefer a safe cruelty to an inconvenient candour. I know it is a most grave problem how to touch so intense an obstinacy, but, observe, if you once touch it, you have done your work. There is but one step between you and success. It is a steep step, but it is one. It is a great thing to know your aim, to be saved from wasting your energies in wrong quarters, to be able to concentrate them on a point. You have but to aim at making men look steadily at you;

when they do this, I do not say they will become Catholics, but they will cease to have the means of making you a by-word and a reproach, of inflicting on you the cross of unpopularity. Wherever Catholicism is known, it is respected, or at least endured, by the people. Politicians and philosophers, and the established clergy, would be against you, but not the people, if it knew you. A religion which comes from God approves itself to the conscience of the people, wherever it is really known.

I am not advocating, as you will see presently, anything rude in your bearing, or turbulent, or offensive; but first I would impress upon you the *end* you have to aim at. Your one and almost sole object, I say, must be, to make yourselves known. This is what will do everything for you: it is what your enemies will try by might and main to hinder. They begin to have a suspicion that Catholicism, known to be what it really is, will be their overthrow. They have hitherto cherished a most monstrous idea about you. They have thought, not only that you were the vilest and basest of men, but that you were fully conscious of it yourselves, and conscious, too, that they knew it. They have fancied that you, or at least your priests, indulged in the lowest sensuality, and practised the most impudent hypocrisy, and were parties to the most stupid and brutish of frauds; and that they dared not look a Protestant in the face. Accordingly, they have considered, and have thought us quite aware ourselves, that we were in the country only on sufferance; that we were like reputed thieves and other bad characters, who, for one reason or another, are not molested in their dens of wickedness, and enjoy a contemptuous toleration, if they keep within bounds. And so, in like manner, they have thought that there was evidence enough at any moment to convict us, if they were provoked to it. What would be their astonishment, if one of the infamous persons I have supposed stood upon his rights, or obtruded himself into the haunts of fashion and good breeding? Fancy, then, how great has been their indignation, that we Catholics should pretend to be Britons; should affect to be their equals; should dare to preach, nay, to controvert; should actually make converts, nay, worse and worse, not only should point out their mistakes, but, prodigious insolence! should absolutely laugh at the absurdity of their assertions, and the imbecility of their arguments. They are at first unable to believe their ears, when they are made sensible that we, who know so well our own worthlessness, and know that they know it, who deserve at the least the hulks or transportation, talk as loudly as we do, refuse to be still, and say that the more we are known, the more we shall be esteemed. We, who ought to go sneaking about, to crouch at their feet, and to keep our eyes on the ground, from the consciousness of their hold upon us,—is it madness, is it plot, what is it, which inspires us with such unutterable presumption? They have the might and the right on their side. They could confiscate our property, they could pack us all out of the kingdom, they could bombard Rome, they could fire St. Peter's, they could batter down the Coliseum, they could abolish the Papacy, if they pleased. Passion succeeds, and then a sort of fear, such as a brutal master might feel, who breaks into fury at the first signs of spirit in the apprentice he has long ill-treated, and then quails before him as he gets older.

And then how white becomes their wrath, when men of their own rank, men of intelligence, men of good connexions, their relations or their friends, leave them to join the despised and dishonoured company! And when, as time goes on, more and more such instances occur, and others are unsettled, and the old landmarks are removed, and all is in confusion, and new questions and parties appear in the distance, and a new world is coming in,—when what they in their ignorance thought to be nothing turns out to be something, they know not what, and the theodolite of Laputa has utterly failed, they quake with apprehension at so mysterious a visitation, and they are mad with themselves for having ever qualified their habitual contempt with some haughty generosity towards us. A proud jealousy, a wild hate, and a perplexed dismay, almost choke them with emotion.

All this because they have not taken the trouble to know us as we are in fact:—however, you would think that they had at last gained an opening for information, when those whom they have known become the witnesses of what we are. Never so little; the friends who have left them are an embarrassment to them, not an illumination; an embarrassment, because they do but interfere with their received rule and practice of dealing with us. It is an easy thing to slander those who come of the old Catholic stock, because such persons are unknown to the world. They have lived all their days in tranquil fidelity to the creed of their forefathers, in their secluded estate, or their obscure mission, or their happy convent; they have cultivated no relations with the affairs or the interests of the day, and have never entered into the public throng of men to gain a character. They are known, in their simplicity and innocence and purity of heart, and in their conscientiousness of life, to their God, to their neighbour and to themselves, not to the world at large. If any one would defame them, he may do it with impunity; their name is not known till it is slandered, and they have no antecedents to serve as a matter for an appeal. Here, then, is the fit work for those prudent slanderers, who would secure themselves from exposure, while they deal a blow in defence of the old Protestant Tradition. Were a recent convert, whose name is before the world, accused of some definite act of tyranny or baseness, he knows how to write and act in his defence, and he has a known reputation to protect him; therefore, ye Protestant champions, if there be an urgent need at the moment for some instance of Catholic duplicity or meanness, be sure to shoot your game sitting; keep yourselves under cover, choose some one who can be struck without striking, whom it is easy to overbear, with whom it is safe to play the bully. Let it be a prelate of advanced age and of retired habits, or some gentle nun, whose profession and habits are pledges that she cannot retaliate. Triumph over the old man and the woman. Open your wide mouth, and collect your rumbling epithets, and round your pretentious sentences, and discharge your concentrated malignity, on the defenceless. Let it come down heavily on them to their confusion; and a host of writers, in print and by the post, will follow up the outrage you have commenced. But beware of the converts, for they are known; and to them you will not be safe in imputing more than the ordinary infirmities of humanity. With them you must deal in the contrary way. Men of rank, men of station, men of ability, in short, men of name, what are we to do with them! Cover them up, bury them; never mention them in print, unless a chance hint can be dropped to their disadvantage. Shake your heads, whisper about in society, and detail in private letters the great change which has come over them. They are not the same persons; they have lost their fine sense of honour, and so suddenly, too; they are under the dominion of new and bad masters. Drop their acquaintance; meet them and pass them by, and tell your friends you were so pained you could not speak to them; be sure you do nothing whatever to learn from them anything about the Catholic faith; know nothing at all about their movements, their objects, or their life. Read none of their books; let no one read them who is under your influence; however, you may usefully insert in your newspapers half sentences from their writings, or any passing report, which can be improved to their disadvantage. Not a word more; let not even their works be advertised. Ignore those who never can be ignored, never can be forgotten; and all for this,—that by the violation of every natural feeling, and every sacred tie, you may keep up that profound ignorance of the Catholic Religion which the ascendency of Protestantism requires.

3.

These are but snatches and glimpses, my Brothers of the Oratory, of the actual state of the case; of the intense determination of Protestants to have nothing to do with us, and nothing true to say of us; and of the extreme arduousness of that task to which I think we should all direct our exertions. The post must be carried; in it lies the fortune of the day. Our opponents are secretly conscious of it too; else why should they so strenuously contest it? They must be made to know us as we are; they must be made to know our religion as it is, not as they fancy it; they must be made to look at us, and they are overcome. This is the work which lies before you in your place and in your measure, and I would advise you about it thus:—

Bear in mind, then, that, as far as defamation and railing go, your enemies have done their worst. There is nothing which they have not said, which they do not daily say, against your religion, your priests, and yourselves. They have exhausted all their weapons and you have nothing to fear, for you have nothing to lose. They call your priests distinctly liars: they can but cry the old fables over and over again, though they are sadly worse for wear. They have put you beyond the pale of civilized society; they have made you the outlaws of public opinion; they treat you, in the way of reproach and slander, worse than they treat the convict or the savage. You cannot in any way move them by smiles, or by tears, or by remonstrance. You can show them no attention; you can give them no scandal. Court them, they are not milder; be rude to them, they cannot be more violent. You cannot make them think better of you, or worse. They hold no terms with you; you have not even the temptation to concede to them. You have not the temptation to give and take; you have not the temptation to disguise or to palter. You have the strength of desperation, and desperation does great things. They have made you turn to bay. Whatever occurs, if there be a change at all, it must be a change for the better: you cannot be disadvantaged by the most atrocious charges, for you are sure to be the objects of such, whatever you do. You are set loose from the fear of man: it is of no use to say to yourselves, "What will people say?" No, the Supreme Being must be your only Fear, as He is your only Reward.

Next, look at the matter more closely; it is not so bad as it seems. Who are these who obstinately refuse to know you? When I say, "They have done their worst," what is their "worst," and who are "they?" This is an all-important question; perhaps I shall have some difficulty in bringing out what I mean, but when you once get into my idea, there will be no degrees in your understanding it. Consider, then, that "they" means, in the main, certain centres of influence in the metropolis; first, a great proportion of members of both Houses of Parliament; next, the press; thirdly, the Societies whose haunt or home is Exeter Hall; fourthly, the pulpits of the Establishment, and of a good part of the Dissenters. These are our accusers; these spread abroad their calumnies; these are meant by "they." Next, what is their "worst?" whom do they influence? They influence the population of the whole of Great Britain, and the British Empire, so far as it is British and not Catholic; and they influence it so as to make it believe that Catholicism and all Catholics are professed and habitual violators of the moral law, of the precepts of truth, honesty, purity and humanity. If this be so, you may ask me what I can mean by saying that the "worst" is not so bad as it looks? but after all, things might be much worse.

Think a moment: what is it to me what people think of me a hundred miles off, compared with what they think of me at home? It is nothing to me what the four ends of the world think of me; I care nought for the British Empire more than for the Celestial in this matter, provided I can be sure what Birmingham thinks of me. The question, I say, is, What does Birmingham think of me? and if I have a satisfactory answer to that, I can bear to be without a satisfactory answer about any other town or district in England. This is a great principle to keep in view.

And now I am coming to a second. I grant the whole power of the Metropolis is against us, and I grant it is quite out of the question to attempt to gain it over on our side. It is true, there are various individual members of Parliament who are our coreligionists or our friends, but they are few among many; there are newspapers which act generously towards us, but they form a small minority; there are a few Protestant clergy who would be not quite carried away by the stream, if left to themselves. Granted: but still, I am forced to allow that the great metropolitan intellect cannot be reached by us, and for this simple reason, because you cannot confront it, you cannot make it know you. I said your victory was to be in forcing upon others a personal knowledge of you, by your standing before your enemies face to face. But what face has a metropolitan journal? How are you to get at it? how are you to look into it? whom are you to look at? who is to look at you? No one is known in London; it is the realm of the incognito and the anonymous; it is not a place, it is a region or a state. There is no such thing as local opinion in the metropolis; mutual personal knowledge, there is none; neighbourhood, good fame, bad repute, there is none; no house knows the next door. You cannot make an impression on such an ocean of units; it has no disposition, no connexion of parts. The great instrument of propagating moral truth is personal knowledge. A man finds himself in a definite place; he grows up in it and into it; he draws persons around him; they know him, he knows them; thus it is that ideas are born which are to live, that works begin which are to last.[5] It is this personal knowledge of each other which is true public opinion; local opinion is real public opinion; but there is not, there cannot be, such in London. How is a man to show what he is, when he is but a grain of sand out of a mass, without relations to others, without a place, without antecedents, without individuality? Crowds pour along the streets, and though each has his own character written on high, they are one and all the same to men below. And this impersonality, as it may be called, pervades the whole metropolitan system. A man, not known, writes a leading article against what?—things? no; but ideas. He writes against Catholicism: what is Catholicism? can you touch it? point at it? no; it is an idea before his mind. He clothes it with certain attributes, and forthwith it goes all over the country that a certain idea or vision, called Catholicism, has certain other ideas, bad ones, connected with it. You see, it is all a matter of ideas, and abstractions, and

[5] *Vide* the author's Oxford University Sermons, No. V.

conceptions. Well, this leading article goes on to speak of certain individual Catholic priests; still, does it see them? point at them? no, it does but give their names; it is a matter, not of persons, but of names; and those names, sure enough, go over the whole country and empire as the names of rogues, or of liars, or of tyrants, as the case may be; while they themselves, the owners of them, in their own persons are not at all the worse for it, but eat, sleep, pray, and do their work, as freely and as easily as before. London cannot touch them, for words hurt no one; words cannot hurt us till—till when? till they are taken up, believed, in the very place where we individually dwell. Ah! this is a very different kind of public opinion; it is local opinion; I spoke of it just now, and it concerns us very nearly.

I say, it is quite another thing when the statements which a metropolitan paper makes about me, and the empire believes, are actually taken up in the place where I live. It is a very different thing, and a very serious matter; but, observe the great principle we have arrived at; it is this:—that popular opinion only acts through local opinion. The opinion of London can only act on an individual through the opinion of his own place; metropolitan opinion can only act on me through Birmingham opinion. London abuses Catholics. "Catholic" is a word; where is the thing? in Liverpool, in Manchester, in Birmingham, in Leeds, in Sheffield, in Nottingham. Did all the London papers prove that all Catholics were traitors, where must this opinion be carried out? Not in the air, not in leading articles, not in an editor's room; but in Liverpool, in Manchester, in Birmingham, in Leeds, in Sheffield, in Nottingham. So, in order to carry out your London manifesto, you must get the people of Birmingham, Manchester, and the rest, to write their names after it; else, nothing comes of its being a metropolitan opinion, or an imperial opinion, or its being any other great idea whatever:—you must get Birmingham to believe it of Birmingham Catholics, and Manchester to believe it of Manchester Catholics. So, you see, these great London leading articles have only done half their work, or rather, have not begun it, by proving to the world that all Catholics are traitors, till they come out of their abstractions and generalities, and for the "world," are able to substitute Birmingham, Manchester, and Liverpool; and for "all Catholics," to substitute Catholics of Birmingham, Manchester, and Liverpool; and to get each place in particular to accept what the great Metropolis says, and the Empire believes, in the general.

And now comes another important consideration: it is not at all easy to get a particular place, at the word of London, to accept about its own neighbourhood in particular what London says of all places in the general. Did London profess to tell us about the price of iron generally, if it gained its information from Birmingham, and other iron markets in particular, well and good; but if it came forward with great general views of its own, I suspect that Birmingham would think it had a prior voice in the question, and would not give up its views at the bidding of any metropolitan journal. And the case is the same as regards Catholicism; London may declaim about Catholics in general, but Birmingham will put in a claim to judge of them in particular; and when Birmingham becomes the judge, London falls into the mere office of accuser, and the accused may be heard in his defence. Thus, a Catholic of Birmingham can act on Birmingham, though he cannot act on London, and this is the important practical point to which I have been coming all along. I wish you to turn your eyes upon that local opinion, which is so much more healthy, English, and Christian than popular or metropolitan opinion; for it is an opinion, not of ideas, but of things; not of words, but of facts; not of names, but of persons; it is perspicuous, real and sure. It is little to me, as far as my personal well-being is concerned, what is thought of Catholicism through the empire, or what is thought of me by the metropolis, if I know what is thought of me in Birmingham. London cannot act on me except through Birmingham, and Birmingham indeed can act on me, but I can act on Birmingham. Birmingham can look on me, and I can look on Birmingham. This is a place of persons, and a place of facts; there is far more fairness in a place like this than in a metropolis, or at least fairness is uppermost. Newspapers are from the nature of the case, and almost in spite of themselves, conducted here on a system more open and fairer than the metropolitan system. A Member of Parliament in London might say that I had two heads, and refuse to retract it, though I solemnly denied it; it would not be believed in Birmingham. All the world might believe it; it might be the theme of country meetings; the Prime Minister might introduce it into the Queen's speech; it might be the subject of most eloquent debates, and most exciting divisions; it might be formally communicated to all the European courts; the stocks might fall, a stream of visitors set in from Russia, Egypt, and the United

States, at the news; it would not be believed in Birmingham; local opinion would carry it hollow against popular opinion.

You see, then, Brothers of the Oratory, where your success lies, and how you are to secure it. Never mind the London press; never mind Exeter Hall; never mind perambulating orators or solemn meetings: let them alone, they do not affect local opinion. They are a blaze amid the stubble; they glare, and they expire. Do not dream of converting the public opinion of London; you cannot, and you need not. Look at home, there lies your work; what you have to do, and what you can do, are one and the same. Prove to the people of Birmingham, as you can prove to them, that your priests and yourselves are not without conscience, or honour, or morality; prove it to them, and it matters not though every man, woman, and child, within the London bills of mortality were of a different opinion. That metropolitan opinion would in that case be powerless, when it attempted to bear upon Birmingham; it would not work; there would be a hitch and a block; you would be a match where you were seen, for a whole world where you were not seen. I do not undervalue the influence of London; many things its press can do; some things it cannot do; it is imprudent when it impinges on facts. If, then, a battle is coming on, stand on your own ground, not on that of others; take care of yourselves; be found where you are known; make yourselves and your religion known more and more, for in that knowledge is your victory. Truth will out; truth is mighty and will prevail. We have an instance of it before our eyes; why is it that some persons here have the hardihood to be maintaining Maria Monk's calumnies? because those calumnies bear upon a place over the ocean; why did they give up Jeffreys? because he spoke of a place close at hand. You cannot go to Montreal; you can go to Whitwick; therefore, as regards Whitwick, the father of lies eats his words and gives up Jeffreys, to get some credit for candour, when he can get nothing else. Who can doubt, that, if that same personage went over to Canada, he would give up Maria Monk as false and take up Jeffreys as true? Yes, depend on it, when he next ships off to New York, he will take the veritable account of the persecuted Jeffreys in his pocket, with an interesting engraving of his face as a frontispiece. So certain, so necessary is all this, my Brothers, that I do not mind giving you this advice in public. An enemy might say in his heart, "Here is a priest fool enough to show his game!" I have no game; I have nothing to conceal; I do not mind who knows what I mark out for you, for nothing can frustrate it. I have an intense feeling in me as to the power and victoriousness of truth. It has a blessing from God upon it. Satan himself can but retard its ascendancy, he cannot prevent it.

4.

This, I would say, Brothers of the Oratory, not only to you, but, if I had a right to do so, to the Catholics of England generally. Let each stand on his own ground; let each approve himself in his own neighbourhood; if each portion is defended, the whole is secured. Take care of the pence, and the pounds will take care of themselves. Let the London press alone; do not appeal to it; do not expostulate with it, do not flatter it; care not for popular opinion, cultivate local. And then if troubled times come on, and the enemy rages, and his many voices go forth from one centre all through England, threatening and reviling us, and muttering, in his cowardly way, about brickbats, bludgeons, and lighted brands, why in that case the Birmingham people will say, "Catholics are, doubtless, an infamous set, and not to be trusted, for the *Times* says so, and Exeter Hall, and the Prime Minister, and the Bishops of the Establishment; and such good authorities cannot be wrong; but somehow an exception must certainly be made for the Catholics of Birmingham. They are not like the rest: they are indeed a shocking set at Manchester, Preston, Blackburn, and Liverpool; but, however you account for it, they are respectable men here. Priests in general are perfect monsters; but here they are certainly unblemished in their lives, and take great pains with their people. Bishops are tyrants, and, as Maria Monk says, cut-throats, always excepting the Bishop of Birmingham, who affects no state or pomp, is simple and unassuming, and always in his work." And in like manner, the Manchester people will say, "Oh, certainly, Popery is horrible, and must be kept down. Still, let us give the devil his due, they are a remarkably excellent body of men here, and we will take care no one does them any harm. It is very different at Birmingham; there they have a Bishop, and that makes all the difference; he is a Wolsey all over; and the priests, too, in Birmingham are at least one in twelve infidels. We do not recollect who ascertained this, but it was some most respectable man, who was far too conscientious and too charitable to slander any one." And thus, my Brothers, the charges against Catholics will become a sort of Hunt-the-slipper, everywhere and nowhere, and will end in "sound and fury, signifying nothing."

Such is that defensive system, which I think is especially the duty of Catholics at this moment. You are attacked on many sides; do not look about for friends on the right hand or on the left. Trust neither Assyria nor Egypt; trust no body of men. Fall back on yourselves, and trust none but yourselves. I do not mean you must not be grateful to individuals who are generous to you, but beware of parties; all parties are your enemies; beware of alliances. You are your own best, and sure, and sufficient friends; no one can really hurt you but yourselves; no one can succour you but yourselves. Be content to have your conscience clear, and your God on your side.

Your strength lies in your God and your conscience; therefore it lies not in your number. It lies not in your number any more than in intrigue, or combination, or worldly wisdom. God saves whether by many or by few; you are to aim at showing forth His light, at diffusing "the sweet odour of His knowledge in every place:" numbers would not secure this. On the contrary, the more you grew, the more you might be thrown back into yourselves, by the increased animosity and jealousy of your enemies. You are enabled in some measure to mix with them while you are few; you might be thrown back upon yourselves, when you became many. The line of demarcation might be more strictly observed; there might be less intercourse and less knowledge. It would be a terrible state of things to be growing in material power, and growing too in a compulsory exclusiveness. Grow you must; I know it; you cannot help it; it is your destiny; it is the necessity of the Catholic name, it is the prerogative of the Apostolic heritage; but a material extension without a corresponding moral manifestation, it is almost awful to anticipate; awful, if there should be the sun of justice within you, with so little power to cast the illumination of its rays upon the multitudes without. On the other hand, even if you did not grow, you might be able to dispense on all sides of you the royal light of Truth, and exert an august moral influence upon the world. This is what I want; I do not want growth, except of course for the sake of the souls of those who are the increment; but I want you to rouse yourselves to understand where you are, to know yourselves. I would aim primarily at organization, edification, cultivation of mind, growth of the reason. It is a moral force, not a material, which will vindicate your profession, and will secure your triumph. It is not giants who do most. How small was the Holy Land! yet it subdued the world. How poor a spot was Attica! yet it has formed the intellect. Moses was one, Elias was one, David was one, Paul was one, Athanasius was one, Leo was one. Grace ever works by few; it is the keen vision, the intense conviction, the indomitable resolve of the few, it is the blood of the martyr, it is the prayer of the saint, it is the heroic deed, it is the momentary crisis, it is the concentrated energy of a word or a look, which is the instrument of heaven. Fear not, little flock, for He is mighty who is in the midst of you, and will do for you great things.

As troubles and trials circle round you, He will give you what you want at present—" a mouth, and wisdom, which all your adversaries shall not be able to resist and gainsay." "There is a time for silence, and a time to speak;" the time for speaking is come. What I desiderate in Catholics is the gift of bringing out what their religion is; it is one of those "better gifts," of which the Apostle bids you be "zealous." You must not hide your talent in a napkin, or your light under a bushel. I want a laity, not arrogant, not rash in speech, not disputatious, but men who know their religion, who enter into it, who know just where they stand, who know what they hold, and what they do not, who know their creed so well, that they can give an account of it, who know so much of history that they can defend it. I want an intelligent, well-instructed laity; I am not denying you are such already: but I mean to be severe, and, as some would say, exorbitant in my demands, I wish you to enlarge your knowledge, to cultivate your reason, to get an insight into the relation of truth to truth, to learn to view things as they are, to understand how faith and reason stand to each other, what are the bases and principles of Catholicism, and where lie the main inconsistences and absurdities of the Protestant theory. I have no apprehension you will be the worse Catholics for familiarity with these subjects, provided you cherish a vivid sense of God above, and keep in mind that you have souls to be judged and to be saved. In all times the laity have been the measure of the Catholic spirit; they saved the Irish Church three centuries ago, and they betrayed the

Church in England. Our rulers were true, our people were cowards. You ought to be able to bring out what you feel and what you mean, as well as to feel and mean it; to expose to the comprehension of others the fictions and fallacies of your opponents; and to explain the charges brought against the Church, to the satisfaction, not, indeed, of bigots, but of men of sense, of whatever cast of opinion. And one immediate effect of your being able to do all this will be your gaining that proper confidence in self which is so necessary for you. You will then not even have the temptation to rely on others, to court political parties or particular men; they will rather have to court you. You will no longer be dispirited or irritated (if such is at present the case), at finding difficulties in your way, in being called names, in not being believed, in being treated with injustice. You will fall back upon yourselves; you will be calm, you will be patient. Ignorance is the root of all littleness; he who can realise the law of moral conflicts, and the incoherence of falsehood, and the issue of perplexities, and the end of all things, and the Presence of the Judge, becomes, from the very necessity of the case, philosophical, long-suffering, and magnanimous.

5.

Cultivation of mind, I know well, is not the same thing as religious principle, but it contributes much to remove from our path the temptation to many lesser forms of moral obliquity. Human nature, left to itself, is susceptible of innumerable feelings, more or less unbecoming, indecorous, petty, and miserable. It is, in no long time, clad and covered by a host of little vices and disgraceful infirmities, jealousies, slynesses, cowardices, frettings, resentments, obstinacies, crookedness in viewing things, vulgar conceit, impertinence, and selfishness. Mental cultivation, though it does not of itself touch the greater wounds of human nature, does a good deal for these lesser defects. In proportion as our intellectual horizon recedes, and we mount up in the knowledge of men and things, so do we make progress in those qualities and that character of mind which we denote by the word "gentleman;" and, if this applies in its measure to the case of all men, whatever their religious principles, much more is it true of a Catholic. Your opponents, my Brothers, are too often emphatically *not* gentlemen: but it will be for you, in spite of whatever provocations you may meet with, to be manly and noble in your bearing towards them; to be straightforward in your dealings with them; to show candour, generosity, honourable feeling, good sense, and forbearance, in spite of provocation; to refrain from taking unfair or small advantages over them; to meet them half way, if they show relentings; not to fret at insults, to bear imputations, and to interpret the actions of all in the best sense you possibly can. It is not only more religious, not only more becoming, not only happier, to have these excellent dispositions of mind, but it is far the most likely way, in the long run, to persuade and succeed. You see I am speaking to you almost in a worldly way; I do not speak to you of Christian charity, lest I should adopt a tone too high for the occasion.

When men see this, they may attempt other weapons; and the more serious you are, they may make the greater efforts to pour contempt and ridicule upon you. But ridicule will not hurt you, as it hurts other religious bodies; they hate and fear Catholicism—they cannot really laugh at it. They may laugh at individuals or at details connected with it, but not at Catholicism itself. Indeed, I am disposed, in one sense, to allow the maxim of the unbeliever, which has before now given rise to so much discussion—viz., that ridicule is the test of truth. Methodism is ridiculous, so is Puritanism; it is not so with the Catholic Religion; it may be, and is, maligned and defamed; ridiculed it cannot be. It is too real, too earnest, too vigorous, to have aught to fear from the most brilliant efforts of the satirist or the wit.

You will not be able to silence your opponents; do not be surprised at it; that will not show that they do not secretly respect you. Men move in parties; what shows on the surface is no index of what is felt within. When they have made assertions, they cannot withdraw them, the shame is so great; so they go on blustering, and wishing themselves out of the awkward position in which they stand. Truth is great: a blow is struck within them: they are unnerved by the secret consciousness of failure; they are angry with themselves; and, though they do not like you at all the better for it, they will be more cautious another time. They speak less confidently henceforth; or, even if they harden themselves, and are as bold as before, others do not go with them; public opinion does not respond to them; and a calumny, which at first was formidable, falls on closed hearts and unwilling ears, and takes no root in the community at large.

This is what I think probable; I will not anticipate it can be otherwise; but still, supposing there is that prejudice existing, which, like a deep soil is able to receive any amount of false witness, of scurrility, of buffoonery, of sophistry, when directed against the Catholic Religion, and that the contempt and hatred at present felt against its adherents is kindled, by their increasing strength and intelligence, into a fiercer, prouder feeling,—what then? *noli æmulari*, be not jealous, fret not. You are not as others; you have that in you which others have not. You have in you an unearthly gift; the gift, not only of contending boldly, but of suffering well. It will not happen, it must not be expected; and yet I confess I have not that confidence on the subject which I had a year since, when I said that Catholics never could be persecuted again in England. It will not be so: yet late events have shown, that though I have never underrated the intense prejudice which prevails against us, I did overrate that Anglo-Saxon love of justice and fair dealing which I thought would be its match. Alas! that I should have to say so, but it is no matter to the Catholic, though much matter to the Englishman. It is no matter to us, because, as I have said, "Greater is He that is in you than he that is in the world." I do not, cannot think a time of serious trial is at hand: I would not willingly use big words, or provoke what is so dreadful, or seem to accomplish it by suggesting it. And for myself, I confess I have no love of suffering at all; nor am I at a time of life when a man commonly loves to risk it. To be quiet and to be undisturbed, to be at peace with all, to live in the sight of my Brethren, to meditate on the future, and to die,—such is the prospect, which is rather suitable to such as me. Yet, my Brothers, I have no doubt at all, either about myself or about Catholics generally, if trial came. I doubt not we should suffer any trial well, not from nature, but from grace; not from what we are in ourselves, but from the wonder-working power which is amongst us, and which fills us as vessels, according to our various dimensions.

6.

Not every age is the age of Saints, but no age is not the age of Martyrs. Look into the history of the Church; you find many instances of men trained up by laborious courses of discipline through a long life, or a period of many years. Slowly, silently, perseveringly, often opposed by their own people, for a while looked on with suspicion even by good Catholics, lest they should be extravagant or intemperate, or self-willed (for time is necessary, as the proof of things), setting about heroic works, acting, suffering with superhuman faith, with superhuman patience, with superhuman love, and then at length dying, not by violence, but in peace,—these are what I have called by pre-eminence Saints, being the great specimens of their kind as contrasted with Martyrs. They are the produce, generally speaking, of the prosperous times of the Church, I mean when the Church is in favour of the world, and is in possession of riches, learning, power, and name. The first in history of these great creations of God, is that glorious name, St. Athanasius; then they follow so thick, that I cannot enumerate them: St. Chrysostom, almost a martyr too, St. Basil, St. Gregory of Nazianzus, St. Augustin, St. Ambrose, St. Jerome; in very distinct spheres of religious duty, but all of them heroes. Such, too, was St. Benedict, such St. Leo, such St. Gregory the First, St. Romuald,

St. Gregory the Seventh, St. Bernard, St. Francis, St. Thomas of Aquinum, St. Ignatius, St. Vincent of Paul. As far as human eyes can see, we have none such on earth at present ; nor again, is our age like their age. Ours is not an age of temporal glory, of dutiful princes, of loyal governments, of large possessions, of ample leisure, of famous schools, of learned foundations, of well-stored libraries, of honoured sanctuaries. Rather, it is like the first age of the Church, when there was little of station, of nobility, of learning, of wealth, in the holy heritage ; when Christians were chiefly of the lower orders ; when we were poor and ignorant, when we were despised and hated by the great and philosophical as a low rabble, or a stupid and obstinate association, or a foul and unprincipled conspiracy. It is like that first age, in which no saint is recorded in history who fills the mind as a great idea, as St. Thomas Aquinas or St. Ignatius fills it, and when the ablest of so-called Christian writers belonged to heretical schools. We certainly have little to show for ourselves ; and the words of the Psalm are fulfilled in us,—" They have set fire to Thy sanctuary ; they have defiled the dwelling-place of Thy name on the earth. Our signs we have not seen ; there is no Prophet and He will know us no more. How long shall the enemy reproach ? is the adversary to provoke Thy name for ever ? " So was it in the first age too : they were scorned and hated as we are ; they were without the effulgence and the celebrity of later times. Yet had they nothing at all to show ? were they without their glory ? it was emphatically the age of Martyrs. The most horrible tortures which imagination can fancy, the most appalling kinds of death were the lot, the accepted portion, the boast and joy, of those abject multitudes. Not a few merely, but by thousands, and of every condition of life, men, women, boys, girls, children, slaves, domestics, they willingly offered their life's blood, their limbs, their senses, their nerves, to the persecutor, rather than soil their faith and their profession with the slightest act which implied the denial of their Lord.

Such was the prowess of the Mother of Saints in her valley of humiliation, when she seemed to have hardly any great thought to show, or spirit, or intellect, or cultivation of mind. And who were these her children who made this sacrifice of blood so freely? what had been their previous lives? how had they been trained? were they special men of fasting, of prayer, and of self-control? No, I repeat it, no; they were for the most part common men; it was not they who did the deed, it was not what was matured in them, it was that unfathomable ocean of faith and sanctity which flowed into, and through, and out of them, unto those tremendous manifestations of divine power. It was the narrow-minded slave, the untaught boy, the gentle maid, as well as the Bishop or the Evangelist, who took on them their cross, and smiled as they entered on their bloody way. It was the soldier of the ranks, it was the jailer or hangman suddenly converted, it was the spectator of a previous martyrdom, nay, it was even the unbaptized heathen, who with a joyful song rose up and washed their robes, and made them white in the blood of the Lamb. Nay, strange to say, in the case of such of them as had been Christians before the persecution, good and religious as they were, yet still we read of disorder and extravagance, and other lesser offences, even while in prison and in expectation of their doom, clearly showing that all of them had not that subdued and disciplined spirit which has distinguished those great lights of after times of whom I was just now speaking. Or take particular instances of martyrdom, or what resembles it, from the first age to the present time;—what was St. Justin? a philosopher, with great secular accomplishments, but assuredly not better grounded in Christian truth than the bulk of our own laity. What was our own St. Alban, again, but a Roman officer, who did a generous action, sheltered a priest, was converted by him, made confession of his faith, and went out to die? And then again, St. Hermenegild, several centuries later; a brave youth, who, by his glorious death, not only gained the crown of martyrdom, but wiped out some rash acts which history imputes to him in the course of the trial which led to it. Who was our own St. Thomas? one who with a true heart had served his Lord and led an ascetic life even when he lived in the world, but who, before his elevation to the Primacy, had indulged in a pomp and magnificence unsuitable to the condition, not only of a priest, which he then was not, but of the inferior orders of the sacred ministry. And so, again in recent times, contemplate the heroic deaths of the martyr-priests of France during the excess of the first bloody Revolution; yet they, although men of clear conscience and good life before, seem to have had no special notes of sanctity on their characters and histories. And so again, the most recent martyr, as he may be called, of the French Church, the late Archbishop of Paris; he, indeed, had in every way adorned and sustained his high dignity, by holiness of conversation and a reputation beyond reproach; and the last glorious act of his life was but in keeping with all which had gone before it. True; but it is to my point to observe that this bright example of self-devotion, and paternal tenderness for his flock, is commonly said to have shrunk in anticipation, by reason of the very gentleness and sweetness of his natural disposition, from such rough contests as that to which he was ultimately called; yet, when his Lord's word came, he calmly went forth into the ranks of his infuriated people, stood between the mortal combatants, with the hope of separating them, and received the wound which suddenly took him off to his eternal reward. This, then, may be said, as a general rule, of the individual members of the "white-robed army;" they have been, for the most part, men of noble zeal and chivalrous prowess, who startled the world, startled their friends, startled themselves by what the grace that is in the Church enabled them to do. They shot up at once to their high stature, and "being perfected in a short space," as the Wise man says, "they fulfilled a long time." Thus they shone forth, and "ran to and fro like sparks among the reeds," like those keen and sudden fires which dart forth from some electric mass, on due provocation, and intimate to us the power and intensity of the awful elements which lie concealed within it.

The Church of God cannot change; what she was that she is. What our forefathers were, such are we; we look like other men, but we have that in us which none others have,—the latent element of an indomitable fortitude. This may not be the age of Saints, but all times are the age of Martyrs. The arrow is on the string, and the arm is drawn back, and, "if the Lord give the word," great will be the multitude of His champions. O my Brothers, it is difficult for you and me to realize this; it is difficult for us to believe that we have it in us, being what we are,—but we have. And it is difficult for us to believe that this can be a time for testing it, nor do I say it is; I think it cannot be; I only say, that if it were to be a time for calling out the Martyr's spirit, you and I, through God's grace, have it in us. I only mean that it is profitable, in such lesser trials as may easily come upon us, to be reminded that we may humbly trust we have that in us which can sustain the greatest. And it would be profitable also for our opponents, high and low, if they too would lay this to heart. It would be well for them to recollect, that there is a certain principle, which we call zeal, and they call fanaticism. Let them beware of awaking what they would, in scoffing, call the fanatical spirit of the Catholic. For years and years the Catholics of England have borne personal slander, and insult, and injustice. In their own persons, and not merely in their religious profession, have they been treated as the adherents of no other creed have been treated, with scorn, hatred, and cruelty. Men have shrunk from coming near them, and have almost discarded from their society those who did; as if inflicting on them the greater excommunication, as upon those who were the extremest reprobates and blasphemers on the face of the earth. They have borne, and they bear, an ill-usage, which, in its mildest and most amiable form, has never risen higher than pity and condescension. They have borne, and they bear, to be "the heathen's jest," waiting till the morning breaks, and a happier day begins.

So has it been with us up to this hour; but let our enemies remember that, while they have their point of honour, we have ours. They have stripped us of power, wealth, name, and station; they have left us nothing but our Apostolical inheritance. And now they wish to take from us the "little ewe-lamb," which is our only treasure. There was a saying of old, "Let alone Camarina, for 'tis best let alone." Let them, as sensible men,—I do not say, accept Catholicism as true, but admit it into their imagination as a fact. A story goes about of a sagacious statesman and monarch of our own time, who, when urged by some of his advisers to come to an open rupture with the Holy See, made answer, "If you can put your finger upon the page of history, and point out any one instance in which any civil power quarrelled with Rome with honour and success in the event, I will accede to your wishes." And it has lately been given to the world, how that sagacious politician, apostate priest as he was, Prince Talleyrand, noted it as one of Napoleon's three great political mistakes, that he quarrelled with the Pope. There is only one way of success over us, possible even in idea,—a wholesale massacre. Let them exterminate us, as they have done before, kill the priests, decimate the laity; and they have for a while defeated the Pope. They have no other way; they may gain a material victory, never a moral one.

7.

These are thoughts to comfort and sustain us, whatever trial lies before us. I might pursue them farther, but it is enough to have suggested them. Nothing more remains for me to do, but, in commending myself to your good thoughts, my Brothers, to thank those also, who, though not of our communion, have honoured me with their attendance. If I might take the liberty of addressing them directly, I would anxiously entreat them to think over what I have said, even though they have not been altogether pleased at my manner of saying it. Minds, and judgments, and tastes, are so very different, that I cannot hope to have approved myself to all, even though they be well disposed towards me, nay, to any one at all so fully, but that he may have thought that some things might have been said better, and some things were better omitted altogether. Yet I entreat them to believe that I have uttered nothing at random, but have had reasons, both for what I said and my manner of saying it. It is easy to fancy a best way of doing things, but very difficult to find it: and often what is called the best way is, in the very nature of things, not positively good, but only better than other ways. And really in the present state of things, it is difficult to say anything in behalf of Catholicism, if it is to make any impression, without incurring grave criticism of one kind or another; and quite impossible so to say it, as not grievously to offend those whom one is opposing. But, after all, in spite of all imperfections, which are incident to the doings of every mortal man, and in spite of the differences of judgments, which will make those imperfections greater than they are, I do trust there is a substance of truth in what I have said, which will last, and produce its effect somewhere or other. Good is never done except at the expense of those who do it: truth is never enforced except at the sacrifice of its propounders. At least they expose their inherent imperfections, if they incur no other penalty; for nothing would be done at all, if a man waited till he could do it so well that no one could find fault with it.

Under these circumstances, then, what can I desire and pray for but this?—that what I have said well may be blest to those who have heard it, and that what I might have said better, may be blest to me by increasing my dissatisfaction with myself: that I may cheerfully resign myself to such trouble or anxiety as necessarily befalls anyone who has spoken boldly on an unpopular subject in a difficult time, with the confidence that no trouble or anxiety but will bring some real good with it in the event, to those who have acted in sincerity, and by no unworthy methods, and with no selfish aim.

NOTES.

Note I. (*p.* 18.)

The following is the passage as it stands in Mr. Blanco White's work, a portion of which is extracted in Lecture I.:—

"The Jesuits, till the abolition of that order, had an almost unrivalled influence over the better classes of Spaniards. They had nearly monopolized the instruction of the Spanish youth, at which they toiled without pecuniary reward; and were equally zealous in promoting devotional feelings both among their pupils and the people at large. It is well known that the most accurate division of labour was observed in the allotment of their various employments. Their candidates, who, by a refinement of ecclesiastical policy, after an unusually long probation, were bound by vows which, depriving them of liberty, yet left a discretionary power of ejection in the Order, were incessantly watched by the penetrating eye of the Master of Novices; a minute description of their character and peculiar turn was forwarded to the superiors, and at the end of the noviciate they were employed to the advantage of the community, without ever thwarting the natural bent of the individual, or diverting his natural powers by a multiplicity of employments. Wherever, as in France and Italy, literature was in high estimation, the Jesuits spared no trouble to raise among themselves men of eminence in that department. In Spain their chief aim was to provide their houses with popular preachers, and zealous, yet prudent and gentle, confessors. Pascal and the Jansenist party, of which he was the organ, accused them of systematic laxity in their moral doctrines; but the charge, I believe, though plausible in theory, was perfectly groundless in practice. If, indeed, ascetic virtue could ever be divested of its connatural evil tendency—if a system of moral perfection, that has for its basis, however disavowed and disguised, the Manichæan doctrine of the two principles, could be applied with any partial advantage as a rule of conduct, it was so in the hands of the

Jesuits. The strict, unbending maxims of the Jansenists, by urging persons of all characters and tempers on to an imaginary goal of perfection, bring quickly their whole system to the decision of experience. They are like those enthusiasts who, venturing upon the practice of some Gospel sayings in the literal sense, have made the absurdity of that interpretation as clear as noonday light. A greater knowledge of mankind made the Jesuits more cautious in the culture of devotional feelings. They well knew that but few can prudently engage in open hostility with what, in ascetic language, is called the world. They now and then trained up a sturdy champion, who, like their founder Loyola, might provoke the enemy to single combat with honour to his leaders; but the crowd of mystic combatants were made to stand upon a kind of jealous truce, which, in spite of all care, often produced some jovial meetings of the advanced parties on both sides. The good fathers came forward, rebuked their soldiers back into the camp, and filled up the place of deserters by their indefatigable industry in engaging recruits.

"The influence of the Jesuits on Spanish morals, from everything I have learned, was undoubtedly favourable. Their kindness attracted the youth from their schools to their Company; and though it must be acknowledged that many arts were practised to decoy the cleverest and the wealthiest into the order, they also greatly contributed to the preservation of virtue in that slippery age, both by ties of affection and the gentle check of example. Their churches were crowded every Sunday with regular attendants, who came to confess and receive the sacrament. The practice of choosing a certain priest, not only to be the occasional confessor but *director of the conscience*, was greatly encouraged by the Jesuits. The ultimate effects of this surrender of the judgment are indeed dangerous and degrading; but in a country where the darkest superstition is constantly impelling the mind into the opposite extremes of religious melancholy and profligacy, weak persons are sometimes preserved from either by the friendly assistance of a prudent *director*, and the Jesuits were generally well qualified for that office. Their conduct was correct, and their manners refined. They kept up a dignified intercourse with the middling and higher classes, and were always ready to help and instruct the poor, without descending to their level. Since the expulsion of the Jesuits, the better classes for the most part avoid the company of monks and friars, except in an official capacity; while the lower ranks, from which these professional saints are generally taken, and where they reappear raised, indeed, into comparative importance, but grown bolder in grossness and vice, suffer more from their influence than they would by being left without any religious ministers."

He adds this note :—

"The profligacy now prevalent among the friars, contrasted with the conduct of the Jesuits, as described by the most credible living witnesses, is excessively striking. Whatever we may think of the political delinquencies of their leaders, their bitterest enemies have never ventured to charge the order of Jesuits with moral irregularities. The internal policy of that body precluded the possibility of gross misconduct. No Jesuit could step out of doors without calling on the superior for leave and a companion, in the choice of whom great care was taken to vary the couples. Never were they allowed to pass a single night out of the convent, except when attending a dying person; and even then they were under the strictest injunctions to return at whatever hour the soul departed."—*Doblado's Letters in the New Monthly Magazine*, 1821, vol. ii. pp. 157, 158.

An objection has been taken to the validity of the argument in the latter part of the same Lecture, in which it is attempted to expose the polemic which Protestants commonly use against the Catholic Church, by comparing it to a supposed tirade of some Russian against England; and that, upon the ground that the maxims of the English Constitution (*e.g.*, the king can do no wrong) are confessedly fictions, whereas the Church's infallibility is a dogma expressing a truth. In this particular respect, certainly, the cases are not parallel; but they need not be parallel for the argument. The point urged against the Protestant is this—That, whereas every science, polity, institution, religion, uses the words and phrases which it employs in *a sense of its own*, or *a technical* sense, Englishmen, allowing and exemplifying this very principle in the case of their own Constitution, will not allow it to the divines of the Catholic Church. *E.g.*, the "Omnipotence of Parliament" is a phrase of English law, in which the word *omnipotence* is taken otherwise than when it is ascribed to Almighty God; and so, too, when used by Catholic divines of the Blessed Virgin. If any one exclaims against its adoption, in the latter case, by Catholics, let him also protest against its adoption, in the former case, by English lawyers; if he rejects explanations, distinctions, limitations, in the latter case, and calls them lame, subtle, evasive, &c., let him do so in the former case also; whereas Protestants denounce such explanations as offered by Catholics, and take a pride in them as laid down by English lawyers. In like manner, "the king can do no wrong" has *a* sense in constitutional law, though not the sense which the words would suggest to a foreigner who heard them for the first time; and "the Pope is infallible" has its **own** sense in theology, but not that which the words suggest to a Protestant, who takes the words in their ordinary meaning. And, as it is the way with Protestants to maintain that the Pope's infallibility is intended by **us as a** guarantee of his **private** and personal exemption from theological error, nay, **even from moral** fault of **every** kind; so a foreigner, **who** knew nothing **of** England, were he equally impatient, prejudiced, and indocile, might at first hearing confound the maxim, "the king **can** do no wrong," with the dogma of some Oriental despotism or theocracy.

For a fuller explanation of the argument, *vid.* Lecture VIII.

I may add that I have **been** informed **since I** published Lecture III., that Mr. Hallam, **in a** later edition than my own of his Middle Ages, has explained his severe **remarks** upon St. Eligius. **Nothing less could be expected from a** person **of** his great reputation.

Note II.

THE question of Ecclesiastical Miracles is treated in Lecture VII. solely with reference to their general verisimilitude, or the antecedent probability or improbability of their occurrence; that is, to the pre-judgment, favourable or otherwise, which spontaneously arises in our minds, upon hearing reports or reading statements of particular miraculous occurrences. This antecedent probability depends on two conditions—viz., first of all, whether there is an existing cause adequate to the production of such phenomena; and next, since there certainly is such—viz., the Creator—whether in the particular case, the alleged miracle sufficiently resembles

His known works in character and object to admit of being ascribed to Him. Two questions remain to be determined, which do not come into discussion in the Lecture; first, whether the fact under consideration *is* really miraculous—that is, such as not to be referable to the operation of ordinary processes of nature or of art; and, secondly, whether it comes to us with such evidence, either from sight or from testimony, as warrants us in accepting it as having really taken place.

Thus the liquefaction of St. Januarius' Blood at Naples, in order to its reception as miraculous—(1) must be possible; (2) must be parallel to God's known works in nature or in revelation, or suitable to Him; (3) must be clearly beyond the operation of chemical or other scientific means, or jugglery of man or evil spirit; and (4) must be wrought publicly.

The antecedent probability of such miracles is, I repeat, all that concerned me in Lecture VII.; but I went on, at the end of it, to avow my own personal belief in some of them as facts, lest I should be suspected of making a sham defence of what I did not in my heart myself accept. Here I subjoin, from the columns of the *Morning Chronicle*, a correspondence on this subject, which took place in 1851, between the late Dr. Hinds and myself, soon after the delivery of the Lecture:—

No. 1.
DR. NEWMAN TO THE BISHOP OF NORWICH.
"THURLES, IRELAND, *October* 2.

"MY DEAR LORD,—A slip of a Norwich paper has been sent me, which purports to give a speech of the 'Bishop of the diocese,' delivered in St. Andrew's Hall, at a meeting of the British and Foreign Bible Society. Though the name of the diocese is not stated, I cannot be mistaken, under the circumstances, in ascribing the speech to your lordship. Yet I know not how to credit that certain words contained in it, which evidently refer to me, should have been uttered by one who is so liberal, so fair, and temperate in his general judgments as your lordship.

"The words are these:—'My friends, I have heard—and I am sure all of you who have heard of it will share with me in the disgust as well as the surprise with which I have heard of it—that there is a publication circulated through this land, the stronghold of Bible Christianity—a publication issuing from that Church against which we are protesting, and which is, on the other hand, the stronghold of human authority—a publication issuing from one of the most learned of its members, a man who, by his zeal as a convert, and by his position and acceptance with that Church, speaks with the authority of the Church itself, and represents its doctrines and feelings—a publication, as I have heard with dismay, read, admired, circulated, which maintains that the legendary stories of those puerile miracles, which I believe until now few Protestants thought that the Roman Catholics themselves believed; that these legends *have a claim to belief equally* with that Word of God which relates the miracles of our God, as recorded in the Gospel, and that *the authority of the one is as the authority of the other, the credibility of the one based on a foundation no less sure than the credibility of the other.*'

"The statements here animadverted on are as contrary to the teaching of the Catholic Church as they can be repugnant to your own views of Christian truth.

"Should I be right in supposing that you did not really impute them to me, I beg to apologise to you for putting you to the trouble of disavowing the newspaper account; but if, contrary to my expectation, you ackowledge them to be yours, I take the liberty of begging your lordship to refer me to the place in any work of mine in which they are contained.

"You will not, I am sure, be surprised if, at a moment like the present, when so many misrepresentations are made of Catholicism and its defenders, I should propose, as I do, to give the same publicity to any answer you shall favour me with, as has been given to the speech the report of which has occasioned my question.

"I am, my dear Lord, yours very faithfully,
"JOHN H. NEWMAN."

No. 2.

THE BISHOP OF NORWICH TO DR. NEWMAN.

"LONDON, *October* 8.

"MY DEAR NEWMAN,—As I have already replied to an inquiry, the same as that which you make, in a letter to the Rev. W. Cobb, Roman Catholic priest in Norwich, I enclose a copy of that letter.

"If I have misrepresented you, you will, I hope, believe me when I say that it has been from misunderstanding you. Permit me to add, that what has misled me is likely, you may be sure, to mislead others. I shall rejoice, therefore, at any public statement from you which may disabuse your readers of false impressions. When you are found to be maintaining (as you appear to do) that the miracles of the apostolic age were only the beginning of a like miraculous development, to be manifested and accredited through succeeding times, and professing your belief in the facts of this further miraculous development, in terms as solemn as those of a creed, it is very difficult to avoid the impression that the scriptural narratives are to be regarded as the beginning only of a series of the like histories, partaking of their credibility and authority, although the one may be called Scripture and the other legend.

"Time and circumstances have so long divided us, that I ought to apologize for the familiar mode in which I have addressed you; but your handwriting has brought back on my mind other days, and some dear friends, who were then friends and associates of both of us; and I would still desire you to believe me very truly yours,

"S. NORWICH."

No. 3 (enclosed in No. 2).
THE BISHOP OF NORWICH TO MR. CORB.

"ATHENÆUM, LONDON, *October* 6.

"REVEREND SIR,—My absence from home when your letter was delivered, and my not having Dr. Newman's publications by me when I received it here, have caused a delay in my making reply to your inquiry. The work to which I alluded, when I stated, in St. Andrew's Hall, that he asserted for certain legendary accounts of miracles the same credibility which is claimed for the Scriptural narratives and statements of miracles, is his 'Lectures on Catholicism in England,' more particularly Lecture VII., p. 298. In this passage, after discriminating between some legends and others, as we discriminate between genuine Scripture and that which is either spurious or doubtful, he professes his faith in those the authority of which he pronounces to be unquestionable in terms such as these :—

"'I think it impossible to withstand the evidence which is brought for the liquefaction of the blood of St. Januarius at Naples, and for the motion of the eyes of the pictures of the Madonna in the Roman States. I firmly believe that saints, in their lifetime, have before now raised the dead to life, crossed the sea without vessels, multiplied grain and bread, cured incurable diseases, and stopped the operation of the laws of the universe in a multitude of ways. Many men, when they hear an educated man so speak, will at once impute the avowal to insanity, or to an idiosyncrasy, or to imbecility of mind, or to decrepitude of powers, or to fanaticism, or to hypocrisy. They have a right to say so if they will; *and we have a right to ask them why they do **not say it of those** who bow down before the mystery of mysteries, the Divine Incarnation.*'

"He pursues the same view in his volume of 'Discourses for Mixed Congregations,' setting aside, as a thing of nought, the essential difference between the claim which Scripture has on our belief in miracles related there, and that of human legends for the like statements, and recognizing no difference but that of the marvellousness of the things related in the one or the other.

"'They (speaking of Protestants) have not in them the principle of faith, and, I repeat it, it is nothing to the purpose to urge that at least they firmly believe Scripture to be the Word of God. In truth, it is much to be feared that their acceptance of Scripture itself is nothing better than a prejudice or inveterate feeling impressed on them when they were children. A proof of this is this—that while they profess to be so shocked at Catholic miracles, and are not slow to call them "lying wonders," *they have no difficulty at all about Scripture narratives, which are quite as difficult to the reason as any miracles recorded in the history of the saints.* I have heard, on the contrary, of Catholics, who have been startled at first reading in Scripture the narrative of the ark in the deluge, of the Tower of Babel, of Balaam and Balak, of the Israelites' flight from Egypt and entrance into the promised land, and of Esau's and of Saul's rejection, which the bulk of Protestants receive without any effort of mind.'—Page 217.

"In his speech at the Birmingham meeting, he propounded the same view, in reference to God's revelation through nature, as he has, in the preceding passages, in reference to God's written word. He said on that occasion, if his words are rightly reported—'We have no higher proof of the doctrines of natural religion—such as the being of a God, a rule of right and wrong, and the like—than we have of the Romish system,' including, I must presume, all those legendary statements which he so strongly represents as part of that system.

"It would be very satisfactory to me to have any authoritative disclaimer of these publications as exponents of your Church's views; for they alarm me, from their tendency to bring into discredit that faith which, notwithstanding the serious differences that unhappily divide us, we still, God be thanked, hold in common, and cherish in common.

"I ought to add that, in giving those last words which you have quoted from the newspapers, the reporters must have heard me imperfectly, or have misapprehended me. I did not say that Dr. Newman asserted, for the miracles related in the Romish legends, a credibility based upon the foundation of divine revelation no less than those of Scripture. What I said was, that he claimed for the miracles related in the legends, the authorship of which was human, the same amount of credibility as for the miracles and divine revelations **recorded in Scripture, the authorship of** which **was divine; thus** leading his readers either to raise the authority of the legends to that of Scripture, or to bring down the authority of Scripture **to** that of the legends, the latter of which **appeared to me to be the more likely result.**

"I am, rev. sir, your faithful servant,

"S. NORWICH."

No. 4.

DR. NEWMAN TO THE BISHOP OF NORWICH.

"ORATORY, BIRMINGHAM, *October* 11.

"MY DEAR LORD,—I thank you for the kind tone of your letter, which it was very pleasant to me to find so like that of former times, and for the copy you enclose of your answer to Mr. Cobb.

"Your lordship's words, as reported in the Norwich paper, were to the effect that I believed the ecclesiastical miracles to have 'a claim to belief *equally* with that Word of God which relates the miracles of our God as recorded in the gospels;' that I made 'the authority of the one as the authority of the other,' and 'the credibility of the one as based on a foundation no less sure than the credibility of the other.'

"You explain this in a letter to Mr. Cobb thus:—'I did not say that Dr. Newman asserted, for the miracles related in the Romish legends, a credibility based upon the foundation of divine revelation no less than those of Scripture. What I said was, that he claimed for the miracles related in the legends, the authorship of which was human, the same amount of *credibility* as for the miracles and divine revelations recorded in Scripture, the authorship of which was divine.'

"Will you allow me to ask you the meaning of your word 'credibility'? for it seems to me a fallacy is involved in it. Archbishop Whately says that controversies are often verbal. I cannot help being quite sure that your lordship's difficulty is of this nature.

"When you speak of a miracle being *credible* you must mean one of two things—either that it is 'antecedently probable,' or *verisimile;* or that it is 'furnished with sufficient evidence,' or *proveable.* In which of these senses do you use the word? If you describe me as saying that the ecclesiastical miracles come to us on the same *evidence* as those of Scripture, you attribute to me what I have never dreamed of asserting; if you understand me to say that the ecclesiastical miracles are on the same level of *antecedent probability* with those of Scripture, you do justice to my meaning, but I do not conceive it is of a nature to raise 'disgust.'

"I am not inventing a distinction for the occasion; it is found in Archbishop Whately's works; and I have pursued it at great length in my 'University Sermons,' and in my 'Essay on Miracles,' published in

1843, which has never been answered as far as I know, and a copy of which I shall beg to present to your lordship.

"1. First, let us suppose you to mean by 'credible' antecedently probable, or *likely (verisimile)*, and you will then accuse me of saying that the ecclesiastical miracles are as *likely* as those of Scripture. What is there extreme or disgusting in such a statement, whether you agree with it or not? I certainly *do* think that the ecclesiastical miracles *are* as credible (in this sense) as the Scripture miracles; nay, more so, because they come after Scripture, and Scripture breaks (as it were) the ice. The miracles of Scripture begin a new law; they innovate on an established order. There is less to surprise in a second miracle than in a first. I do not see how it can be denied that ecclesiastical miracles, as coming *after* Scripture miracles, have not to bear the brunt of that antecedent improbability which attaches, as Hume objects, to the idea of a violation of nature. Ecclesiastical miracles are *probable*, because Scripture miracles are *true*. This is all I have said or implied in the two passages you have quoted from me, as is evident from both text and context.

"As to the former passage of the two, I there say, that if Protestants are surprised at my having no *difficulty* in believing ecclesiastical miracles, I have a right to ask them why they have no difficulty in believing the Incarnation. Protestants find a difficulty in even listening to evidence adduced for ecclesiastical miracles. I have none. Why? Because the admitted fact of the Scripture miracles has taken away whatever *prima facie* unlikelihood attaches to them as a violation of the laws of nature. My whole Lecture is on the one idea of 'Assumed Principles,' or antecedent judgments or theories; it has nothing to do with proof or evidence. And so of the second passage. I have but said that Protestants 'have no *difficulty* at all about Scripture miracles, which are quite as difficult to the *reason* as any miracle recorded in the history of the saints.' Now, I really cannot conceive a thoughtful person denying that the history of the ark at the deluge is as difficult to reason as a saint floating on his cloak. As to the third passage you quote as mine, about 'revelation through nature,' and 'legendary statements,' I know nothing about it. I cannot even guess of what words of mine it is the distortion. Tell me the when and where, and I will try to make out what I really said. If it professes to come from my recent lectures, all I can say is that what I spoke I read from a printed copy, and what I printed I published, and what is not in the printed volume I did not say.

"2. But now for the second sense of the word 'credible.' Do you understand me to say that the ecclesiastical miracles come to us on as good *proof* or grounds as those of Scripture? If so, I answer distinctly, I have said no such thing anywhere. The Scripture miracles are credible, *i.e.*, proveable, on a ground peculiar to themselves on the authority of God's Word. Observe my expressions: I think it '*impossible to withstand the evidence* which is brought for the **liquefaction of the blood of** St. Januarius.' Should I thus speak of **the** resurrection of Lazarus? should **I** say, '**I** think it impossible to *withstand the evidence* for his resurrection?' I cannot tell how Protestants would **speak,** but a Catholic would say, '**I believe it** with a certainty beyond **all** other certainty, *for* **God has spoken.**' Moreover, I believe with a like **certainty** every **one of the** Scripture miracles, not only that apostles and **prophets 'in** their lifetime have *before now* raised the dead to life,' &c., but that **Elias** did this, and St. Peter did that, and just as related, and so **all** through the whole catalogue of their miracles. On the other hand, ecclesiastical miracles may be believed, one more than another, and **more or** less by different **persons.** This I have expressed in words which **occur** in the passage from which you quote, for, after saying of one, '**I think it** *impossible to withstand the evidence* for' it, I say of another extraordinary fact no more than, ' **I see** *no reason to doubt*' it; and of a third, still less, '*I do not see why it may not*' be; whereas, whatever God has said is to be believed **absolutely and by all.** This applies to the account of the ark; I believe it, though *more* difficult to the reason, with a firmness quite different from **that with which I** believe the account **of a** saint's crossing the sea on his cloak, though *less* difficult to the **reason; for the one comes** to me on **the** Word of God, **the other on the word of man.**

"The whole of what I have said in **my recent Lecture comes to this;** that **Protestants are most** inconsistent and one-sided, in *refusing to go into the evidence* for ecclesiastical miracles, which, **on the** first blush of the matter, are not stranger than those miracles of **Scripture** which they happily profess to admit. How is this the same **as saying** that *when* the grounds for believing those ecclesiastical miracles *are* entered on, **God's Word through His Church, on which the Catholic rests the** miracles of **the Law** and the Gospel, is not a firmer evidence **than man's** word, on which rest the miracles of ecclesiastical history?

"So very clear is this distinction between verisimilitude **and evidence, and so very** clearly **(as** I consider) is my own line **of argument founded on it, that** I should really for my own satisfaction like **your lordship's** assurance that you had carefully read, not **merely dipped into, my** Lecture, before you delivered your speech. Certain it is, that most people, though they **are** not the fit parallels **of a** person of your dispassionate and candid **mind,** do judge **of my meaning** by bits of sentences, mine or not mine, inserted in letters in the newspapers.

"Under these circumstances, I entertain the most **lively confidence that your** lordship will find yourself able to reconsider the word 'disgust,' as unsuitable to be applied to statements which, if you do not approve, at least you cannot very readily refute. I am, my dear lord,

"With every kind feeling personally to **your lordship,**

"Very truly yours,

"JOHN H. NEWMAN."

No. 5.

THE BISHOP OF NORWICH TO DR. NEWMAN.

"NORWICH, *October* 17.

"MY DEAR NEWMAN,—One of the secretaries of the Bible Society has asked my permission to reprint what I said as **Chairman** of the meeting at Norwich. I will most readily avail myself of this reprint to withdraw the expression 'disgust,' as it appears to be offensive. I will also, as is due to you, have a note appended, referring to the passages in your writings to which my observations were more particularly directed, **and** stating **that** you disavow the construction which **I put** on them.

"At the same time I am unable still to come to any other conclusion than that of the dangerous tendency which I have represented them to have. **If** you maintain, as you distinctly do, not only the *antecedent probability* (*credulity* in that sense) of the legendary miracles, but your firm belief **in** certain of them, specifically stated as *facts proved*, and **if you further** contend that these miracles are only a continuation **of those** recorded **in Scripture, the** impression appears **to me inevitable, that the** legendary channel through which God must have appointed them **to be attested and** preserved has a **purpose and** authority the same with Scripture. What I should fear **is, not indeed that the** generality of your **readers will** exalt legends **into Scripture;** but that, seeing grounds for **discrediting the** legends, **they will look on** all narratives of miracles, scriptural and **legendary, as alike doubtful, and** more than doubtful. In **short,** your **view, as I see it,** tends to a scepticism and infidelity of which I fully acquit **you.**

"The **report of your** speech at Birmingham **I read in the *Times*, but** the quotation **which I sent** to Mr. Cobb, **I** took from a letter in the *Spectator* **of Sept. 27, the** writer's quotation, according with my impression of your **speech as reported,** containing words **to** that effect.

"The **kind present** which you propose **for me** will, I assure you, be valued, **if for no more, as a** token that we are still friends, notwithstanding a wide severance in matters of faith, and that we may still believe all things and hope all things for one **another.**

"My dear Newman, yours **truly,**

"S. NORWICH."

No. 6.

DR. NEWMAN **TO THE** BISHOP **OF NORWICH.**

"ORATORY, BIRMINGHAM, *October* 19.

"MY DEAR LORD,—I thank your lordship with all my heart for your **very** kind and friendly letter just received, and **for your most** frank and ready compliance with the request which I felt it my duty to make to you.

"It is a great satisfaction to me to have been able to remove a misapprehension of my meaning from your mind. There still remains, I confess, what is no misapprehension, though I grieve it should be a cause of uneasiness to you—my avowal, first, that the miraculous gift has never left the Church since the time of the Apostles, though displaying itself under different circumstances, and next that certain reputed miracles are real instances of its exhibition. The former of these two points I hold in common with all Catholics; the latter on my own private judgment, which I impose on no one.

"If I keep to my intention of making our correspondence public it is, I assure you, not only as wishing to clear myself of the imputation which has in various quarters been cast upon my Lecture, but also in no slight measure, because I am able to present to the world the specimen of an anti-Catholic disputant, as fair and honourable in his treatment of an opponent, and as mindful of old recollections, as he is firm and distinct in the enunciation of his own theological view.

"That the Eternal Mercy may ever watch over you and guide you, and fill you with all knowledge and with all peace, is, my dear lord, the sincere prayer of

"Yours most truly,
"JOHN H. NEWMAN."

THE END.

THE ABERDEEN UNIVERSITY PRESS.

A SELECT LIST OF WORKS

PUBLISHED BY

LONGMANS, GREEN, & CO.

LONDON AND NEW YORK.

MESSRS. LONGMANS, GREEN, & CO.

Issue the undermentioned Lists of their Publications, which may be had post free on application to them at 39 Paternoster Row, London, E.C.:

1. **Monthly List of New Works and New Editions.**
2. **Quarterly List of Announcements and New Works.**
3. **Notes on Books:** being an Analysis of the Works published during each Quarter.
4. **Catalogue of Scientific Works.**
5. **Catalogue of Medical and Surgical Works.**
6. **Catalogue of School Books and Educational Works.**
7. **Catalogue of Books for Elementary Schools and Pupil Teachers.**
8. **Catalogue of Theological Works by Divines and Members of the Church of England.**
9. **Catalogue of Works in General Literature.**

CARDINAL NEWMAN'S WORKS.

Parochial and Plain Sermons. Edited by REV. W. J. COPELAND, B.D., late Rector of Farnham, Essex. 8 vols. Sold separately. Crown 8vo. Cabinet Edition, 5s. each; Popular Edition, 3s. 6d. each.

CONTENTS OF VOL. I.:—Holiness necessary for Future Blessedness—The Immortality of the Soul—Knowledge of God's Will without Obedience—Secret Faults—Self-Denial the Test of Religious Earnestness—The Spiritual Mind—Sins of Ignorance and Weakness—God's Commandments not Grievous—The Religious Use of Excited Feelings—Profession without Practice—Profession without Hypocrisy—Profession without Ostentation—Promising without Doing—Religious Emotion—Religious Faith Rational—The Christian Mysteries—The Self-Wise Inquirer—Obedience the Remedy for Religious Perplexity—Times of Private Prayer—Forms of Private Prayer—The Resurrection of the Body—Witnesses of the Resurrection—Christian Reverence—The Religion of the Day—Scripture a Record of Human Sorrow—Christian Manhood.

CONTENTS OF VOL. II.:—The World's Benefactors—Faith without Sight—The Incarnation—Martyrdom—Love of Relations and Friends—The Mind of Little Children—Ceremonies of the Church—The Glory of the Christian Church—St. Paul's Conversion viewed in Reference to his Office—Secrecy and Suddenness of Divine Visitations—Divine Decrees—The Reverence Due to the Blessed Virgin Mary—Christ, a Quickening Spirit—Saving Knowledge—Self-Contemplation—Religious Cowardice—The Gospel Witnesses—Mysteries in Religion—The Indwelling Spirit—The Kingdom of the Saints—The Gospel, a Trust Committed to us—Tolerance of Religious Error—Rebuking Sin—The Christian Ministry—Human Responsibility—Guilelessness—The Danger of Riches—The Powers of Nature—The Danger of Accomplishments—Christian Zeal—Use of Saints' Days.

CARDINAL NEWMAN'S WORKS.

Parochial and Plain Sermons.—*Continued.*

CONTENTS OF VOL. III.:—Abraham and Lot—Wilfulness of Israel in Rejecting Samuel—Saul—Early Years of David—Jeroboam—Faith and Obedience—Christian Repentance—Contracted Views in Religion—A particular Providence as revealed in the Gospel—Tears of Christ at the Grave of Lazarus—Bodily Suffering—The Humiliation of the Eternal Son—Jewish Zeal a Pattern to Christians—Submission to Church Authority—Contest between Truth and Falsehood in the Church—The Church Visible and Invisible—The Visible Church an Encouragement to Faith—The Gift of the Spirit—Regenerating Baptism—Infant Baptism—The Daily Service—The Good Part of Mary—Religious Worship a Remedy for Excitements—Intercession—The Intermediate State.

CONTENTS OF VOL. IV.:—The Strictness of the Law of Christ—Obedience without Love, as instanced in the Character of Balaam—Moral Consequences of Single Sins—Acceptance of Religious Privileges Compulsory—Reliance on Religious Observances—The Individuality of the Soul—Chastisement amid Mercy—Peace and Joy amid Chastisement—The State of Grace—The Visible Church for the Sake of the Elect—The Communion of Saints—The Church a Home for the Lonely—The Invisible World—The Greatness and Littleness of Human Life—Moral Effects of Communion with God—Christ Hidden from the World—Christ Manifested in Remembrance—The Gainsaying of Korah—The Mysteriousness of our Present Being—The Ventures of Faith—Faith and Love—Watching—Keeping Fast and Festival.

CONTENTS OF VOL. V.:—Worship, a Preparation for Christ's Coming—Reverence, a Belief in God's Presence—Unreal Words—Shrinking from Christ's Coming—Equanimity—Remembrance of Past Mercies—The Mystery of Godliness—The State of Innocence—Christian Sympathy—Righteousness not of us, but in us—The Law of the Spirit—The New Works of the Gospel—The State of Salvation—Transgressions and Infirmities—Sins of Infirmity—Sincerity and Hypocrisy—The Testimony of Conscience—Many called, Few chosen—Present Blessings—Endurance, the Christian's Portion—Affliction, a School of Comfort—The Thought of God, the Stay of the Soul—Love, the One Thing Needful—The Power of the Will.

CONTENTS OF VOL. VI.:—Fasting, a Source of Trial—Life, the Season of Repentance—Apostolic Abstinence, a Pattern for Christians—Christ's Privations, a Meditation for Christians—Christ the Son of God made Man—The Incarnate Son, a Sufferer and Sacrifice—The Cross of Christ the Measure of the World—Difficulty of realising Sacred Privileges—The Gospel Sign Addressed to Faith—The Spiritual Presence of Christ in the Church—The Eucharistic Presence—Faith the Title for Justification—Judaism of the Present Day—The Fellowship of the Apostles—Rising with Christ—Warfare the Condition of Victory—Waiting for Christ—Subjection of the Reason and Feelings to the Revealed Word—The Gospel Palaces—The Visible Temple—Offerings for the Sanctuary—The Weapons of Saints—Faith Without Demonstration—The Mystery of the Holy Trinity—Peace in Believing.

CONTENTS OF VOL. VII.:—The Lapse of Time—Religion, a Weariness to the Natural Man—The World our Enemy—The Praise of Men—Temporal Advantages—The Season of Epiphany—The Duty of Self-Denial—The Yoke of Christ—Moses the Type of Christ—The Crucifixion—Attendance on Holy Communion—The Gospel Feast—Love of Religion, a new Nature—Religion Pleasant to the Religious—Mental Prayer—Infant Baptism—The Unity of the Church—Steadfastness in the Old Paths.

CONTENTS OF VOL. VIII.:—Reverence in Worship—Divine Calls—The Trial of Saul—The Call of David—Curiosity, a Temptation to Sin—Miracles no Remedy for Unbelief—Josiah, a Pattern for the Ignorant—Inward Witness to the Truth of the Gospel—Jeremiah, a Lesson for the Disappointed—Endurance of the World's Censure—Doing Glory to God in Pursuits of the World—Vanity of Human Glory—Truth Hidden when not Sought after—Obedience to God the Way to Faith in Christ—Sudden Conversions—The Shepherd of our Souls—Religious Joy—Ignorance of Evil.

Sermons Preached on Various Occasions. Crown 8vo. Cabinet Edition, 6s.; Popular Edition, 3s. 6d.

CONTENTS:—Intellect the Instrument of Religious Training—The Religion of the Pharisee and the Religion of Mankind—Waiting for Christ—The Secret Power of Divine Grace—Dispositions for Faith—Omnipotence in Bonds—St. Paul's Characteristic Gift—St. Paul's Gift of Sympathy—Christ upon the Waters—The Second Spring—Order, the Witness and Instrument of Unity—The Mission of St. Philip Neri—The Tree beside the Waters—In the World, but not of the World—The Pope and the Revolution.

PUBLISHED BY LONGMANS, GREEN, & CO.   3

CARDINAL NEWMAN'S WORKS.

Selection, Adapted to the Seasons of the Ecclesiastical Year, from the 'Parochial and Plain Sermons.' Edited by the REV. W. J. COPELAND, B.D. Crown 8vo. Cabinet Edition, 5s.; Popular Edition, 3s. 6d.

> CONTENTS :—*Advent:* Self-Denial the Test of Religious Earnestness—Divine Calls—The **Ventures of** Faith—Watching. *Christmas Day:* Religious Joy. *New Year's Sunday:* The **Lapse of** Time. *Epiphany:* Remembrance of Past Mercies—Equanimity—The Immortality **of** the Soul—Christian Manhood—Sincerity and Hypocrisy—Christian Sympathy. *Septuagesima:* **Present** Blessings. *Sexagesima:* Endurance, the Christian's Portion. *Quinquagesima:* Love, the One Thing Needful. *Lent:* The Individuality **of** the Soul—Life the Season of Repentance—Bodily Suffering—Tears of Christ at the Grave of Lazarus—Christ's Privations, a Meditation for Christians—The Cross of Christ the **Measure** of the World. *Good Friday:* The Crucifixion. *Easter Day:* Keeping Fast and **Festival.** *Easter Tide:* Witnesses of the Resurrection—A Particular **Providence as** Revealed in the Gospel—Christ Manifested in Remembrance—The Invisible **World—**Waiting **for Christ.** *Ascension:* Warfare the Condition of Victory. *Sunday after Ascension:* Rising with Christ. *Whitsun Day:* The Weapons of Saints. *Trinity Sunday:* The **Mysteriousness** of Our Present Being. *Sundays after Trinity:* Holiness Necessary **for Future Blessedness**—The Religious Use of Excited Feelings—The Self-Wise Inquirer—Scripture **a Record of** Human Sorrow—The Danger **of** Riches—Obedience without Love, **as** instanced in the Character of Balaam—Moral Consequences of Single Sins—The Greatness **and Littleness** of Human Life—Moral Effects of Communion with God—The Thought **of God the Stay of** the Soul—The Power of the Will—The Gospel Palaces—Religion **a Weariness to the** Natural Man—The World **our** Enemy—The Praise of Men—Religion **Pleasant to the** Religious—Mental Prayer—Curiosity a Temptation **to** Sin—Miracles **no Remedy for Unbelief—**Jeremiah, a Lesson for the Disappointed—The **Shepherd of our Souls—** Doing Glory to God **in** Pursuits of the World.

Sermons Bearing upon Subjects of the Day. Edited by the REV. W. J. COPELAND, B.D., late Rector of Farnham, Essex. Crown 8vo. Cabinet Edition, 5s.; Popular Edition, 3s. 6d.

> CONTENTS :—The Work of the Christian—Saintliness not Forfeited by the Penitent—Our Lord's Last Supper and His First—Dangers to the Penitent—The Three Offices of Christ—Faith and Experience—Faith unto the World—The Church and the World—Indulgence in Religious Privileges—Connection between Personal and Public Improvement—Christian Nobleness—Joshua a Type of Christ and His Followers—Elisha a Type of Christ and His Followers—The Christian Church a Continuation of the Jewish—The Principles of Continuity between the Jewish and Christian Churches—The Christian Church an Imperial Power—Sanctity the Token of the Christian Empire—Condition of the Members of the Christian Empire—The Apostolic Christian—Wisdom and Innocence—Invisible Presence of Christ—Outward and Inward Notes of the Church—Grounds for Steadfastness in our Religious Profession—Elijah the Prophet of the Latter Days—Feasting in Captivity—The Parting of Friends.

Fifteen Sermons Preached before the University of Oxford, between A.D. 1826 and 1843. Crown 8vo. Cabinet Edition, 5s.; Popular Edition, 3s. 6d.

> CONTENTS :—The Philosophical Temper, first enjoined by the Gospel—The Influence of Natural and Revealed Religion respectively—Evangelical Sanctity the Perfection of Natural Virtue—The Usurpations of Reason—Personal Influence, the Means of Propagating the Truth—On Justice as a Principle of Divine Governance—Contest between Faith and Sight—Human Responsibility, as independent of Circumstances—Wilfulness, the Sin of Saul—Faith and Reason, contrasted as Habits of Mind—The Nature of Faith in Relation to Reason—Love, the Safeguard of Faith against Superstition—Implicit and Explicit Reason—Wisdom, as contrasted with Faith and with Bigotry—The Theory of Developments in Religious Doctrine.

CARDINAL NEWMAN'S WORKS.

Discourses Addressed to Mixed Congregations. Crown 8vo. Cabinet Edition, 6s.; Popular Edition, 3s. 6d.

CONTENTS :—The Salvation of the Hearer the Motive of the Preacher—Neglect of Divine Calls and Warnings—Men not Angels—The Priests of the Gospel—Purity and Love—Saintliness the Standard of Christian Principle—God's Will the End of Life—Perseverance in Grace—Nature and Grace—Illuminating Grace—Faith and Private Judgment—Faith and Doubt—Prospects of the Catholic Missioner—Mysteries of Nature and of Grace—The Mystery of Divine Condescension—The Infinitude of Divine Attributes—Mental Sufferings of Our Lord in His Passion—The Glories of Mary for the Sake of Her Son—On the Fitness of the Glories of Mary.

Lectures on the Doctrine of Justification. Crown 8vo. Cabinet Edition, 5s.; Popular Edition, 3s. 6d.

CONTENTS :—Faith considered as the Instrumental Cause of Justification—Love considered as the Formal Cause of Justification—Primary Sense of the term 'Justification'—Secondary Senses of the term 'Justification'—Misuse of the term 'Just' or 'Righteous'—The Gift of Righteousness—The Characteristics of the Gift of Righteousness—Righteousness viewed as a Gift and as a Quality—Righteousness the Fruit of our Lord's Resurrection—The Office of Justifying Faith—The Nature of Justifying Faith—Faith viewed relatively to Rites and Works—On Preaching the Gospel—Appendix.

On the Development of Christian Doctrine. Crown 8vo. Cabinet Edition, 6s.; Popular Edition, 3s. 6d.

On the Idea of a University. Crown 8vo. Cabinet Edition, 7s.; Popular Edition, 3s. 6d.

An Essay in Aid of a Grammar of Assent. Crown 8vo. Cabinet Edition, 7s. 6d.; Popular Edition, 3s. 6d.

Two Essays on Miracles. 1. Of Scripture. 2. Of Ecclesiastical History. Crown 8vo. Cabinet Edition, 6s.; Popular Edition, 3s. 6d.

Discussions and Arguments. Crown 8vo. Cabinet Edition, 6s.; Popular Edition, 3s. 6d.

1. How to accomplish it. 2. The Antichrist of the Fathers. 3. Scripture and the Creed. 4. Tamworth Reading-room. 5. Who's to Blame? 6. An Argument for Christianity.

Essays, Critical and Historical. 2 vols. Crown 8vo. Cabinet Edition, 12s.; Popular Edition, 7s.

1. Poetry. 2. Rationalism. 3. Apostolic Tradition. 4. De la Mennais. 5. Palmer on Faith and Unity. 6. St. Ignatius. 7. Prospects of the Anglican Church. 8. The Anglo-American Church. 9. Countess of Huntingdon. 10. Catholicity of the Anglican Church. 11. The Antichrist of Protestants. 12. Milman's Christianity. 13. Reformation of the XI. Century. 14. Private Judgment. 15. Davison. 16. Keble.

Apologia Pro Vita Sua. Crown 8vo. Cabinet Edition, 6s.; Popular Edition, 3s. 6d.

CARDINAL NEWMAN'S WORKS.

Verses on Various Occasions. Crown 8vo. Cabinet Edition, 6s.; Popular Edition, 3s. 6d.

Historical Sketches. 3 vols. Crown 8vo. Cabinet Edition, 6s. each; Popular Edition, 3s. 6d. each.
1. The Turks. 2. Cicero. 3. Apollonius. 4. Primitive Christianity. 5. Church of the Fathers. 6. St. Chrysostom. 7. Theodoret. 8. St. Benedict. 9. Benedictine Schools. 10. Universities. 11. Northmen and Normans. 12. Mediæval Oxford. 13. Convocation of Canterbury.

The Arians of the Fourth Century. Crown 8vo. Cabinet Edition, 6s.; Popular Edition, 3s. 6d.

Select Treatises of St. Athanasius in Controversy with the Arians. Freely translated. 2 vols. Crown 8vo. Cabinet Edition, 15s.; Popular Edition, 7s.

Theological Tracts. Crown 8vo. Cabinet Edition, 8s.; Popular Edition, 3s. 6d.
1. Dissertatiunculæ. 2. On the Text of the Seven Epistles of St. Ignatius. 3. Doctrinal Causes of Arianism. 4. Apollinarianism. 5. St. Cyril's Formula. 6. Ordo de Tempore. 7. Douay Version of Scriptures.

The Via Media of the Anglican Church. 2 vols. Crown 8vo. Cabinet Edition, 6s. each; Popular Edition, 3s. 6d. each.
  Vol. I. Prophetical Office of the Church.
  Vol. II. Occasional Letters and Tracts.

Certain Difficulties felt by Anglicans in Catholic Teaching Considered. 2 vols.
  Vol. I. Twelve Lectures. Crown 8vo. Cabinet Edition, 7s. 6d.; Popular Edition, 3s. 6d.
  Vol. II. Letters to Dr. Pusey concerning the Blessed Virgin, and to the Duke of Norfolk in defence of the Pope and Council. Crown 8vo. Cabinet Edition, 5s. 6d.; Popular Edition, 3s. 6d.

Present Position of Catholics in England. Crown 8vo. Cabinet Edition, 7s. 6d.; Popular Edition, 3s. 6d.

Loss and Gain. The Story of a Convert. Crown 8vo. Cabinet Edition, 6s.; Popular Edition, 3s. 6d.

Callista. A Tale of the Third Century. Crown 8vo. Cabinet Edition, 6s.; Popular Edition, 3s. 6d.

The Dream of Gerontius. 16mo, sewed, 6d.; cloth, 1s.

Meditations and Devotions. Part I. Meditations for the Month of May. Novena of St. Philip. Part II. The Stations of the Cross. Meditations and Intercessions for Good Friday. Litanies, etc. Part III. Meditations on Christan Doctrine. Conclusion. Oblong Crown 8vo. 5s. *net*.

CARDINAL NEWMAN'S WORKS.

COMPLETION OF THE POPULAR EDITION.

Parochial and Plain Sermons. 8 vols. Each	3s. 6d.
Sermons preached on Various Occasions	3s. 6d.
Selection, from the Parochial and Plain **Sermons**	3s. 6d.
Sermons bearing on Subjects of the Day	3s. 6d.
Sermons preached before the University of Oxford	3s. 6d.
Discourses addressed to Mixed Congregations	3s. 6d.
Lectures on the Doctrine of Justification	3s. 6d.
On the Development of Christian Doctrine	3s. 6d.
On the Idea of a University	3s. 6d.
An Essay in Aid of a Grammar of Assent	3s. 6d.
Biblical and Ecclesiastical Miracles	3s. 6d.
Discussions and Arguments on Various Subjects	3s. 6d.
Essays, Critical and Historical. 2 vols.	7s. 0d.
Historical Sketches. 3 vols. Each	3s. 6d.
The Arians of the Fourth Century	3s. 6d.
The Via Media of the Anglican Church. 2 vols. Each	3s. 6d.
Difficulties felt by Anglicans considered. 2 vols. Each	3s. 6d.
Present Position **of** Catholics in England	3s. 6d.
Apologia **pro** Vita Sua	3s. 6d.
Theological **Tracts**	3s. 6d.
Select Treatises of St. Athanasius. 2 vols.	7s. 0d.
Verses on Various Occasions	3s. 6d.
Loss and Gain	3s. 6d.
Callista	3s. 6d.

FOUARD.—The Christ, The Son of God. A Life of Our Lord and Saviour **Jesus** Christ. By the ABBÉ CONSTANT FOUARD, Honorary Cathedral Canon, Professor of the Faculty of Theology at Rouen, etc., etc. Translated from the Fifth Edition with the Author's sanction. By GEORGE F. X. GRIFFITH. With an Introduction by CARDINAL MANNING. Third Edition. With 3 Maps. 2 vols. Crown 8vo. **14s.**

'In erudition the author is to the full up to the level of any writers, Catholic or Protestant, who have as yet attempted the same task, while his reliableness in matters of dogma gives him an enormous scientific advantage over non-Catholics.'—*Dublin Review.*

Saint Peter and the First Years of Christianity. By the ABBÉ CONSTANT FOUARD. Translated by GEORGE F. X. GRIFFITH. Crown 8vo. 9s.

St. Paul and His Missions. By the ABBÉ CONSTANT FOUARD. Translated, with the Author's sanction and co-operation, by GEORGE F. X. GRIFFITH. With 2 Maps. Crown 8vo. 9s.

LYONS.—Christianity or **Infallibility**—Both or Neither. By the Rev. DANIEL LYONS. Crown 8vo. 5s.

'His method is thoroughly popular, and while he has admirably succeeded in avoiding that didactic and argumentative style which is apt to repel the ordinary reader of our day, he nevertheless leaves the distinct impression that his reasoning is based on sound logic, and strengthened by such authorities as would command the attention of every theological student.

'The work is full of erudition, as is shown by the numerous notes indicating a wide range of pertinent and careful reading. . . . The book is a solid and timely contribution to the theological literature of the day.'—*American Ecclesiastical Review.*

CHRISTIAN BIOGRAPHIES:

Henri Dominique Lacordaire. A Biographical Sketch. By H. L. SIDNEY LEAR. With Frontispiece. Crown 8vo. 3s. 6d.

A **Christian Painter of the Nineteenth Century;** being the Life of Hippolyte Flandrin. By H. L. SIDNEY LEAR. Crown 8vo. 3s. 6d.

Bossuet and his **Contemporaries.** By H. L. SIDNEY LEAR. Crown 8vo. 3s. 6d.

Fénelon, Archbishop of **Cambrai.** A Biographical Sketch. By H. L. SIDNEY LEAR. Crown 8vo. 3s. 6d.

A Dominican Artist. A Sketch of the Life of the Rev. Père Besson, of the Order of St. Dominic. By H. L. SIDNEY LEAR. Crown 8vo. 3s. 6d.

The Life of Madame Louise de France, Daughter of Louis XV., also known as the Mother Thérèse de S. Augustin. By H. L. SIDNEY LEAR. Crown 8vo. 3s. 6d.

The Revival of Priestly Life in the Seventeenth Century in France. Charles de Condren—S. Philip **Neri** and Cardinal de Berulle—S. **Vincent** de Paul—S. Sulpice and Jean Jacques **Olier.** By H. L. SIDNEY LEAR. Crown 8vo. 3s. 6d.

Life **of S.** Francis de Sales, Bishop and Prince of Geneva. By H. L. SIDNEY LEAR. Crown 8vo. 3s. 6d.

Henri Perreyve. By A. GRATRY, PRÊTRE DE L'ORATOIRE, Professeur de Morale Evangélique à la Sorbonne, et Membre de l'Académie Française. Translated, by special permission, by H. L. SIDNEY LEAR. With Portrait. Crown 8vo. 3s. 6d.

FÉNELON.—Spiritual Letters to Men. By ARCHBISHOP FÉNELON. Translated by H. L. SIDNEY LEAR, author of 'Life of Fénelon,' 'Life of S. Francis de Sales,' etc. etc. 16mo. 2s. 6d.

FÉNELON. — Spiritual Letters **to** Women.—By ARCHBISHOP FÉNELON. Translated by H. L. SIDNEY LEAR, author of 'Life of Fénelon,' 'Life of S. Francis de Sales,' etc. etc. 16mo. 2s. 6d.

DRANE.—The **History of St. Dominic, Founder of the Friar Preachers.** By AUGUSTA THEODORA DRANE, author of 'The History of St. Catherine of Siena and her Companions.' With 32 Illustrations. 8vo. 15s.

JAMESON—Works by MRS. JAMESON:
  Sacred and Legendary Art. With 19 Etchings and 197 Woodcuts. 2 vols. Cloth, gilt top. 20s. *net.*
  Legends of the Madonna: The Virgin Mary as Represented in Sacred and Legendary Art. With 27 Etchings and 165 Woodcuts. 1 vol. Cloth, gilt top. 10s. *net.*
  Legends of the Monastic Orders. With 11 Etchings and 88 Woodcuts. 1 vol. Cloth, gilt top. 10s. *net.*
  History of the Saviour, His Types and Precursors. Completed by LADY EASTLAKE. With 13 Etchings and 281 Woodcuts. 2 vols. Cloth, gilt top. 20s. *net.*

MANUALS OF CATHOLIC PHILOSOPHY.
(*Stonyhurst Series.*)
EDITED BY RICHARD F. CLARKE, S.J.

Logic. By RICHARD F. CLARKE, S.J. Crown 8vo. 5s.

First Principles of Knowledge. By JOHN RICKABY, S.J. Crown 8vo. 5s.

Moral Philosophy (Ethics and Natural Law). By JOSEPH RICKABY, S.J. Crown 8vo. 5s.

General Metaphysics. By JOHN RICKABY, S.J. Crown 8vo. 5s.

Psychology. By MICHAEL MAHER, S.J. Crown 8vo. 6s. 6d.

Natural Theology. By BERNARD BOEDDER, S.J. Crown 8vo. 6s. 6d.

Political Economy. By CHARLES S. DEVAS. Crown 8vo. 6s. 6d.

ENGLISH MANUALS OF CATHOLIC THEOLOGY.

Outlines of Dogmatic Theology. By SYLVESTER JOSEPH HUNTER, of the Society of Jesus. Crown 8vo. 3 vols., 6s. 6d. each. Vol. I. *now ready.* Vols. II. and III. *nearly ready.*

LONDON AND NEW YORK: LONGMANS, GREEN, & CO.

www.ingramcontent.com/pod-product-compliance
Lightning Source LLC
Chambersburg PA
CBHW032140010526
44111CB00035B/633